Praise for *Never Silent*

"*Never Silent* is a powerful and poignant remembrance of love and loss, fear and fury. It's also an inspiring call to action, showing the power of protest and of people coming together, educating themselves, and demanding change. It is fierce and funny, and a critical account of what it was like to be in the trenches of a war against a virus that was also a fight against silence, and greed, and hate."

—**Anderson Cooper**,
from the foreword

"In this moving and compassionate book, one of the heroes of our recent history looks back on the brilliant brashness of his youth with a wisdom won through unexpected survival. Gay men of my generation owe ACT UP our lives; with his riveting memoir, Peter Staley offers a vital account of how activism transformed fear, desperation, and rage into power."

—**Garth Greenwell**,
author of *Cleanness* and *What Belongs to You*

"Forty years after the onset of the pandemic, Peter Staley's book is an important addition to the growing canon of AIDS memoirs. As a veteran organizer of many protests over the decades, I particularly enjoyed learning the intricate backstories of some of ACT UP New York's most celebrated and controversial exploits. From civil disobedience with radical activists to private dinners with the nation's leading HIV researchers and scientists, Peter shares remarkable memories from his bold, complicated, and passionate life."

—**Cleve Jones**,
author of *When We Rise*

NEVER SILENT

ACT UP and My Life in Activism

PETER STALEY

CHICAGO
REVIEW
PRESS

Published by Chicago Review Press Incorporated
814 North Franklin Street
Chicago, Illinois 60610
ISBN 978-1-64160-142-9

Library of Congress Control Number: 2021941694

Typesetting: Nord Compo
Unless otherwise indicated, all images are from the author's collection

Printed in the United States of America
5 4 3 2 1

To my dad and mom, Paul & Kit Staley,
and my gay brother Rich DeNagel
Recent losses, dearly missed, from my two families

CONTENTS

FOREWORD

BY ANDERSON COOPER

PETER STALEY IS A HERO TO ME. I first heard about him in 2004 when he paid to put up a half dozen ads on phones booths in a gay neighborhood in New York, warning of the dangers of crystal meth. They looked like sleek ads for a gay dating app, but their tagline was startling: HUGE SALE! BUY CRYSTAL, GET HIV FREE! They were, no doubt, offensive to some, but they certainly got your attention, and made you think. I'd heard a famous HIV/AIDS activist was behind them, but it wasn't until years later, when I watched David France's remarkable documentary *How to Survive a Plague*, that I actually saw Peter in action and came to understand what he, and his band of brothers and sisters in ACT UP and TAG, accomplished during the darkest days of the AIDS epidemic. I was so moved by what Peter did that I reached out to him to thank him, and we've been friends ever since.

Peter jokingly says he blames me for this book. He claims I was the first to push him to write a memoir, though I'm quite sure many others suggested it before me. Now, having read the book, I am so glad that I did push. The plague that killed a generation of gay men cannot be forgotten, and Peter saw it all from the front lines. *Never Silent* is a powerful and poignant remembrance of love and loss, fear and fury. It's also an inspiring call to action, showing the power of protest and of people coming together, educating themselves, and demanding change. It is fierce and funny, and a critical account of what it was like to be in the trenches of a war against a virus that was also a fight against silence, and greed, and hate.

Peter found out he was HIV positive in November 1985. Back then, there was no effective treatment. AIDS was a likely death sentence. Peter was a twenty-four-year-old bond trader on Wall Street; still in the closet, he had only just begun to explore gay life in New York. It is hard for many to imagine what that time was like for LGBTQ people—the fear of getting sick, the loss of so many friends and loved ones, the stigma surrounding the disease, the discrimination, and the hate. Peter could have stayed silent about his diagnosis. He could have tried to take care of his health and enjoy life for as long as he could. But that is not what he did. It is not who he is. Peter Staley is a warrior, and it wasn't long after his diagnosis that he began to fight.

In a speech Peter gave in 1990 at an international AIDS conference, he quoted Vito Russo, saying, "AIDS is a test of who we are as a people. When future generations ask what we did in the war, we have to be able to tell them that we were out here fighting. And we have to leave a legacy to the generations of people who will come after us. Remember, that someday, the AIDS crisis will be over. And when that day has come and gone, there will be a people alive on this earth—gay people and straight people, Black people and White people, men and women—who will hear the story, that once, there was a terrible disease, and that a brave group of people stood up and fought and in some cases died so that others might live and be free."

That is what Peter Staley did—that is what he chose to do in the face of death and discrimination. He wasn't the only one, but he was a key member of a brave group of people who stood up and fought back so that others, you and I, might live and be free.

1

WALL STREET CATHARSIS

H IS EYES LOCKED WITH MINE for that beat longer than straight guys' do. What was a young gay stud in 501 Levi's and a black leather jacket doing on Wall Street at 7:30 AM? He handed me a sheet of paper as our eyes kept meeting, eyes that could undress my crisp suit and tie. But it would have to be a passing thrill, or I'd miss the market briefing that always started my workday on the US government bonds trading floor at Morgan Guaranty.

It was the morning of March 24, 1987. The flyer in my hand was about AIDS, the six-year-old epidemic that was terrifying and repulsing Americans. They had ignored the disease and its rising death toll for years, until headlines blared ROCK HUDSON HAS AIDS, followed closely by ROCK HUDSON IS GAY. The news launched a fear-based backlash and forced Americans to think about homosexuality, toward which repulsion was still the social norm.

No one at the bank knew I was gay. I had carefully cultivated the straight macho persona required of US government bond traders, kings of Wall Street at the time. We made millions for the fastest-growing firms, like Salomon Brothers and Goldman Sachs, by churning "Reagan's debt"—all the new bonds needed to finance President Ronald Reagan's huge tax cuts for the rich, which included those very same bond traders.

The flyer was announcing a MASSIVE AIDS DEMONSTRATION that morning in front of Trinity Church, just a block from my trading floor. It included a bulleted list of demands targeting Reagan, the US government, and the Food and Drug Administration. It mentioned both AIDS and AIDS-related complex (ARC), a kind of pre-AIDS diagnosis that is no longer used today. The flyer resonated: less than two years before, I had received my own terrifying diagnosis of ARC just after Rock Hudson's death. Only my family and a few gay friends knew.

The other traders surrounding me on the floor received the same flyer from the handsome guy in leather, whose piercing eyes they likely looked away from.

Mark Werner, the senior trader on our floor and my mentor since I started there in 1984, with his tall, muscular build, short-cropped blond hair, and blue eyes—eyes that were too risky for me to stare at—quickly shut down the conversation about the flyers. "If you ask me," he said, "they all deserve to die for taking it up the butt."

"I hear ya," another trader replied.

Me? I showed no emotion, having perfected this non-reaction along with a safer subtle, self-loathing grin. These were my default responses to the locker-room banter that filled our days on the trading floor, which included abundant use of the word *faggot*. But inside, I died a little more. The guy I looked up to had just said I deserved to die, and no one seemed to care.

After work, however, my unexpressed anger was given voice by men and women far braver than me. The AIDS demonstration had made national news, and the story focused on our government's slow response to the epidemic. One week later, I would join these men and women at their weekly meetings of the newly named group ACT UP, the AIDS Coalition To Unleash Power. A year after that, I would leave my job on disability and devote what time I had left to the activism I had watched on TV that night.

The Corinthian columns of the New York Stock Exchange stand like sentinels guarding the inner sanctum of its trading floor from the commoners outside. Civil disobedience had never breached those columns, with the exception of a legendary prank in the visitors' gallery organized by antiwar activist Abbie Hoffman in 1967.

Hoffman had cofounded the Yippie movement, a group of countercultural revolutionaries who staged theatrical antiauthoritarian demonstrations and events. The Yippies made their first big splash when Hoffman and about a dozen of his friends threw handfuls of dollar bills onto the trading floor of the New York Stock Exchange during a regularly scheduled tour. The traders below became desperate game show contestants in Hoffman's performance piece, leaping into the air to snatch the falling cash. No one was arrested, but the anti-capitalistic stunt got international press.

I got a phone call out of the blue from Hoffman in late 1988. He was living in Pennsylvania but had been following ACT UP's ascension in New York and around the nation. I had become one of ACT UP's poster boys by this time, appearing often in the press, as he once had. He offered to help us if we could think of some way to use him. I was still the clueless twentysomething who was only vaguely aware of his significance, and I'll forever regret not following up with him. He died a year later, and his *New York Times* obit mentioned the stock exchange action in passing.

ACT UP would soon find a way to pay Hoffman its respects. Our war against Burroughs Wellcome over the price of AZT was about to heat up. In August, the National Institutes of Health announced the results of a study showing that AZT helped a larger group of HIV patients, and the company's stock price rose accordingly. ACT UP joined a coalition of AIDS and LGBT rights groups to push for a price reduction on what was still the most expensive drug on the market for any disease. The company agreed to meet, but since we had recently invaded their headquarters, they thought better of inviting us back. Instead, they ponied up for a hotel conference room in Raleigh to keep us far away from their besieged employees.

Once again, the company stonewalled us on the price, and most of the activists left feeling that their time had been wasted. After the meeting, I walked up to Lisa Behrens, Wellcome's public affairs director, and gave them a deadline: ACT UP was going to stage a huge demonstration in front of the New York Stock Exchange on September 14, but we'd gladly cancel it if they announced a price reduction before then. She thanked me for the heads-up but offered no indication that our increasing pressure was going to make them blink.

On the flight home, I kept wondering how we could turn the upcoming demo at the stock exchange from a simple New York City media event into a national—or, better yet, international—story. The ghost of Abbie Hoffman had the answer. Get inside. Disrupt trading.

Unfortunately Hoffman's method—the visitors' gallery—was no longer an option. After the Yippies' stunt, the stock exchange walled off the gallery behind bulletproof Plexiglas. However, ACT UP always had gay eyes and gay ears inside the targets we hit, from pharmaceutical companies to St. Patrick's Cathedral. Sure enough, there was a regular member of ACT UP who worked at the exchange. I plied him endlessly for details about the trading floor and, more specifically, the entrances and security that led to it.

Our insider started using different entryways to work in the morning, taking notes on each. One of them stood out as their weakest link. It offered the shortest path from the sidewalk to the trading floor—remarkably short, about four yards total, with only one security guard in the way. It was an entrance door just below those famous Corinthian columns on Broad Street, leading directly into a small vestibule to the left where the guard stood, followed by three steps on the right leading up to the trading floor.

Getting past this guard became our next challenge. Fortunately for us, since no one previously had attempted to sneak onto the *actual* trading floor, the exchange had become very lax with its entrance security procedures. Our inside informant was pretty sure that as long as you looked like a floor trader, you could walk right in. The traders were all issued picture ID cards but weren't required to show them—this was before most buildings started using digital swipe cards and turnstiles.

I was happily stunned. The exchange was practically rolling out a red carpet for our performance.

But looking like a floor trader wasn't as easy as throwing on a coat and tie. They all wore white rectangular numbered badges with a large three- or four-digit number covering most of the badge, and the trader's name along with their firm's name in smaller type just below it. Where was I going to get a half dozen of these unique badges? Our insider didn't have one that matched; he worked on the options trading floor in an annex connected to the exchange, and the options traders had completely different badges from the stock traders. While our insider's badge allowed him to traverse the stock exchange and use its exits, he would raise suspicion if he lingered there.

So on a bright, sunny lunch hour in August, my videographer boyfriend and I pretended to be tourists outside the exchange. Robert Hilferty used his camcorder to surreptitiously zoom in on traders during their quick lunch breaks. We studied this footage to get close-enough measurements, fonts, and font sizes for a standard trader's badge. They were hard, white plastic, about an eighth of an inch thick, with the black numbers and letters engraved into the plastic.

New York City is filled with expert craftsmen for highly sought fake IDs used by underage visitors wanting to party. We used partying as our excuse, too. Charlie Franchino, my closest friend and confidant in ACT UP, walked into a small shop near his West Village apartment that made IDs and handed the craftsman our mocked-up design and specs. "We're doing a skit at our Bear Stearns office party with singing stock traders, and want to look the part." The craftsman didn't care, saying only, "When do you need them?"

Within a few days, we had seven badges, each with its own number, and all from BEAR STEARNS & CO., our supposed employer. Charlie and I had fun making up alias names for each activist. Mine was Philip Lord.

As I reassembled the team that had invaded Burroughs Wellcome's headquarters a few months earlier, finding new members to replace those not available for another scrape with the legal system, we decided to attempt a test run to see if the badges would get us

past security. Besides, I wanted to see the trading floor with my own eyes—we had to find the perfect spot for our planned disruption.

On Monday, September 11, just three days before the scheduled protest, Robert and I stood near a group of stock traders getting in their last cigarettes just minutes before the opening bell. We wore our best corporate drag and counterfeit badges, and carried small pads of paper with pens to record our pretend trades. We knew there would be a rush for the door to beat the bell, and following the smokers would lower the odds of drawing attention from the sole security guard on duty.

All our planning had worked. We walked right in.

We were on the edge of the busiest trading floor in the world, looking out over a vast cathedral of capital. It was a beehive of energy and noise, with hundreds of traders crisscrossing its expanse, weaving around large round trading stations that dotted the scuffed wood floor.

Robert and I walked toward the center of the room, pretending to check the latest stock prices on the stacks of video displays the trading desks wore like crowns, lest we make eye contact with an actual trader. Where could we deploy our disruptive action that would be just out of reach of hundreds of angry traders? A balcony along the west wall, often used by the press, was only accessible from the side offices on the upper floors. The famous ornate balcony with its opening bell, centered on the south wall, had the same issue: some unknown intricate path to get there. We walked to the other side of the floor, then circled around its circumference.

And then, there it was, an unused relic from the past, right next to the door we first entered: an old one-story gallery lined in dark oak paneling, topped with a shiny brass balustrade where a simple classic tote board showed the day's date. For our purposes, what mattered most was the small opening on the ground floor that led to a skinny wooden staircase, up to the gallery's balcony. Once a day, before the traders arrived for work, an exchange employee would climb these stairs to change the large, square white cards showing the date. This beautiful balcony seemed to serve no other purpose that we could discern, except as an inviting and safe stage for angry AIDS activists.

"Well, hello. You must be new here."

My startled eyes moved down from the balcony to an outstretched hand attached to a smiling, portly older man who had probably been trading at the exchange for decades. I started to sweat. I had not expected a welcoming committee. Robert stood frozen a few feet behind me.

"Hi," I blurted out, then quickly grabbed the man's hand and gave it a good firm shake, like Wall Street men expect. *Don't look nervous. Play along.* "Yes, I'm brand new here."

"Bear Stearns, eh?" as he looked at my fake badge.

"Yup," I replied, hoping this would be his last question. *Please, dear god, don't ask me about your best friend from Bear Stearns who works here too and might be standing a few feet away.*

"Your ID number is weird," he said. "There are only about twelve hundred of us here."

Fuck. My badge number was 5794. I had failed to ask our informant if there was a numerical range we should stick to when designing the badges. My interrogator's badge number was in the low hundreds. *Can he see the beading sweat on my forehead?*

"Really?" I asked, as I tried to feign innocence. *Play dumb.* "I guess it's a new system," I said, definitely sounding dumb.

"I guess so," he said, looking baffled.

End this, end this now, I thought. "Well, I better get to it. Nice meeting you."

"You too," he replied, still looking baffled.

And with that, I pulled away, and Robert followed. We walked until we were out of our interrogator's sightline. "Let's get out of here," I said.

"Jesus Christ, I'm shitting my pants," said Robert, as we made a hasty exit.

Within an hour, Charlie had returned to his local ID shop for another set of badges, telling the craftsman, who still didn't care, that "our crew of dancing traders has doubled." This time, he provided a new set of names and picked numbers for each badge that were all in the 1200s. He paid extra for a rush order, saying the skit was happening the following night. We had our corrected badges in time.

I got little sleep the night before the demo. This was becoming typical for actions I planned. The mind would race endlessly, playing out various scenarios. There were always a few weak spots during deployment when a little bit of bad luck could bring the action to a screeching halt, and no amount of strategizing could eliminate these vulnerabilities. You just had to roll the dice.

At 8:00 AM on Thursday, September 14, nine members of ACT UP sat nervously around two tables at a McDonald's on Nassau Street, about five blocks north of the exchange. As we downed our coffees and Egg McMuffins, we ran through the game plan a few more times, making sure everyone's questions were answered and roles defined. Seven of us would be going inside. Five of the seven would stage the disruption in the balcony: me, Gregg Bordowitz, James McGrath, Lee Arsenault, and Scott Robbe. The other two, Robert Hilferty and Richard Elovich, would hang back on the exchange floor and attempt to take pictures of our disruption. The two additional members of our crew would provide logistical support outside.

We couldn't count on there being any press in the room, and giving the press a heads-up was out of the question, since they'd have to arrange access with the exchange. We'd have to be our own press—not an easy thing in a time before iPhones. Hilferty and Elovich had small disposable cameras with high-speed film that could take a decent picture inside a building without a flash. Still, taking those pictures while surrounded by dozens of pissed-off traders would be dangerous work, even without the flash. It was our hope that everyone's eyes would be looking up toward the balcony, leaving our photographers in peace.

The five of us who hoped to climb those balcony stairs had dressed carefully that morning. We were loaded down with hidden gear strapped to our bellies beneath the buttoned-down shirts, jackets, and ties that fleshed out our corporate cosplay, much like the padding a drag queen would attentively prepare before her show. There was a large banner, carefully folded down to a thick square, and eight feet of steel chain, a padlock, handcuffs, and extra goodies that would spice up the show. We appeared to be slightly pudgy stock traders, at least on the way in.

My wristwatch was accurately set so that I could see the minutes and seconds count down to the opening bell at 9:30 AM. We left the McDonald's around 9:05 for the walk down Nassau Street toward the corner of Broad and Wall Streets, then mingled near the tourists under George Washington's statue in front of Federal Hall, watching the traders smoking cigarettes in front of the exchange.

The last cluster of traders started making their way onto the floor around 9:27 AM, and we merged up against them from behind as they each held the door open for the next guy. We had decided in advance it was probably better to acknowledge the guard with at least a grin of recognition, however false, but avoided any vocal greetings. It was the one choke-point moment where everything could go wrong. We had to look like we belonged there while our hearts were racing.

I passed the guard first. Our eyes locked for a split second while I curled a grin, then looked forward toward the backs of the traders we were following. The guard glanced down at my badge. None of us broke our stride, keeping pace with the real traders who did this every morning just before the opening bell. I resisted looking back at my comrades until safely out of view of the guard. We regrouped on the edge of one of the most foreign and frenetic environments these boys had ever seen—all of us were in.

We had less than two minutes to find our places and prepare our show. "Ready?" I asked. Everyone nodded. Robert and Richard started walking onto the floor, looking for good camera sight lines of the balcony from two different angles. The other four followed me to the old wooden staircase. My first steps up felt victorious. From this point, there was little chance anything or anyone could stop us from doing what we came to do.

As the five of us reached the top of the stairs, we crawled on all fours to the balustrade, hoping not to be spotted before the opening bell. We untucked our shirts and emptied our pockets as we gathered our protest contraband. Next, we looped the chain over the top rail and padlocked its two ends together, forming a long loop. Five steel handcuffs were used to lock each of us onto the chain. The banner was unfolded and stretched between us, still out of sight. I looked at my watch. It was 9:29 and 15 seconds—45 seconds until the opening bell.

We each pulled out one more item from our coat pockets, our guarantee for maximum impact that would stop everything else on the trading floor and announce our enemy incursion with a bang. Our thumbs were on the triggers of five pocket-sized air horns with their warning labels saying, Do Not Use near Ears.

At 9:29 and 45 seconds I said, "Ready," and then, "Go." We stood up and lifted the black eight-foot banner over the balustrade. It had a simple two-word warning that could clearly be read from the far corners of the trading floor: Sell Wellcome, a reference to the company that had ignored our warnings. Each of us had an arm raised high in an amplified power salute. Our air horn blasts became a what-the-fuck moment for the hundreds of traders below. No one heard the opening bell.

For the first few seconds, it seemed like the trading floor was frozen. Traders stopped walking and talking. Everything stopped while our horns became a piercing new reality. As all heads turned our way, they soon put two and two together. They read the banner and knew that over a thousand AIDS activists would be protesting just outside later that morning. Yet somehow, inconceivably, we'd invaded their turf. They exploded in anger.

The traders surged toward the balcony. Many of them pointed at us, yelling for security guards. Before our horns died out, Gregg Bordowitz and Lee Arsenault had one more surprise in their pockets. In homage to Abbie Hoffman, they threw fistfuls of fake hundred-dollar bills onto the mob below. Many of the traders noticed something printed on the backs of the bills. They picked them up or grabbed them midair and read the provocation: "FUCK YOUR PROFITEERING. People are dying while you play business."

At this point they became rabid. As security guards made their way toward the balcony, traders started throwing wads of paper at us, yelling, "Mace the faggots!" I looked for Robert and Richard, but they had quickly taken pictures during the first seconds of the disruption and had exited the exchange as planned. One of our support team outside ran the cameras up to the Midtown offices of the Associated Press, which promptly developed the film and found one usable picture, perfectly angled to capture the stock exchange's logo on a banner hanging behind us. The AP quickly ran the picture with a story on its newswire.

In any other circumstance, a large crowd of angry heterosexual men yelling "Faggots!" with their fists raised would fill me with justifiable fear. But after years of hearing this word used almost daily at my job on a bond trading floor, and years of suppressing my closeted rage and feeling the sting of powerlessness against hate, this moment became the most cathartic of my life. The faggots had the power now, and the haters were merely our pawns.

The redder their faces got and the more they cursed, the bigger my smile grew. Nothing they could do now would diminish our success. The action would likely get front-page coverage in the *New York Times* and the *Wall Street Journal*. Their hatred would only feed the public's sympathy for our cause.

At the NYSE balustrade, (left to right) James McGrath, Lee Arsenault, Scott Robbe, and me, September 14, 1989.

Three security guards finally climbed to our balcony and tried to pull us away, only to find that we were locked to the balustrade. One of them yelled into his walkie-talkie, "We need a bolt cutter."

A scuffle broke out below us. I saw Robert running toward the exit with a half dozen traders chasing him yelling, "Get that faggot!" After he and Richard had exited the exchange to hand off their cameras, they foolishly came back inside to see if we were OK. Some of the traders were scouring the floor for possible collaborators, and had pounced on both of them. Richard's jacket was pulled off in the scuffle, and then a shirtsleeve was ripped from his shoulder. Fortunately, additional security guards intervened, and both of them were whisked off the floor.

The crowd below us continued to jeer as we waited for the bolt cutter. Every time a trader yelled a slur at us, I looked right at him and widened my smile. This made them angrier. The bolt cutter arrived and a burly guard made quick work of our lightweight chain. With one guard assigned to each of us, we were escorted down the stairs toward the angry mob that I'd been relentlessly taunting.

After witnessing the roughing up that Robert and Richard had received, the security team realized they had a logistical problem of getting us from point A to point B—from the balcony, past hundreds of traders, to the elevator banks just off the floor, and finally to their security office on one of the upper floors. This was already a deeply embarrassing news event for the exchange. Any violence, especially against a person with AIDS, would only make things worse. They smartly decided to protect us.

With all the manpower they could muster, a human chain of security guards and exchange personnel had been deployed, stretching from the bottom of the stairwell, along the east wall of the trading floor, to a corridor that led to the elevators. They needed every man. The traders pushed up against them, trying to grab us, spitting insults and throwing more wads of paper at our heads. It was like a Hollywood scene in a medieval fortress, where the captured bronzed invaders are marched to the dungeon through a mob of bloodthirsty villagers. But in our film, the righteous invaders were rescued by their own army, and welcomed back as conquering heroes.

We made it, unharmed, to the elevators. The guards took us to a small office on an upper floor, where one wall was filled with live feeds from various security cameras. We joined Robert and Richard around a rectangular folding table where I imagined the guards ate most of their meals.

"What are you guys doing here?" I joked to Robert and Richard.

"We thought they were going to kill you guys, so we came back in," said Robert.

Turning serious, I asked about the cameras, whispering, "Did you make the hand-off?"

"Yes," he quietly replied.

"Were you both able to get some shots?" I asked.

"We think so," he said.

All of us were smiling from the sheer relief of having pulled off our mission impossible. The guards looked distraught as they quietly discussed their next steps and who would carry them out. An executive type, probably the head of security, approached us and started the interrogation.

He was holding Richard's fake badge, and asked, "Where did you get these?"

"We had them made," I said, still smiling.

"Where?" he asked.

"A place that could make them," I answered.

"OK, guys, we're going to need the rest of those badges," he demanded.

"Sure," I said, and removed mine, leading my comrades to do the same.

Badges in hand, our interrogator apparently didn't need to know more, and said, "Hang tight, guys."

We waited, and then waited some more. Finally, a New York City police officer came forward and told us they'd be driving us to a local precinct for processing. "There's a situation outside, so sit tight while we work on getting you out of here," he said.

We knew what the situation outside was. Hundreds of AIDS activists were beginning to arrive for the lunchtime demonstration, and our support team was spreading the news about our preemptive strike.

We waited some more. Eventually, a bunch of cops squeezed into the room—one for each of us. They handcuffed us together like a chain gang, then led us to the elevators. Once the doors opened, we began the most exhilarating perp walk any of us had experienced in our combined histories of arrests.

The NYPD not only wanted to protect us from revenge-minded stock traders we passed in the building, they also wanted to prevent any mingling between us and the crowd of press and activists outside.

We were greeted by a tunnel of blue, about fifty cops forming two lines on either side of the elevator that led all the way to a police van, just past the waiting camera crews and photographers on the sidewalk. You'd think we committed the crime of the century to warrant such handling.

As we exited the exchange, we all raised our fists in victory, while gathered activists chanted "ACT UP! Fight Back! Fight AIDS!" as the cameras clicked.

Years later, I saw a film clip of our perp walk. It zoomed in on Robert Hilferty and me as we were about to get into the police van. For a brief second, I looked up, across the street. The bond trading floor I had worked on just two years earlier was directly above me now on the sixth floor of J. P. Morgan's headquarters. I had looked down on the exchange's iconic columns for the four years I had worked there, four years in my stifling closet, smiling at homophobic jokes, telling

NYSE perp walk: (left to right) Scott Robbe, Robert Hilferty, and me, September 14, 1989. *New York Post Archives via Getty*

a thousand lies, and fighting the inevitable depression from living alone with my secrets. And now, my former colleagues were pressed against those sixth-floor windows, wanting to see the disrupters of the opening bell.

They would read about us on the front page of the *Wall Street Journal* the next day, and on the front page of the *New York Times* the day after that. And they would read another front-page story in the *Times* five days later, titled AIDS DRUG'S MAKER CUTS PRICE BY 20%.

Before entering the van, I let them have a good look. I was exactly where I was meant to be: with my people, proudly and openly fighting for our lives.

With that quick look up, the circle was now closed, and the pain erased.

2

TROUBLEMAKER

MY KITE GOT AWAY FROM ME, plunging into the transformer on the telephone pole behind our house, and somehow ignited the voltage-filled bucket like a bomb. As sparks filled the sky, I could feel the concussive force from the blast. To this seven-year-old, it seemed like those exploding kegs of black powder that toasted Wile E. Coyote.

But this was no Saturday-morning cartoon, and there would be no escaping the blame—no *beep-beep* and I'm gone, like the Road Runner. My mom was too quick.

"WHAT JUST HAPPENED?" she yelled as she ran out of the house.

Only fifteen minutes earlier I was an innocent kid flying a kite on the street. It wasn't my fault that the kite got wet after it plunged into a sidewalk puddle. It wasn't my fault that my older brother Jes didn't tie the end of the kite's line to the Lincoln Log I used to spool out the string, so that when I tested how high the kite could go, the last of the line whipped off, surrendering the kite to the whims of wind and gravity. It wasn't my fault that the transformer was constructed so delicately that a seven-year-old's flimsy kite could make it explode.

The Staley kids, (top) Jes and Chris,
(bottom) Janet and me, 1967.

And it surely wasn't my fault that this blast caused some freak chain reaction, as a nearby transformer exploded, then another, and another, and another, each boom farther and farther away.

After about twenty seconds, the sound of electrical carnage ended. Thankfully, my kite didn't cause an entire power plant to explode, tragically killing dozens, just because my big brother couldn't tie a knot.

None of my innocence mattered. I was fingered as the kid who caused the major blackout in our Long Beach neighborhood, where everyone used candles that night. Electric cables, blasted off their poles, lay draped over various plantings and play areas in all the backyards on our block. Kids in my elementary school taunted me with a false rumor that an elderly man had been killed during his afternoon swim when a wire fell into his pool.

At first, my mother was furious, yelling at my father when he got home from work, insisting that he discipline me with a grounding. "Sorry, Pedro," he said, using his nickname for me, "No TV tonight." But Mom quickly pivoted after news of it appeared in our local paper. It was notoriety, the kind that could be counted on for good laughs. She eagerly shared the new family lore with friends and relatives near and far.

A couple of weeks later, two lawyers from Southern California Edison Company arrived at our house for prescheduled interrogations of all involved. I was promised ice cream if I told the men in suits the truth. Jes and my mom were interviewed as well. Then, as the team wrapped up, the lawyers told my dad that there still might be legal repercussions, at which point Dad stopped being cordial.

"Are you really telling me your multimillion-dollar corporation would sue a kid with a kite?" he mockingly asked.

I was witnessing my first tough-talk between businessmen, along with an impressive display of paternal protection. Dad had my back. The lawyers soon left, and we never heard from them again.

The Night the Lights Went Out in Long Beach wasn't the first time I worked my mom's nerves. As a five-year-old, I'd become fascinated with our lawnmower, especially after my dad taught me how to start it—yanking the pull-cord two or more times and finding the sweet spot for the choke. The engine's roar and the smell of exhaust provided a heady power trip, a kind of high I wanted to tap more than my weekly mowing chore provided. So one morning, after starting our mower, I tested my pull-cord skills on all the other mowers on our street. I would open a neighbor's garage door, get the mower going, and move on to the next, until a chorus of mowers echoed down the block.

This happened more than once until my mom, in exasperation, advised our neighbors to remove the spark plugs from their mowers until needed.

Problem solved.

Well, *that* problem, at least. My budding pyromania proved more difficult to snuff out. As before, I took a worthwhile lesson from my dad—in this case, starting a fire in our fireplace—and took it way too far.

Successfully burning something to ashes while controlling the process was intoxicating. It was beautiful and dramatic and tapped my ever-present rebelliousness and curiosity. And boy, did I have questions. How did other things burn besides paper and wood? Why did different items produce different-colored flames or different odors? Conducting these experiments in less-trafficked rooms of our home became my new obsession.

My mom, already stretched thin by the full-time job of running a home with four often misbehaving children, had developed her own habits for coping, honing drinking skills from her college years into a nightly gin and tonic routine. Like me with my fire experiments, she handled it well, for the most part. But on rare occasions, when one too many drinks met one too many problems, watch out—like the time that mom opened the door to my bedroom and caught me torching a plastic toy truck centered carefully on a metal platter.

"You're going to burn down this house with everyone in it!" she screamed. "I'm going to teach you not to play with fire . . ." After blowing out the flames, she pulled me down to the floor. I squirmed to get away, but she pinned me down with her knees on both my arms while sitting on my torso. Her hands were free now, so she grabbed my box of matches. Her reddened face leaned into mine as she lit a match and brought it close to my nose.

"This is what it feels like when you play with fire," she said, as she slowly moved the flame to my right arm, briefly touching its skin.

I screamed. Having made her point, she blew out the match and released me. "That better be the last time you play with fire in this house," she said.

And it was.

To be fair, violence was exceedingly rare in the Staley house. My younger sister, Janet, and my two older brothers, Jes and Chris, all recall a few moments each, from a head slap to my first-degree burn.

Except for Mom's highly effective, albeit controversial anti-pyromania lesson, I got off relatively easy. Truth be told, I was the momma's boy of the Staley house during the first fifteen years of my life. Despite my antics, she seemed to favor me over my siblings with attention, and I enjoyed it, until I didn't.

But why me? Janet says I was the most precocious of the four of us, while Jes says I seemed to live in my own, more cerebral world, lonely but openly creative and opinionated.

I do remember feeling apart from my peers, more mature than they were, wanting to be an adult as soon as possible. I loved science, math, classical music, Broadway musicals, *Star Trek* reruns, bird-watching, building forts in the woods, catching tadpoles and tending to them until they turned into frogs. I could also stare down bullies with a look that could kill, an important skill for a kid with an affinity for Broadway and tadpoles.

I also remember charming my maternal grandparents, especially my granddad, whom my mom and our entire family revered. Maybe my mom saw a bit of her dad in me. Maybe that's why she favored me, hoping I'd follow in his footsteps.

When Dr. James R. Killian Jr., my maternal grandfather, died in 1988, his obituary in the *New York Times* filled half a page, everything above the fold. My granddad, the obit starts, was "the first Presidential assistant for science and technology, an architect of the National Aeronautics and Space Administration, and a president of Massachusetts Institute of Technology."

He was a southerner, born in South Carolina, with a hard-driving father who worked as a superintendent of a cotton mill. His parents called him by his middle name, Rhyne, which was his mother's maiden name.

When President Eisenhower tried to calm the nation after the Russians launched Sputnik in 1957, he asked the president of MIT to be his science adviser. The Cold War press dubbed my granddad the country's missile czar. Within a few years of his appointment, we had intercontinental ballistic missiles, and NASA.

During Eisenhower's final days as president, granddad Killian returned to Cambridge, Massachusetts, and my mother was rushed to Sutter Memorial Hospital in Sacramento, California, for the birth of her third son. I was apparently in a hurry, crowning before the doctor could get scrubbed and ready. My ambitious arrival was rewarded when my mom gave me her beloved dad's same middle name, Rhyne.

As I grew old enough to earn the *precocious child* label, I also earned my mom's attention, along with that coin's flip side, her growing expectations. Whatever hobbies I took an interest in, be it birdwatching or judo, I was fully supported. When I became obsessed with my twenty-six-key toy piano, I was quickly given an upgrade. An upright piano arrived, and weekly lessons commenced. Two years later, I wowed all the parents at my elementary school's Christmas show as I accompanied the school choir. Three years after that, a six-foot Yamaha grand piano arrived for my thirteenth birthday.

By then, I was already practicing Brahms, Bach, Gershwin, and Ives with a renowned local teacher, Benjamin Whitten, who was a professor of music at West Chester State College. When my parents took a two-week, four-country vacation through Europe not long after the grand piano arrived, I was the only child invited along, with a tour of Beethoven's Vienna apartment to spoil me further.

I started competing in regional piano competitions, even winning a few. I added bass clarinet to my practice schedule so I could join the school orchestra, added tuba to join the marching band, and got a standing ovation after performing Gershwin's "Rhapsody in Blue"

The Staley family, 1973.

with my junior high school orchestra, forever confirmed by my mom yelling "A standing ovation!" into the tape recorder on her lap. And I was trotted out to play "Bridge over Troubled Water" and "My Way" at every cocktail party my parents threw. During Sinatra's classic, my mom would sing along, tearing up every time with a defiant, "I did it *myyyy waaaay!*"

This symbiotic relationship between mother and son—she liked bragging about my accomplishments, and I liked the attention—was probably doomed from the start. My rebellious nature would eventually have its way.

After reaching top music geekdom in junior high and weathering through the concomitant verbal bullying from the jocks, I grew weary of the endless hours of solitude at the piano. I was self-aware enough to know a career playing classical piano was unlikely—I wasn't the next Glenn Gould—and immature enough to desire more popularity with my peers, especially since I was starting my first year of high school. So, in a leap of logic, I slashed my time at the piano bench and started hanging out with some of the school stoners.

My new stoner friends certainly spurred my rebellious streak. True to form, they suggested that I make full use of my family's spacious home by hosting a keg party when my parents were away on one of my dad's business trips.

Before moving, when I was eight years old, to the Main Line, Philadelphia's ritzy suburbs, we had lived a largely middle-class existence. My dad worked as a plant manager for Procter & Gamble, and the company moved him around the country from plant to plant every few years. My siblings and I were born all over the place—Chris and Jes in Boston, Janet in Kansas City, and me in Sacramento. Berwyn, Pennsylvania, was Chris and Jes's sixth hometown, my fourth, and Janet's third.

But the move to Pennsylvania was distinctly different. Dad had been hired away from Procter & Gamble by a family-owned chemical company based in Philadelphia, to be groomed as their first non-family CEO. His salary took an instant leap up.

All our previous moves, even the cross-country ones, were done in our beat-up station wagon. This time, we flew (my first airline trip) and went from upper middle class to lower upper class in a flash. Dad's big raise afforded a newly built home, all glass and high ceilings, at the top of a long, steep driveway in the woodsy hills near our schools. This hip-looking house became an attractive staging area for a teenage boy determined to join his high school in-crowd.

Conestoga High School's weekend social scene revolved around beer keg parties at some cool kid's house. Flouting Pennsylvania's drinking age of twenty-one was considered a coming-of-age challenge to all in their midteens. Older siblings, cool parents, and craft knife–altered driver's licenses were all deployed to thwart this foolish prohibition.

Small-town cops, at the behest of their local PTAs, would drive through neighborhoods on Friday and Saturday nights looking for telltale signs of keg parties: dozens of tightly parked cars on a residential street with a thumping bass coming from a nearby home. Our revelries were often busted by these cops, but in a slap-on-the-privileged-wrist way. No arrests, just a firm "Party's over, kids," as we were allowed, amazingly, to drunkenly return to our cars and drive home, or to other, smaller parties.

Breaking free from my music-geek status to the in-crowd would be accomplished in just one eventful night. My stoner friends helped me procure two kegs of beer the day my parents left town. It was not unheard-of to collect a modest door fee for covering party costs, so we advertised it as an "open party": no invitation needed, with a two-dollar cover. Word of mouth did the rest.

Apparently, there were no other parties competing for attention that night. In addition, there was a fascination that I, the piano nerd, was attempting to throw a kegger. My street quickly turned into a crowded parking lot. It seemed like the entire school showed up. Even though I had only spent about $40 on beer, I collected over $250 at the door in short order, and the house was packed. But I didn't anticipate my immediate demand and supply problem. About an hour into the party, as my guests began to run wild, the kegs ran dry.

Disaster.

Just as I was strategizing with my stoned party advisers over how to procure more beer, one of the popular kickline girls—our marching band featured over fifty skimpily clad girls that did Rockettes-style kickline routines—ran up to me in a panic. Frank Pitts, a six-foot-four, 230-pound defensive tackle on our football team, was "destroying" the house. He had only recently arrived and was livid at paying two bucks for kegs of beer that only hissed air when he tried to fill his plastic cup. So he snapped.

Pitts began his destruction by throwing all the second-floor deck furniture into the woods below. As he reentered the house, he punched his fist through the dining room wall, then stomped downstairs, grabbed someone else's beer, and poured it on the pool table. By the time we caught up with him, the damage was done. Three kickline girls helped me kick the behemoth out, convincing Pitts to leave the house and go climb up the Empire State Building to swat at fighter planes.

I was drunk and almost in tears, but the cool girls were in rescue mode. The four of us quickly shut down the party and started planning and implementing Operation Clean-Up: we blow-dried the pool table, recovered furniture, spackled, sanded, and repainted the damaged wall. We were still blow-drying the wall less than a half hour before my parents got home at eleven the next morning. Thankfully, most of the paint smell was gone and the house was spotless when they arrived. My parents seemed oblivious to the war zone that had existed just twelve hours earlier.

If only the town's rumor mill could be as easily cleaned. Within forty-eight hours, my mom overheard two other moms at the local pharmacy discussing the big party at the Staley residence that weekend. The details eluded her, including the ham-fisted hole in the wall, which remained my secret for years. Regardless, I was grounded for a week.

Chastened but not defeated, I was still on a mission to make my mark in high school. And a big dumb jock and his testosterone weren't going to ruin my moment to shine.

So I started planning another party. Only this time, there would be major adjustments to avoid the unpredictability of a standard kegger. It would be invitation-only for thirty or so of the most popular members of our marching band and its kickline, my new bouncers. Embossed invites were handed out, promising THE ULTIMATE PARTY and featuring what I billed as THE SHOW, a multimedia extravaganza crafted for a thoroughly stoned audience. If there's a gay gene for throwing parties, mine was on splashy overdrive.

I periodically stole my mom's credit card for printing the invites and other expenses, hoping she wouldn't notice one or two extra charges on her monthly bill. In addition to a keg of beer, I secured a case of champagne, copious amounts of marijuana, and a two-foot-tall stainless steel bong.

When the night arrived, our living room's large pit-like sectional sofa was surrounded by hidden wires and platforms for the surprises to come. After a few hours of laughing, drinking, bonding, and bong-smoking, everyone sank into the sofa or sprawled out on the shag carpet as I readied myself behind a makeshift table of equipment near the back of the room.

My friends were familiar with the Konica C35 Automatic camera that often hung from my neck at school, but they had never seen its handiwork. Projected on the wall above the fireplace, here we all were: our parties, our Friday-night football games, our homecoming float prep, our band trip through Florida's best tourist stops, all synced with a mixtape of our favorite music from the past year. It was a trippy stroll down memory lane, capturing the silliness and bonding that had gotten us through high school.

I saved the best pics for last, the ones with hugs and smiles, as Dan Fogelberg's "Nether Lands" crescendoed on the mixtape. Dozens of small votive candles on both sides of the room lit up all at once, and before the stoners' "*Whoas*" and "*Oooohs*" could die down, the dormant wood-burning fireplace burst into flames. Fogelberg's string section soared as he sang of "anthems to glory and anthems to love." My handiwork, busily connecting wires to a car battery at my feet, set off well-placed electric matches throughout the room. My inner pyromaniac was in heaven.

I had hoped that this party's invite-only secrecy and lack of property damage might keep it off my parents' radar. But no such luck. Maybe it was the fireworks I set off from the roof after the slideshow? Regardless, they grounded me again. But it was worth it, because my transition to a loftier social status had finally taken off.

Shortly after turning sixteen, I tested how much freedom came with my new learner's permit. While my mom and dad were away for a quick trip, I convinced a couple of friends to join me for a joy ride in Mom's car. Philadelphia was only thirty minutes away, and we had never explored the big city without our parents. The trip did not end well. I almost totaled my mom's car during a downtown collision that—spoiler alert!—wasn't the other guy's fault.

I left the deeply battered evidence of my crime, still drivable, in the family's garage and curled up in my bed downstairs, holding back tears, waiting for my parents to return. I heard them drive up, heard the automatic garage door open, and cringed at what my parents were about to see. They ran into the house, my dad calling my name.

"Peter, are you OK?" he asked. I burst into tears while answering, "Yes, I'm so sorry."

"What did you do to my car?" my mom asked, as the grilling commenced.

I managed to get out the whole story through my tears, with my dad looking concerned and my mom looking increasingly furious.

As they finally left my bedroom, my mom chided my dad, "Do something, Paul!"

"Can you wait?" he replied. "He's just been in a bad car accident."

But she had had enough. My rebellion had been well underway at this point, with my grades tanking, my new stoner friends, and that unapproved keg party. In her mind, I was out of control, and my dad was complicit. His empathy and patience were not meshing with her anger and frustration. Add two glasses of gin, and this tension snapped.

They argued loudly upstairs while she drank. And then it seemed to be over. But after a few minutes of quiet, I could hear my mom coming down the stairs, past my room, and into the garage. I could hear her get into her car and start the engine. I thought she might be leaving in a huff. But why hadn't she opened the garage door?

Hearing all of this from my bed, I froze. What was happening? It made no sense to me. Was she trying to kill herself?

My dad came down the stairs, past my room, and opened the door to the garage. I finally got up to follow him, stopping short in the laundry room. I saw my dad's back just inside the garage.

"What the fuck are you doing?" he asked my mom as he pushed the button that opened the garage door. The gears drowned out my mom's response.

Incoming fresh air slightly reduced my panic. Mom turned off the car, got out, walked past Dad and then past me, her face red, her eyes wet. My dad told me to go back to my room and try to sleep. We all collapsed. Exhaustion had finally quieted the house.

My mom would turn on the car in our closed garage two more times before I graduated from high school, including once after I almost failed a class. All three episodes followed arguments between my parents. All three followed the glasses of gin my mom would start at around 5:00 PM. All three were stopped by my dad.

Even back then, my dad and I thought these were more staged than serious suicide attempts. She knew we could hear them and stop her. Was she lashing out at what was by then a failed marriage? Was it a cry for help from a woman who felt increasingly isolated, over-whelmed, and unsupported? Was it just an example of how alcoholics always damage those they love most?

I love my mom. She is surely flawed, and I can blame her for an unwillingness to confront those flaws, for failing to examine what damaged her and how she damaged others. Her generation seemed ill equipped for self-reflection. But she did spend most of her life trying to raise four kids, mostly without help—mostly without my dad, who either deferred to her or avoided her, and had long ago stopped loving her. I am my mom's son and was molded both by her and by surviving her flaws.

Shortly after the car accident and my mom's meltdown, my dad sat me down for a talk. My grades had tanked, I had lost interest in the piano, I was getting into trouble with parties and the car, and I was warring with Mom. My life was falling apart, and he could tell I was miserable.

So he threw me a lifeline. "Do you want to see a professional for some help?" he asked.

"Yes!" I said, surprising myself with how quickly and desperately I latched on to his offer. A teenager in the 1970s who needed a shrink was still something both parents and kids only whispered about. Only the most fucked-up kids were sent to one, or so it was thought.

But I was truly confused at the state of my life, how I had gone from the best musician in the school district to flunking classes. My dad seemed as confused as I was. Why not ask someone trained to help kids in crisis?

My parents found a reputable psychiatrist at a mental health clinic associated with the local hospital in Bryn Mawr. He was straight from central casting: a middle-aged White guy with a reserved manner and, I swear to god, an Austrian or German accent. My parents had found a facsimile of Sigmund Freud, at least in my imagination. Since I've long ago forgotten his name, I'll just call him my Dr. Freud.

Our first few sessions were methodical and uneventful. He asked lots of questions, took notes, and offered little if any feedback. Unlike Judd Hirsch in *Ordinary People*, which became my favorite film a few years later, Dr. Freud wasn't going to become my best friend. But like the film, we'd have our own Hollywood moment, a session with a short, crisp monologue that would change my life.

There were a couple of scenes before the breakthrough, where the tension built. After seeing me once a week for about a month, Dr. Freud ended a session by informing me that he wanted to spend an hour the following week with my dad and mom, alone. My mom had never been to a shrink in her life and considered the need for one to be a sign of weakness. I warned Dr. Freud that she might have to be dragged in kicking and screaming. "Good luck with that," I said.

Sure enough, my mom complained, but at my dad's insistence, they visited my shrink the following week. I'll never know what was asked or said. Regardless, he apparently gained enough insight into the causes of my crisis to loosen his tongue at our very next session. He didn't show his cards right away and started by quickly brushing aside the momentous hour with my parents, more specifically, my mom. "We had a helpful session," he said drily.

Dr. Freud then strung me along for another fifteen minutes, asking questions and taking notes. After I finished describing yet another argument with my mom, he surprised me with a long pause before asking his next question.

"Do you want to know what I think is going on between you and your mom?" he asked.

"Sure," I said.

"You and your mom are having a battle of control," he said. "She wants you to follow in her father's footsteps, to reach a high level of renown and success, as she measures it. She's trying to control your life so that it stays on course to achieve this success."

He continued. "You want to control your own life, so you are rebelling against her efforts to control you. What we have to figure out in this room is how you can win this battle of control. We just need to change your methods. You are rebelling against her control with acts that are self-destructive." He then ended, "We have to figure out how you can rebel with acts that aren't self-destructive, with acts that help you more than hurt you."

Holy fuck, I thought, as I stared at him with my mouth open. *Holy fucking bingo. It all made perfect sense.*

"Wow, I hadn't looked at it this way," I feebly replied while my mind exploded.

And he was on my side! Dr. Freud was willing to conspire with me to win a battle of control with my mom.

In the Hollywood version, this is where I'd break into tears as the music swelled, but I was too in my head for that, plotting new tactics and leaving the session exhilarated and determined to break free of my mother's control.

A few days later, I described the entire session to my piano teacher, Ben Whitten. While studying with him through most of my teens, we had become more than just teacher and student. Ben had become the most significant mentor in my life.

Born in Mississippi, trained at the Peabody Conservatory, and married with three kids, Ben and his large house in West Chester became my weekly refuge. Ostensibly straight, Ben was the campiest mentor a closeted gay boy could dream of bonding with.

Even though Big Ben—the nickname his wife, kids, and ultimately his students used—won many teaching awards before his retirement, his eccentric mentoring style would likely have gotten him thrown in jail today. He didn't just teach piano technique, he would transform often socially stifled teenagers into expressive and self-aware artists, using his frank sexual humor to shock the timid and create a no-limits space where life's issues could be discussed. I owe my lewd sense of humor and my sometimes boundary-pushing frankness to Big Ben. For example, imagine a thirteen-year-old boy being asked by his piano teacher, after playing a passage of music at the wrong speed, "How do you masturbate—adagio, allegro, or prestissimo?" I was shocked and thrilled that an adult was willing to talk to me like this.

Ben's response to hearing about my shrink's take on things? An immediate willingness to join my new, healthier rebellion against

Mom's control. And he had a brilliant escape plan. West Chester State College, where he was a professor, had a program that allowed early admissions to high school students before their senior year. These students could take courses during their first year at the college to satisfy required classes for their high school degree, which they'd receive at the end of their freshman year.

Ben's plan was offering me a way out of the house a year early, since I'd be able to move into one of the college's dormitories. With the target of September 1978 less than six months away, I'd finally be free from my mom's immediate oversight in short order.

Dr. Freud loved the idea.

When I announced to my parents that I intended to apply to West Chester's early admissions program, my mom was horrified that I was picking a state college instead of MIT or an equally prestigious school. She even threatened to withhold payment for my tuition, but I called her bluff by invoking the person who inspired her lofty goals for me. "Well, I'll just ask your dad for the money," I said. Letting Granddad Killian know about our family crisis would be something she'd avoid at all costs. She never repeated the threat.

Once West Chester accepted me, I noticed that their entrance paperwork had an option for having my grades mailed to my college mailbox. I promptly informed my mom that she would never see another report card or class grade of mine again, and surprise, surprise, I started getting good grades. Because when the grades were mine, and only mine to see, my classwork became a personal measure of progress, rather than a hurdle of meeting other people's expectations. In just a few months after Dr. Freud's profound diagnosis, and with a big assist from Big Ben, I had started to win control of my life in ways that helped me rather than hurt me.

This began a very slow process of raising my expectations. Even though I had a miserable 2.3 grade point average, barely equivalent to a C+, from my two years at Conestoga High School, I was hoping my piano skills could get me into a better school of music.

After a half-hour audition with some Bach, Brahms, and Ives, I was accepted at Oberlin Conservatory of Music the following year. But a few weeks before my first semester at Oberlin, I checked in with my brother Jes on the phone. This call would further shift the now ever-changing course of my life.

Jes was four years my senior and had recently graduated from Bowdoin College, quickly nabbing a job on Wall Street. As we caught up, Jes described his new life in New York City, working at Morgan Guaranty and riding his motorcycle over the Brooklyn Bridge to work. I thought I'd won my independence, but Jes's new young adult life was the pure freedom I craved.

"What are you going to be studying at Oberlin?" he asked.

"I guess music education," I replied. "I could be a high school band director . . ."

"Why would you pick that?" he asked, annoyed.

"Because It's probably the only thing I'd be good at," I said, only half joking.

"That's bullshit, Peter." His voice was rising. And serious. "You could do anything you want. I see these guys at the bank trading millions of dollars of bonds or currencies, and you're ten times smarter than any of them. Most of them are fucking idiots, and they're still making money hand over fist. You'd run rings around them."

Jes was delivering the epic pep talk I didn't know I needed. Everything had pointed down during high school—my grades, my self-confidence, and ultimately my ambition. I had forgotten my younger self . . . creative, cocky, and full of limitless dreams. Those memories came flooding back. Maybe Jes was right. Maybe I did have endless options in front of me.

"Oh, come on, Pete," he implored. "If I can do this, you can do this. You're one of the smartest guys I know."

With that simple call, my life's direction pivoted sharply. I started to dream again. And big.

Maybe I could follow my increasing passion for politics. Ever since I could remember, my parents and older brothers had discussed politics over dinner each night. As a kid, I avoided these debates, but as a teenager, I finally caught the political bug after Jimmy Carter was elected president in 1976, during my first year in high school. My dad, a lifelong Republican, had backed President Ford's reelection. My mom, a lifelong Democrat, had backed Carter. I'm forever grateful that my parents' split political leanings allowed me and my siblings to develop our own views from a far wider political spectrum than most of our peers, who just seemed to parrot their parents' one-sided opinions.

Carter's 1976 campaign had a Bernie Sanders–like feel to America's cynical youth after the political chaos the country had witnessed between Kennedy's assassination and Nixon's resignation. Carter was the guy with graying temples who came out of nowhere with talk of changing Washington's culture and our nation's direction. I adored him, and got hooked on all the twists and turns of his tumultuous years in office. Fully inspired, I leaped into our family's nightly dinner debates, and soon enough held my own against equally strong opinions.

I was developing my own political instincts and dreamed of using them someday, perhaps becoming an adviser to a president, a future version of, say, Carter adviser Hamilton Jordan, or . . . well, hell . . . maybe even being elected president myself.

Between the phone call with Jes and my first days at Oberlin, I dreamed up an entirely new life plan. I'd apply for a transfer from the conservatory to the college starting the following semester, major in economics, follow my brother to Wall Street, make a small fortune there in my twenties, self-finance my first congressional campaign in my early thirties, then the Senate in my late thirties or early forties, and finally the White House in my late forties. Kennedy had become president at forty-three, so my timeline seemed perfectly reasonable.

President Staley. Crazy, eh?

Amazingly, I would manage to stay on this new path, on schedule, for the next six years. Everything was going according to plan. And then a virus changed everything. But even if it hadn't, another monkey wrench was in my political future: that small issue of being homosexual.

3

SEVEN NIGHTS, EIGHT MEN

CAPTAIN KIRK WAS THE FIRST MAN to beam me up. Right around puberty, when I was about ten years old, *Star Trek* had gained new popularity in reruns. The occasional shirtless scenes with James Tiberius Kirk caught my attention. The even rarer shirtless scenes with Spock stirred me even more. And that scene with Sulu and his sword? Oh my!

How did I know I was gay? Pretty simple. A man's body gave me a boner. A woman's body didn't. The men of *Star Trek*, the boys in bathing suits on *Flipper*, and even the Professor on *Gilligan's Island* quickened my breathing just enough to let me know I liked men.

At the same time, the world around me was in total opposition to these thoughts. Boys liked girls, and girls liked boys, and men married women who had babies that would grow up to do the same thing. Period. And unfortunately it didn't end there: boys hated boys who liked boys. They used the word *fag* as a slur, and a fag was a boy who liked boys. All of this was taught on playgrounds from about third grade on.

It was obvious to me that my thoughts were so different that I should keep them to myself. They'd be my secret, then and for years to come. But it was a secret without shame. My logical mind—yet another reason to love Spock—saved me from the typical inner turmoil a young closeted gay boy feels. I knew that my attractions were immutable, a baked-in trait that I did not choose. Why feel shame or guilt about something I was born with? My quickened breathing at the sight of a shirtless man seemed as unchangeable to me as my brown eyes.

I was also protected by how shut I kept my closet door, sealed as tightly as the docking port to the USS *Enterprise.* I never told a soul. I didn't even act on the tantalizing thoughts orbiting my imagination. The opportunity never presented itself anyway, either because of my terribly bad luck—none of my close teenage friends turned out to be gay—or because I was unwilling to risk exposure in what seemed like a universally heterosexual world.

I've always had the ability to compartmentalize troublesome thoughts. I knew I liked boys, and would visualize a man's body when I masturbated. But I didn't waste time worrying about how society viewed my thoughts, or what would happen to me if someone found out. If I wasn't acting on it, how could they?

The secrecy and inaction inoculated me from paying a price. And on a good day, I might barely pass as straight. I was a music geek and had a subtle lisp, but those were the only clues. Then again, the Marlboro Man never had a flair for throwing parties. I covered by dabbling in sports—judo, wrestling—and dating girls. Karen Rettew was my first kiss, in junior high school. We even got to second base, awkwardly. The first time she saw a penis, it was mine. But as soon as she saw it, she raised her hands to both sides of her head and squealed, "I hate it!" Now *that* was traumatic.

After high school, and proms, and more girlfriends, and more awkward sex, it was obvious that only a change of location would save me. Thankfully, once I got to Oberlin College I went from a world that felt completely heterosexual to a world that was about 80 percent heterosexual, leaving plenty of room for exploration.

By the fall of 1979, Oberlin's Gay Union was a firmly entrenched student organization, and the college was already considered one of the most gay-friendly in the country. The union's Lesbian & Gay Dance was considered one of the social highlights of each semester, for gay and straight students alike.

During my first year, I tried to find my social footing among twenty-eight hundred students, but I kept my closet door firmly shut. Then in the fall of 1980, I saw some flyers around campus that caught my eye.

The Gay Union was advertising a night of LGBT videos and short films in one of the lecture halls that doubled as a movie theater. I figured I could sneak in after the lights were turned down, find a seat in the back, and see what I had been missing out on most of my life.

Courtesy of Oberlin College Archives

Boy, did I ever. Shortly after I slipped into a row of empty seats, a short educational film started called *Nick and Jon*. It was like a David Attenborough documentary describing the mating habits of chimpanzees, except it explicitly showed how gay men have sex, all explained by a narrator with an exaggerated baritone.

It started with a staged scene of a crowded cocktail party, with well-dressed twentysomethings of both sexes. One male actor held the gaze of another man standing across the room. The narrator explained the coded way gay men show interest in each other, by locking eyes far longer than straight men ever would. One of the men then crossed the room, and they had a quick chat and left the lame party for you-know-what. Cut to the next scene: a bedroom, where the two actors started kissing. The play-by-play commentary continued as they undressed each other, engaged in some oral sex, and topped it all off with—*Wait, are they really showing this in a schoolroom?*—a lovely moment of anal intercourse.

I had hit pay dirt.

The passionate kissing was enough. Once they started unbuttoning each other's shirts, I folded my legs and crossed my arms over my lap. *I have got to try this*, I thought. The decision was made, and it was as firm as my cock. But where? And with whom? How could I have sex with a man and still keep it secret?

I decided to apply to the London School of Economics for my junior year abroad, and asked my parents if I could visit London by myself over winter break to see the school and be interviewed by the admissions office.

Ever since I transferred to Oberlin, things with my mom had smoothed over somewhat, and she was thrilled with my plans to follow Jes to Wall Street. My parents quickly agreed to pay for my airfare to London. This one-week trip offered the total anonymity and independence I needed for a highly secretive mission of sexual exploration. I was determined to find a gay man and have sex with him.

With my mission set, I landed in London on the morning of January 8, 1981, one day before my twentieth birthday. After checking into a cheap bed-and-breakfast near Victoria Station, I set out on foot to explore the city. I kept my eyes peeled for something—anything—that might be gay or gay-related, like a bookstore or a pub. And I walked *for hours*. Around midafternoon, my fold-out map said I was in the Soho neighborhood. It was there I struck gold: a gay porn shop. I took a deep breath and walked in. It was empty except for a middle-aged guy behind the cash register. The shop was small, just a rectangular room lined with porn magazines and Betamax videotapes, and a turnstile in the back that led downstairs to who-knows-what.

I slowly browsed the magazines while working up the courage to chat with that guy behind the register. Each magazine would give me a hard-on, which kept me from turning toward him, so I stared at two pages filled with type instead of photos and tried to visualize dead babies until things were under control. Even though my jeans probably had a wet spot from precum, I turned toward the first probable homosexual I had ever met. I'll call him Nigel.

"Excuse me, sir. I'm new here and was wondering if you could recommend any places I could go dancing tonight."

Nigel smiled and with his lovely British accent said, "Well, it depends on what you're looking for. Are you looking for guys *my* age? Are you looking for guys *your* age?"

Nigel looked old to nineteen-year-old me, probably over thirty. Still, he was a handsome bloke. "Um, maybe my age, I guess," I said with an innocent and lost look, trying not to offend.

"Oh, well I know the perfect place. You'll want to go to Heaven. It's the hottest gay dance club in Europe, and it's filled with guys your age."

My eyes widened. "Sounds great!" I started to open my map. "Can you show me how to get there?"

"It's a little tricky to find. If you'd like, I was thinking of going myself tonight. We could meet up around 11:00 PM at a pub nearby, have some pints, and then walk over to the club together."

Well gosh golly, these Brits are friendly, I thought. "Really? I'd love that!" I said as we both smiled broadly.

Heaven is literally on the other side of the tracks—the underside, to be exact, in the Adelphi Arches beneath Charing Cross railway station. Nigel wasn't lying: Heaven was hard to find. I remember walking down the steps past its front door like it was yesterday. After paying our entrance fee, Nigel and I waited in a long coat-check line. Here I was, a teenage Yank, surrounded by sweaty, shirtless young Brits walking off the dance floor to take a piss. The stares and locked eyes and glistening pecs thrilled me. I was new meat, fresh off the plane. I couldn't stop smiling. I was in heaven at Heaven.

Before long, I was shirtless and sweaty, feeling the beats, raising my arms with hundreds of other men, singing along with Diana Ross to "I'm Coming Out." A gay dance floor can summon magic—a tribal sense of communal love.

I had found my people.

Less than twenty-four hours after landing in London, some extraordinary traveler's luck had brought me just one step away from accomplishing my goal of sleeping with a man. And I had so many men to choose from! Even though I had stuck pretty close to Nigel most of the night, he didn't seem to mind at all when other guys showed interest, chatted me up, or sidled up to me on the dance floor. This is probably why I had grown so comfortable with Nigel. *He* brought me here. His hospitality had been so lovely, and I figured that a handsome older man who worked in a porn shop was guaranteed to have the required experience to make my first time special. So I, gentleman that I can sometimes be, went home with the man who brung me.

As we were climbing the stairs to his flat, Nigel warned me about the mess. "My main occupation is a dressmaker. I make dresses for drag queens," he said.

His small living room had a couple of dresses in production, with pieces and half forms strewn about, patterns on the floor, and sequins and glitter everywhere. It looked like a fairy had thrown up. Any way you cut it, I was in the gayest flat in London. But before I could even start worrying about what moves to make to accomplish my mission, Nigel took charge.

"Hey, you," he said with a mischievous smile.

Nigel put his arm around my waist, pulling me toward him, then the other hand went behind my neck as he moved in for a kiss. Nothing felt forced. His hands and mouth could sense my eagerness, and every move thrilled me. His tongue—a man's tongue—had none of the awkwardness or hesitations of the girls I had French-kissed in high school. His kiss was penetration, a new and ecstatic sensation that we tried to keep going, uninterrupted, all the while pulling off each other's clothes, our giggling filling the room as we fumbled with a button . . . or a buckle . . . or a shoe . . .

Nigel pulled me close, shuffling us backward into his bedroom, which was as wonderfully gay as his living room, filled with more dresses and sequins, and a queen-sized bed with a plush, red velvet Victorian headboard. I got a master class in frottage as we merged, naked on that bed. By the time he went down on my cock, I was going nuts. He looked up at my reaction, bringing me close, then slowed down to prolong the ecstasy. "I'm going to come," I said, arching my back. He wanted to watch and finished me with his hand. The first spurt surprised us both, vaulting past my head and hitting the velvet on his headboard.

"My, my," he chuckled.

"Oops," I laughed.

"Hmm, how old are you?" he asked.

"Oh shit, what time is it?" I asked back.

"It's about one thirty."

"I'm twenty! I just turned twenty at midnight."

"Happy birthday!" he said. "I hope you don't mind me asking, but was this your first time?"

"Um, yeah, was I that obvious?"

"No, no, no, you were wonderful. I just had an inkling. You seemed to enjoy it."

"Well, duh. I hope we're not done," I said.

"Would you like to spend the night?"

I nodded, and this time I leaned in to kiss him.

In the morning, Nigel gave me a short list of other gay pubs to visit during my stay and wished me good luck with exploring gay London.

My second day was busy. I had an appointment at the London School of Economics, which went fine, but I had also set up time to visit with one of Ben Whitten's former piano students. Robert was studying at a prestigious music school in London and was about five years my senior. When we made the arrangements to meet, he had suggested afternoon tea in his single-room flat in a residence hall for graduates and postdocs.

After the night before, I arrived with a skip in my step. My gaydar was on high alert, and within a minute or two of chatting with Robert, I felt comfortable enough to come out to him, blabbing about my sexual escapades the night before. I was right to trust him. He was on my team, and warmly embraced my need for a friendly ear. I had found even more than I'd set out to on this trip: my first gay mentor, and Robert kept pace with my bold revelations.

He even pushed them further. "Have you had anal sex yet?" he asked.

"No—it kinda scares me."

"Well, don't deny yourself for long. When done right, it can be a beautiful way to bond."

"Wow, tell me more," I said.

Robert pressed on, offering a gentle and specific verbal lesson on how to get fucked for the first time. He was teaching about something he obviously loved, and I couldn't believe my luck. With the mission to have sex with a man accomplished earlier than expected, I was now embarking on what would be a seven-night crash course in gay sex.

Armed with Robert's knowledge, I returned to Heaven that night for more lessons. Another man. Another flat. He wanted me inside him, so I topped for the first time. I liked it, he *loved* it. Another lesson learned.

I visited Nigel every afternoon in the porn shop, where he graciously gave me more dating advice as I entertained him with my dishy exploits from the night before. Nigel soon introduced me to a gorgeous redhead from Ireland. Tall, lanky, and in his late twenties, he became Number 3. He wanted to fuck me. But, as my mentor advised, I told him it was my first time. He went slow. *Breathe. Relax. More.* . . . I could hear my mentor's sage words. *Thank you, Robert*, I thought. And boy, was he right.

The next night, at a pub of Nigel's recommending, I saw my first drag performer. At any other time, that would have been the highlight of my day, but I also found man Number 4, and learned a new position and new techniques.

Every night, another lesson.

Another man.

Another flat.

On my final night in London, I returned to Heaven. After working up a sweat on the dance floor, I fixed my eyes on a rare sight in the UK in 1981: a very buff young gay man who obviously lived half his days in a gym.

John Taylor returned my stare. He was shirtless, slightly hairy, joyously sweaty—and, my god, those pecs! Unlike the six sexy men before him, John had a car and lived on the outskirts of London. "By the way, I have a boyfriend at home," he said during the drive there.

"Oh," I replied.

"Don't worry—we have a guest bedroom. We'll use that tonight, and I'll introduce you to Paul in the morning."

"I'll follow your lead," I said.

This was novel—tiptoeing into a house with a guy I had just met so as not to wake his boyfriend. None of my new mentors in London had prepared me for this. Still, the sex with John was great, even though we had to keep our volume in check.

In the morning, we slowly unspooned. "Let me get the kettle going for tea and wake Paul up," John said. "I'll come and get you once he's ready." Delightful. Until I soon heard the muffled domestic negotiations in the next room, none of which sounded happy.

John returned to the guest bedroom quickly. I tensed up.

"All right, then, you ready to meet Paul?"

Not really, I thought.

"He's a little grumpy this morning, but I'm sure you can cheer him up. No need to get dressed. Just your underwear is enough."

I slipped on my white briefs and followed John. We entered the adjoining bedroom together.

"Paul, this is Peter. Peter, this is Paul," John announced.

"So you're the Yank John snagged last night, are you?" Paul asked.

"The very one," I said as he looked me up and down. Then down again.

"Jump in," John said, as he lifted the bed covers. "You'll freeze standing there in just your knickers. We'll warm you up." Paul looked OK with it. He was slightly older than John, with a handsome head of prematurely gray hair. And unlike John, he had a traditional English body: slender, pale, undefined.

My incredible week in London was coming to an end, but it was hard to feel sorry for myself while I was sandwiched between

Number 7 and Number 8. And they had one more lesson to teach
me—how to make a threesome work. Even to a newb like me, the
rules seemed clear enough: Don't play favorites, even if you have one.
Beyond that, just enjoy the ride. And who doesn't enjoy being the
center of attention?

I was, at that moment, something fresh in *their* sex life, too. The
ingredient that could either ruin the stew or spice it up. But this
meal sated us all. Not only was the sex great, but by the time we all
climaxed there were smiles and giggles all around.

During the post-romp tea and cigarettes, I found that the once-
intimidating Number 8 shared my love of politics. We even bonded
over our negative views of Thatcher and Reagan.

Sadly, I had a flight to catch, or I would have stayed in that bed
for days. I'd departed Oberlin in December as a homosexual virgin,
and one month later I returned to Oberlin as a horny and experienced
gay slut, though still a closeted one.

When I returned to London in September for my junior year
abroad, I picked up where I left off: the threesome with Number 7
and Number . . .

With John and Paul.

For six days and nights a week, I was the joke-cracking, straight-
pretending Yank who drank pints of lager and pub-hopped with my
straight buddies from LSE's Rosebery Hall. But on most Saturday
nights, I slipped away and took a long Tube ride to rejoin the threesome. John and Paul would save that week's episode of *Brideshead
Revisited* on their Betamax VCR, and slowly coaxed me into loving
spicy Indian curry from the local takeout—bhuna, then Madras, and
finally vindaloo. We'd watch the flirtations between a very young
Jeremy Irons and Anthony Andrews, and once the show ended, while
our endorphins were still high from the vindaloo, we'd start kissing
and undressing on the couch, eventually moving to the bedroom. I'd
always spend the night between them, often triple-spooned.

A year earlier, if you'd told me that my youthful, yearning fantasy would become a reality, I'd have told you that you were high. Several years after those tender, formative encounters, a sudden, inexplicably cruel intruder would shift my reality again.

John would die from AIDS. But Paul survived him and has a new partner now. We have remained in touch ever since. Our origin story was beautiful, as were the mentors and one-night stands, and dancing with my new tribe at Heaven.

On that London trip, I became the adult realization of my being, transforming from an inquisitive kid who could only dream of being accepted in the ways I now was, and have been since.

4

INNOCENCE LOST

—————

MY LAST WEEKS AT OBERLIN WERE PURE JOY. It was the college's winter term, when they let students pick a project to work on during the month of January. I have no memory of whatever project I did (or most likely didn't do). But I remember a lot of weed and sex.

Having lived, since my first year, in one of Oberlin's ugliest dorms, East Hall, I was determined to experience one of the campus's alternative housing options during winter term. We had a hippie-dippie, student-run not-for-profit called the Oberlin Student Cooperative Association that ran housing and dining options, called co-ops, for nearly one quarter of the student body. With a Queen Anne–style turret and wraparound porch, Tank Hall was the college's most beautiful co-op, and also its hippiest, as if frozen in time from Oberlin's late '60s / early '70s counterculture years. Built in 1897 to house the children of missionaries traveling abroad, it still had the feel of an unstaffed orphanage, with its musty air and tiny rooms.

I was finally coming out as gay to some of my close school friends, including Tracey Tanenbaum, my closest. With long, gorgeous brown hair on a slender frame, she was confident, outspoken, and Jewish.

Born and raised in New York City, she was a portent of the vast majority of my future friends. And now I was looking for her to share my amazing news.

With less than two weeks before I was set to return home to an uncertain future in Pennsylvania, I'd gotten one last letter from the handful of Wall Street firms I had interviewed with in the fall—all the previous letters had been rejections. Now I was running across campus to show Tracey the job offer letter from Morgan Guaranty Trust Co. of New York, considered the Harvard of Wall Street— old, stuffy, and full of itself, but revered by all the other banks.

Tracey and I clasped hands in the air and danced around the circular living room under that gorgeous turret, reading the letter again and again.

"What are you two celebrating?"

I locked eyes with the young man who must have been on his way somewhere until our joy stopped him in his tracks, leaving genuine bemusement in those gorgeous dark brown eyes. Instead of looking away, his eyes locked with mine in a knowing intensity.

Jef Mittleman, still in his junior year, was tall and lean, with a thick mop of straight brown hair that covered his forehead—like the early Beatles—and lengthy sideburns that framed a long face with thin lips, which often formed a guilty-looking smile.

As we explained our celebration, he sat down to join us, pretending to be enthralled. We kept locking eyes. When I looked over at Tracey, she gave me a knowing smile, realizing a connection was afoot. She made up some excuse about work she needed to do in her room. Tracey hugged me and then our new friend before leaving us alone, knowing she'd get all the details later.

"You wanna get stoned?" Jef asked.

His pot was back in his dorm room at Dascomb Hall, another sterile three-story brick dormitory, much like East Hall. But Jef's room was a surprising oasis. His brick walls were covered with his own art:

simple silkscreens of abstract torsos, black-and-white photos of places in Oberlin that caught his eye, and a few self-portraits, close-ups of his face with its handsome contours. There were hanging printed fabrics, candles, beads, and clutter—the room of a stoner artist, equipped with a comforter-covered mattress on the carpeted floor. It was warm, lived-in, and inviting.

We got very stoned and took our time. Jef was guiding me into his free-spirited world, so I gladly let him lead. We very slowly explored each other's bodies, with running commentary that would make us both giggle, pausing only to flip the mixtapes of his laid-back favorites—Guthrie, Janis Joplin, Simon & Garfunkel, and the like.

I loved his torso—very lean, nothing built up, but still highly defined, like a swimmer's. It was mostly hairless, except for faint curly patches around his nipples and a thin line, starting slightly above his belly button, down to his pubic hair.

The exploration lasted three hours. By the end, we were covered in sweat. Jef gave me an extra bathrobe, grabbed his toiletry bag, and pulled me along for a speedy, giggle-filled walk to the coed bathroom down the hall. With the curtain pulled, our shower added another hour of bliss. Whenever someone else entered the bathroom, we'd just quietly kiss.

My strongest memory from that steam-filled shower was brushing each other's teeth—his suggestion, of course. We skipped spitting out the toothpaste, and simply kissed under the water until it was all gone.

I couldn't see Jef enough during my last week at Oberlin. We were the epitome of young lust, spending every night together, and most of our days. I even met his parents; they lived just off campus. Jef's father was a science professor at the college.

The day before I left, Jef asked me to help him with one of his art projects. It had just snowed, and he wanted some black-and-white pictures of himself in the secluded woods of the Oberlin Arboretum. We found a large fallen tree that crossed Plum Creek, its trunk now carpeted with snow. Once I was in position, Jef quickly stripped off all his clothes and his boots. As I snapped the camera's shutter, he slowly made his way across the creek, like a folklore fairy, unaffected by the cold, at peace with his world.

In April 1983, when I started the first intimidating days inside the hermetically sealed offices at Morgan's headquarters, I yearned to relive those dreamlike moments with Jef, if only as an escape. But first I had to learn how to make a living in a cutthroat industry and explore my new home city.

It helped that I felt rich and independent. My starting salary was $25,970 a year, which felt like a fortune. I found a studio apartment for $661 a month, just a five-minute walk from work. My childhood grand piano gobbled up one-third of my new living space, though I seldom had the time or energy to play it.

My first few months at the bank were filled with textbooks and professors from Harvard and Yale. Morgan's six-month commercial bank training program was like a master's degree in business, focused on the financial sector. Everyone was guaranteed placement within one of the bank's divisions after the program ended. But you had to do another round of interviews, rejections and all, to find your first job within the bank. It was competitive and grueling. I usually rebelled against textbooks and reading assignments, but this was time-limited and crucial to my future, so I knuckled down.

Thankfully, the weekends were still my own. I'd often spend Saturdays exploring Lower Manhattan by foot, from Maiden Lane to the shops beneath the World Trade Center, up through Tribeca and SoHo, and every shop and bar along both sides of Christopher Street. But my favorite stretch was the three blocks of St. Mark's Place between Third Avenue and Avenue A, from Boy Bar—my second favorite gay bar after a dive called the Bar—and Tompkins Square Park, where I'd lie out in the sun and people-watch.

With a nice beer buzz from the Bar, I'd head south past all the restaurant supply stores, then the lighting stores along the Bowery, with a side trip to Little Italy, and finally through the bustle of Chinatown toward the smells of the Fulton Fish Market, just blocks from home. After dinner and some rest, I'd often set out again, this time to Greenwich Village and the East Village, where I'd drink, play some pool, flirt, and find someone's bed.

On one of those nighttime walks, near the end of my first summer, some joyous sounds drew me to a new experience. I was walking up Seventh Avenue, just before Christopher Street, and heard a crowd of people singing a raucous version of "As Long as He Needs Me" from *Oliver!*, led by a talented pianist. They were belting their hearts out, but in tune and with harmonies.

I walked toward the singing, and for a few minutes, I felt like Ingrid Bergman walking into Rick's Café Américain in *Casablanca*, gliding down the steps into a smoke-filled piano bar. The Duplex was old New York, from Greenwich Village's glory days in the 1950s. The spirits were high, the ceiling was low, and a hardwood bar ran along the wall to the right. Round, tightly packed café tables dotted the room. The slightly elevated stage in the back was scarcely big enough for the upright piano, stool, and mic stand that filled it.

I found a seat in the corner farthest from the stage and soaked it all in. It was open mic night, and folks from the crowd randomly took turns trying to best each other in front of a very discerning audience packed with theater queens. The singing was thrilling, which made sense when I later learned that most of them were Broadway chorus members hoping for their breakout moment.

When my first beer ran low, another arrived. The waitress told me it was on the house, compliments of the bartender, Curtis, whom she pointed to. He was gorgeous in a goofy way, with light brown hair, dimples, and a sexy, bigger-than-average nose. I raised my glass to him and mouthed a thank-you, and he winked back at me while preparing someone's cocktail.

The drink and wink practically made my year. I downed a few gulps, then weaved my way to the bar to thank him up close. After some flirtatious chitchat, he asked if I could hang around until closing. It was around 11:00 PM, but they wouldn't close until 2:00 AM. I would have waited until 7:00 AM if asked.

Curtis lived only two blocks away on West Fourth Street, between West Tenth and Charles. One of the Village's cute quirks is that Fourth and Tenth Streets intersect, and one of Curtis's cute quirks is that he not only worked at the Duplex, he lived in one, too. Thankfully, his roommate from the loft at the top of the stairs was away.

Curtis Randall was his stage name; unbeknownst to me, I was hooking up with my first of many struggling caterer/waiter/bartender/actors in New York, a special breed that offers drama and beauty to the city's unique gay scene. His real name was Curtis Randel Oetjen, and we were both twenty-two years old. Over the next two weeks we attempted every position imaginable in every non-loft inch of his apartment, including the stairs, which were conveniently bordered by a mirrored wall that allowed us to watch our own gymnastics.

Alas, our half-month relationship ended abruptly after our umpteenth political argument. Curtis was a dedicated socialist, and I loved our semi-heated debates—he was heated, I wasn't—which reminded me of Oberlin. But with an ideological red line I could only admire, Curtis told me he couldn't become boyfriends with a Wall Street banker.

It was great while it lasted. I hadn't fallen in love yet, so the parting was easy if you don't count the painful sores from some sort of sexually transmitted disease that emerged soon after. Even though Morgan Guaranty had an in-house doctor, there was no way I was going to risk outing myself to see him for this.

Over the summer, I met an older gay guy who lived just around the corner from me. Rick Gillette was my first gay mentor, back when our community's collective closet necessitated a beautiful cross-generational pollination of knowledge. Younger guys would learn the ropes from the older guys, and Rick was often my guide, along with Stephen Racaza, a gentle Filipino man who introduced me to the gay Hamptons. Rick survived the AIDS years. Stephen did not.

With my undiagnosed STD, I asked Rick if he knew of any gay doctors in the city. Thankfully, his own doctor was, and in no time, I was being poked and prodded by Dr. Daniel William.

My brief but spectacular sex life in New York City came crashing down with my herpes diagnosis. There was a new prescription cream to treat it, but that only reduced the duration of my monthly outbreaks. Fearing I could spread the infection to others, I stopped bottoming. Dr. William said that an oral version of the drug was in human studies, so I hung my future sexual hopes on those.

Meanwhile, Morgan Guaranty kept me on my toes. As the training program wound down, I started interviewing at all the major market trading desks—foreign exchange, equities, municipal bonds, and US government bonds. The timing was perfect. President Reagan was running up huge budget deficits, and the Federal Reserve was trying to snuff out inflation, resulting in highly volatile interest rates. The US government bond market had become Wall Street's rowdiest and most profitable sandbox to play in.

I was still viewing my banking job as a financial stepping-stone to a career in politics, so bond trading, with its huge bonuses, looked like the fastest way to make that step. The top bond traders on the street were paid more than their CEOs. They were the kings of Wall Street in the '80s, placing multibillion-dollar bets with borrowed money. And the good ones were poached between firms like professional baseball players.

My interview with Tommy Kalaris, the new head of Morgan's US government bond trading floor, went well. We clicked. Maybe it was his age. At twenty-seven, he was only five years older than I was—a quickly rising star within the bank.

I got the job. Now I just had to figure out how to actually make money trading bonds.

———— ————

Morgan Guaranty's bond traders and sales force worked in a kind of amphitheater on the sixth floor of 15 Broad Street, with windows we rarely looked out of facing the New York Stock Exchange. The lowest level of the trading floor was in the middle—we called it the pit. It was where the highest-volume, most profitable traders had their desks. Behind them, one level up, were intermediate-volume traders, and on another level behind them, like the cheap seats at a baseball stadium, were the traders with low-volume portfolios. More rows of desks were a step up from the pit on the other side, with all the salespeople facing the traders, like competing armies. And in a sense they were. The traders wanted to make profits on all their trades and positions, and the salespeople wanted to get the best possible price for their clients.

You'd think there would be some sort of rarefied training program for new bond traders before they start playing with millions of dollars of the bank's money. Not back then. I was given a trading desk in the back row and told to watch and learn from the guy sitting next to me.

At thirty-nine, Bill Schreiner was one of the oldest traders on the floor and seemed perfectly content placing arbitrage trades from the quieter row. To me, he seemed like the calmest person in the room, with his big, nerdy eyeglasses and constant dry-witted quips about the "dumb jocks" down in the pit.

Schreiner explained the shortest end of the yield curve to me—all the notes and bonds that had less than one year until they matured, which were called short-shorts. It was the quietest end of the market and a perfect place to learn things without taking huge risks. Bill was welcoming.

My new trading desk was intimidating. On its left side were stacked six small green CRT screens filled with bid and ask prices on all the short-short bonds. Below those sat a Monroe Bond Trader, which was just a huge calculator that crunched yields based on price, and vice versa. Dozens of direct-line phone buttons lined the back wall of the desk like a giant switchboard, along with two black phone handsets for managing a couple of calls at once, one in each ear. An early IBM personal desktop computer—an XT—sat on the right side of the desk.

Given the low volume of trades I started with, I kept myself busy by geeking out on some of the textbooks on the floor, including Marcia Stigum's *Money Market Calculations*, and this led to an aha moment. Buried in her dense chapters, Stigum described a small flaw in the standard street formula for calculating yields on soon-to-mature bonds—the stuff I was learning to trade. Amazingly, the flawed formula was built into the Monroe Bond Traders on every trader's desk.

I asked Schreiner if he or anyone else in the bond market tried to profit off these small miscalculations. He said no. The short-shorts are considered the graveyard of the bond market—too sleepy to bother with. "Pitch the idea to Kalaris," Schreiner suggested.

So I spent a few days creating a program on my IBM desktop that used Stigum's more accurate yield formula, allowing me to bypass my flawed Monroe calculator, then wrote up a five-page memo to Kalaris describing my find and my fix and how we could profit from both.

Kalaris was surprised and impressed. "Place some bets," he said.

Over time, my arbitrage trades started paying off, adding a few million dollars each year to the bank's bottom line. I had my choice of four boutique bond-brokerage firms to choose from to make these trades. Each of these firms supplied the little green screens stacked on my desk and provided an assigned broker that I had a direct phone line to. They all charged the same fractional commissions, so the service they provided was basically identical. That's where each broker's expense account came into play. Traders were wined and dined and lavished with other freebies, each broker trying to out-wine and out-dine the other, hoping to lure the trader into using the most generous broker when it was time to place big trades. Somehow this was all legal.

When I started placing my first trades, all four of my assigned brokers asked me out to glad-handing dinners at expensive downtown restaurants. Three were like the dumb jocks I couldn't relate to in junior high. The fourth, Lou Olivieri at Garban, was all sweetness and dry humor. Italian and married with two kids, Lou had an effortless conversational style, the opposite to the other brokers' used-car-salesmen approach. Only later would we understand why we had bonded so effortlessly—we were both closeted gay men. As I started trading exclusively through Garban, Lou and I spent hours on the phone together, dishing about our new work lives, sharing theater and movie tips, and quickly falling into a friendship limited only by our similar secrets.

Our careers rose in tandem. As I placed ever-larger trades, Lou's star rose within Garban. Short-short traders and their assigned brokers rarely made much money, but we were breaking that mold. Even though our friendship sealed the deal for which brokerage house I would place trades through, Garban kept refilling Lou's expense account to let us both know they appreciated the business.

Lou and I viewed his growing piggy bank as our ultimate Wall Street perk. Other traders visited strip clubs with their brokers, ordering bottles of Cristal champagne and doing lines of cocaine, but Lou and I would dine at the city's most glamorous restaurants, like our favorite, the Quilted Giraffe. And while other traders would attend the Super Bowl, I'd take Ben Whitten, my former piano teacher, to see the last performance of Leontyne Price in *Aida*, or double-date with Lou and his wife to Bruce Springsteen's Born in the U.S.A. Tour, or the Live Aid concert in Philadelphia.

But by late 1984, regardless of the perks, I was hating my Wall Street life. The toxic masculinity on the trading floor felt Darwinian. Adapt or die.

If you didn't tell a salesman to fuck off after he screamed at you for not giving him a better price, then the entire sales force would walk all over you. If you didn't play along with the sexism and homophobia that stunk up the trading floor like a high school locker room, you'd soon find yourself becoming that quiet guy on the bench whom the football team picked on.

So I adapted. I yelled back. I slammed my phone on the desk when a trade went sour. I told others to fuck off. And when I got back to my apartment at night, I'd replay moments from that day when I was the kind of asshole I abhorred. To counter it all, I looked for otherworldly escapes, moments when I could completely wash away the Wall Street dirt from my skin.

After Jef Mittleman graduated from Oberlin in '84, he found odd jobs around the country and then he'd invite me to explore his temporary, new surroundings for a weekend. As soon as the market closed on a Friday, I'd grab the bus to Newark Airport. People Express Airlines was my carrier of choice—you'd just jump on the next available flight to one of its many destinations, grab any seat, and pay the flight attendant fifty dollars cash after you were in the air.

That's how I found myself skinny-dipping with Jef at Hardscrabble Falls in the wooded hills outside Cookeville, Tennessee. He was doing an internship with a local herbalist named Hector Black, a closeted fifty-year-old Quaker. God knows how or where they met.

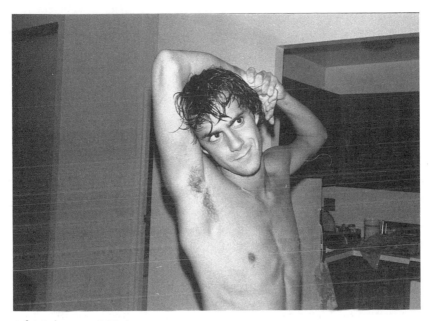

Jef Mittleman, 1984.

After flying into Nashville, I rented a car for the drive to Jef's cabin in the woods. We popped some Quaaludes—my first time, his umpteenth—then walked to the hidden falls up the hill, far from any roads. Quaaludes had just been internationally banned and soon vanished from the underground market. Little did I know we were enjoying their good-bye party.

Alone at the base of the falls, we made love near its spray on an outcrop of sun-warmed limestone. Then we took turns snapping pictures of each other climbing up the falls, naked, some with cold water shrinkage, some with youthful erections. I still have these captured memories in a shoebox at home.

A few months later, after further soul-suffering on the caustic trading floor, laughing along to jokes belittling everyone who wasn't us, including fags, and defending my turf with more fuck-yous, I sought out Jef even more. He had moved on to his next dead-end job, this one on Martha's Vineyard. This time, Jef introduced me to mescaline, a psychedelic found naturally in the peyote cactus.

As the sun set on the white-and-orange clay slopes of the Aquinnah Cliffs bordering Gay Head beach, we were naked again, painting each other's faces, limbs, and torsos with the clay's various shades, like two hippies at a gay version of Woodstock. We were invited to a bonfire just down the beach, joining a dozen other nudists for beer, grilled fish, and vegetables.

We overslept the next day, and I almost missed my sad flight home. These drug-filled escapes with Jef are some of the most beautiful memories of my youth—shedding my straight guy's coat and tie on the walk home from Morgan, then finding my naked, flower-child self the next day, lying beside a beautiful man amid nature's trippy wonders. Our liberated explorations got me through those otherwise stifling years.

In August 1985, another Oberlin fave, Tracey, helped me reclaim some self and sanity as well. We traveled to Amsterdam and Copenhagen together, falling in love with both cities. I fell hard for a Dutch guy my same age and with my same name. Peter vowed to visit me back in New York in the months ahead. And as most American gay men who travel to Europe quickly find out, if you invite your new lust to visit you, they'll show up at your doorstep within weeks, often with no return date in mind.

Peter Launy arrived in early November and hoped to stay at least a month. He wasn't a typical Dutchman. He was Jewish, for one, on his mother's side, and his father was from Spain. Peter had black hair, a dark complexion, and sexy facial stubble, tight and uniform, between shaves.

Although I loved coming home to Peter after work, I kept the relationship hidden. Letting my colleagues know was out of the question— I'd lose my job. And since I didn't know how long the relationship would last, it was too easy to push back a day of reckoning with my family.

Thanksgiving was approaching. I'd have to leave Peter in New York for the annual family gathering in Pennsylvania. So, to lessen the sting, I booked mid-November airline tickets to Orlando. Peter was dying to see Disney World, and that would more than make up for missing out on all the fun of watching my siblings stuff their faces with mashed potatoes.

On the Monday before we left, we joined thirty-four million Americans to watch the first television movie about AIDS. NBC's *An Early Frost* had caused a huge public stir before it aired. Rock Hudson had died of AIDS a month before, and the country was going through waves of stigma and fear about the not-so-new virus. Before the Hudson shocker, HIV had seemed as hidden as homosexuality was supposed to be. But now? AIDS seemed to be everywhere, and it was always fatal. Advertisers refused to purchase commercial time for the broadcast, worried about associating their brand with a disease killing the country's most despised minority, gay men. The controversy and morbid curiosity led to blockbuster ratings. Everyone wanted to see what the advertisers were too afraid to touch.

Peter and I certainly did. AIDS still seemed distant to us both. We didn't know anyone who was ill or had died. We were much more interested in seeing how gay men would be portrayed on network TV. Frankly, we were so young and dismissive of larger concerns that the one big takeaway we agreed on was that Aidan Quinn, who portrayed the closeted gay man who faced an AIDS diagnosis, was drop-dead gorgeous.

A seemingly less important takeaway was that the bad cough I had mimicked Quinn's foreboding cough from PCP pneumonia. As I broke into a bad hack of my own, Peter joked, "You sound just like him," pointing to the TV.

"OK, OK, I'll go see my doctor," I replied, having ignored the persistent cough for long enough.

Dan William's office was as quiet and efficient as it had been since finding him two years earlier. Little did I know, it was one of the many ground zero spaces in the city for treating AIDS patients. He had already lost dozens of gay men in his care, and dozens more were dealing with the various illnesses that killed people with AIDS.

So, when any of his previously healthy gay patients came in for an appointment with any issue, even a cold, William discovered a way to identify early signs of HIV, just in case. He'd run a CBC, a complete blood count test, the most basic and common blood work used to judge a person's overall health. If it came back showing a low white blood cell count, it set off an alarm for him. HIV attacks and kills off T4 cells, a kind of white blood cell.

Less than forty-eight hours after the prompt from Aidan Quinn's cough, I was saying "Ah" as Dr. William held my tongue down with his depressor, followed by a blood draw for the CBC.

"It's probably just a bad cold," he said.

Two days later, on Friday, November 15, I was at my trading desk, counting down the hours until Peter and I would take off from La Guardia Airport for our Florida minivacation. Then, the phone rang. It was Bob Freedman, Dr. William's office manager and boyfriend. There was an abnormality in my blood work, he said, and they wanted me back for more tests.

I was in my no-bullshit bond trader mode and pressed for more info. Freedman said I had a low white blood cell count. I pressed further: What might that mean?

He told me the doctor would discuss all that when I came in. "I'm a big boy, Bob," I replied. "You can tell me now." Finally, he caved, admitting that the low white blood cell count they saw in my results was the same thing that they saw in their patients with HIV.

In an instant, years of easy dismissiveness about my chance of getting HIV just vanished. *That's it*, I thought. *That's what I have.* My prior sense of invulnerability was swallowed by the humble realization that of course this could happen to me. I was a gay man. In New York City. In 1985.

Little warnings quickly came flooding back, like when my brother Chris asked me about AIDS two years earlier, about a week before I arrived in New York. In fact, he asked me if I was gay, and I flatly denied it. He knew someone at the Rhode Island School of Design who had just died from the disease, and he had harbored some suspicions about my sexuality.

I remembered the wild sex with Curtis and the STD that shut me down sexually. *Was that when it happened?*

I told Kalaris I had to leave work early for a family emergency and jumped on the subway to Dr. William's office. One vial of blood was drawn for a T lymphocyte subset assay to see if I had a low T4 cell count. Another vial was drawn and handed back to me. I was told to deliver it to the New York City Department of Health's retrovirology and immunobiology laboratory across from Bellevue Hospital on First Avenue.

The T4 count would come back in a few days. The second blood vial was for the new test that looked for antibodies to HTLV-III/LAV, the two acronyms given by the American and French scientists who both claimed to have discovered the virus that causes AIDS.

After dropping off the vial of blood, I returned to my apartment and told Peter I probably had HIV. He had heard even less about AIDS in Amsterdam than I had here, and he wasn't sure how to react at first. He realized it was serious, but only because I sounded panicked. I wasn't sure if he even believed me when I told him it might kill me, until he asked if we should cancel our trip to Florida.

"No," I replied. "We need the distraction until my next test results come back."

After we arrived at La Guardia, I scanned the newsstand there for stories about AIDS and caught a lucky break. The just-released December issue of *Discover* magazine had a cover story titled "Special Report: AIDS, the Latest Scientific Facts," which I devoured on the flight down, rereading each paragraph until fully understood before proceeding to the next. The article was remarkably comprehensive, heavy on the science, but written for the magazine's general audience. Within hours of finding out I might have HIV, I had learned it was a retrovirus, meaning its genetic code was stored in RNA, not DNA. It was coated with proteins that could latch onto specific receptors on T4 cells (later called CD4 cells), considered the master cells of the immune system, like a conductor that tells all the other immune cells what to do.

I learned about reverse transcriptase, the enzyme used by the virus to copy its RNA into DNA before splicing itself into the T4 cell's DNA. At this point, the cell is turned into a virus factory, flooding your body with HIV, overrunning all the conductors, and destroying your immune system. Other diseases and pathogens, like *Pneumocystis carinii* pneumonia (PCP), toxoplasmosis, and Kaposi's sarcoma (KS), would then swoop in for the kill. It was presumed that AIDS was nearly 100 percent fatal. More than fourteen thousand Americans had been diagnosed with it by the time the article went to press. Over half of them had already died.

It was dark when we landed in Orlando. After checking into our hotel just outside Disney World, we ritualistically unpacked and moved our toiletry bags to either side of the bathroom sink. I sat on the end of the bed, and the day finally sunk in. My eyes welled up. Even though Peter certainly knew, he gently asked me what was wrong. I broke down sobbing in his arms, telling him my worst fears: that I'd lose everything—him, my job, my life.

If I had HIV, there was no getting rid of it. The one thought I couldn't shake was that the virus genetically integrated itself into your cells. It became part of you. Gene therapy didn't exist outside of sci-fi novels. I would not live long enough to see a cure.

But the hopelessness frightened me, too. It could only make things worse. *No more tears*, I thought. *Compartmentalize death. Search for ways to live a bit longer.*

The next day Peter and I strolled through the Magic Kingdom. We rode some rides and took pictures of each other, gamely smiling with Snow White, Mickey Mouse, and two of the Three Little Pigs. And two days later, we stood outside the Kennedy Space Center Visitor Complex while I dialed my doctor's office from a pay phone next to the Rocket Garden. I stared at Delta, Mercury, and Gemini rockets while Bob Freedman read and explained my lab results.

My fears were confirmed: I had only 351 T4 cells per cubic millimeter of blood. Healthy people have counts between 500 and 1,500. Another lymphocyte, called T8 cells, often surges during HIV infection. A healthy person usually has fewer of these cells than T4 cells. I had 823 T8 cells. This inverted ratio of T4 and T8 cells was a distinct marker of HIV infection.

The antibody test result that came back two weeks later was anticlimactic, showing positive for HIV. Dr. William diagnosed me with AIDS-related complex. The now-defunct diagnosis signified that the patient was showing signs of immunosuppression. Along with the low T4 count, I had swollen lymph nodes.

Thanksgiving loomed. I never debated whether or not to tell my family. They'd find out eventually and deserved to know now. Besides, I felt desperate for their emotional support. Peter had been wonderful, but I could see the fear and confusion in his eyes. I needed the kind of consistent support only a family could provide.

I decided to tell them one at a time, starting with who I thought might be easiest. My oldest brother, Chris, the ceramic artist who had already lost a friend to AIDS and had previously asked me if I might be gay, seemed like the safest bet for an understanding response. So the night before Thanksgiving, I walked into his bedroom, where he was settling in for the night with his first wife, Amy.

"Can I talk to you about something serious?" I asked, the first time Chris had ever heard me preface a conversation this way. He and Amy immediately looked worried. I had practiced this in my head, deciding that a short, factual, and calm delivery would be best. The outline was simple: I have HIV, my immune system is already weakened, I will need your support, and yes, I'm gay.

Chris looked stunned, but he was immediately supportive. After I left the room, he broke down, sobbing in Amy's arms. It was the first time she'd ever seen him cry.

I then went to Janet's room, then Jes's, each disclosure no easier than the first. I knew from their identical stunned expressions that my siblings would need time to process it all. But all three of them immediately offered love and support. I was sure, with whatever laid ahead, I would need it.

The next night, after Thanksgiving dinner, I drove to my dad's place. He had separated from my mom just a year before. My father's shock was deeper than my siblings', and he seemed lost in it at first. I could tell he'd need help and told him it was OK to discuss it with his new partner, Joan.

By the next morning, Dad had turned a page. He asked me back for another talk and had a lined yellow notepad out when I arrived, ready to brainstorm our next moves. And for the months and years ahead, my dad's notepad was always present when we talked, filled with strategies to beat the challenges that faced his youngest son.

My mother surprised me the most. Since our battles throughout high school, I had kept her at an emotional distance, rarely calling her and only visiting about twice a year. That's why I told her the news last, and not until Christmas: I have HIV and I'm gay—the *Early Frost* double whammy. Without blinking, Mom absorbed the news like a champ and was fearless and loving with all her questions. Since she had not suspected I was gay, we freely discussed all the clues she had missed. When I asked all the Staleys to embrace my new boyfriend as a member of the family, Mom's welcoming of Peter, and all the crazy boyfriends after him, was the most genuine of all. "How is Peter?" she would ask near the top of our phone calls, which went from rare to frequent.

The Staleys became my core support group, their stoicism more an asset than a liability. I would lean on them often in the months ahead, especially for mental ballast. I could compartmentalize sickness and death to an extent, choosing not to dwell on them, but their seriousness still crept into my life.

After my diagnosis, there was an immediate sense of loss. My mind no longer imagined trippy nudist weekends with Jef or falling in love with a man while traveling through Europe. Youth itself seemed to vanish, and my innocence with it.

5

SEARCHING FOR ACT UP

———

MY NEW MISSION WAS BUYING TIME. How could I forestall what seemed inevitable—dying from AIDS as a young man? Could I bolster my immune system or take an experimental drug that would add months, or even years, to the running estimate in my head of how much time I had left?

Based on what I was reading about the HIV life cycle, I knew my three-hundred-odd T cell count wasn't in the danger zone, yet . . . but it wasn't that far from it either. Below two hundred is when your chances of getting an opportunistic disease rise significantly, so I figured that as long as I stayed above that, I had at least two years ahead of me. If I dropped below that? Then the two-year clock would start ticking down.

HIV itself doesn't kill you. Instead, it slowly depletes your T cells. And once your immune system is severely weakened, some other bug or cancer takes advantage and knocks you off, grabbing the opportunity that HIV has cleared the way for.

Many of these diseases were considered rare before HIV came along. Kaposi's sarcoma, the skin cancer with its purple blotches that became a defining characteristic of a dying AIDS patient, and *Pneumocystis carinii* pneumonia (PCP) were the two biggest killers. If I was going to buy some time and a few extra ticks on my doomsday clock, I'd have to learn about KS and PCP, and much more.

But first, I made an emotional detour that almost led me astray: I came very close to moving to Amsterdam. I was so terrified of the possibility of not having a partner during the hard months and years ahead, someone who would be there during those scary nights when I'd wake up having soaked the sheets with sweat, that I desperately latched on to my relationship with Peter, who was back in Amsterdam attending law school.

I begged him to move to New York. I even offered to pay his tuition at one of the city's law schools. He rightly hedged, knowing that if the relationship floundered, he might be left high and dry. Since luring Peter to New York didn't work, maybe I could move to Amsterdam—the bank had an office there.

After consulting with Jes, I marched into my boss's office and told him a story that had a touch of truth to it, wrapped in a bunch of lies. I had fallen in love during my vacation in Amsterdam, and we were now engaged to be married. My future wife was a Dutch lawyer, and she and I had decided it was probably easier for me to get a job there than the other way around. So could I transfer to Morgan's Amsterdam office?

Kalaris had always been a great boss, and he didn't let me down this time. He worked the phones, convincing our Amsterdam branch to let me transfer there, while setting up a one-month training program for me at our London office. By April 1986, I had moved into the five-star Brown's Hotel in London on Morgan's dime and was training in the European markets.

But London had lost all the joy I experienced during my junior year abroad. The city hadn't changed much in five years, but I sure had. No longer the young explorer living, for the first time, in a big and vibrant city, I was now there for desperate reasons, ripping up roots, fighting off the depressing effects of London's drizzly, sunless days. I spent each night alone in the hotel, and worked each day on a windowless trading floor with other miserable traders who viewed me as an annoying outsider whom they didn't have time to train.

I quickly felt overwhelmed.

And that was *before* I got sick.

When the night sweats woke me in my hotel room, it was a cruel reminder that my body was being overrun by a deadly virus. In the morning, I had a high fever, so I called in sick. It felt like a terrible flu, but what if it was something worse than that?

The hotel kept a doctor on call for its guests. Should I reach out? What would I even tell this doctor? It felt too risky to tell someone I didn't know that I had the world's scariest disease. So instead, I just laid there in bed, on sheets still damp from sweat, feeling the full burden of fear and loneliness that AIDS might bring me in the years ahead.

I eventually asked the hotel to send its doctor. But I kept my secret, and without the full picture, he gave me some prescription-level acetaminophen. I called in sick for a second day, and hoped my "flu" was just a flu. And thankfully, it was. But I would be hit by random night sweats for years to come, my constant reminder of the millions of virions attacking my T cells.

After I finished my training in London, I returned to New York to begin packing for the move to Amsterdam. But then one man's decision thwarted my plans.

Kalaris called me into his office, saying, "I've got some bad news." The bank's CEO, Lewis Preston, had announced an international restructuring that would focus on cities with the largest trading markets—New York, London, Frankfurt, and Tokyo—while downsizing the bank's footprint in smaller markets. They'd be reducing staff in Amsterdam, and there was no way the branch could bring in an expat while it was laying off locals.

Just like that, my plans for living with Peter in Amsterdam were dashed. I called my brother Jes and started to sob. It was only the second time I had broken down in tears after my diagnosis—it was all finally sinking in. For the first time in my life, I had lost control of my fate. I knew I couldn't control when AIDS would kill me, but I had compartmentalized that fear and stayed focused on everything I could control: my career, my love life, the months or year or two years in front of me. I was losing grip on all of those things.

Within months, the relationship with Peter unraveled. We were both twentysomethings and too immature to handle the stress that my diagnosis was putting on our long-distance, on-again-off-again romance. In retrospect, I had dodged a bullet. If I had moved to Amsterdam, I would have missed the life-changing events that started happening in New York City during the months ahead.

Without a boyfriend, and with none of my immediate family living in New York, I had a woefully small support network. Tracey was a godsend, shouldering most of my sadness and fears. But I needed to find fellowship with those who were facing my same fate. I was still in the closet, not knowing a single person living with HIV, when I walked into an AIDS support group in the West Village run by Gay Men's Health Crisis, hoping to be inspired and meet others who, like me, were actively fighting for more time.

There were about twenty gay men seated in a circle, along with a counselor from GMHC. Again and again, I heard fear and resignation from the health scares and stigma the men had experienced. Many lamented that they would never have sex again. Then a wild-looking guy across from me chimed in. "I'm sorry, but I'm not about to stop having sex," he said. "Just use a condom!"

I chuckled at his boldness while others squirmed. He noticed my reaction and continued with a campy rant on how there was no way in hell he was going to stop living to the fullest.

What a sight he was: spiky blond hair, a black leather biker jacket and blue jeans, black boots, and too many piercings to count. He was a lesson in contrasts, with a defiantly effeminate voice and mannerisms and don't-fuck-with-me looks. I was instantly drawn to this fiercest of queens, so as the meeting ended, I made a beeline toward him. I explained that this was my first time meeting others who were infected. "I loved a lot of the things you said tonight. Can I buy you a cup of coffee so we can talk some more?"

His name was Griffin Gold. He was an activist—a cofounder of the People with AIDS Coalition (PWAC)—and I latched on to him for dear life. Within a week, we had slept together, otherwise known as a gay handshake. Griff's funky one-room basement apartment was at the corner of Christopher Street and Gay Street in Greenwich Village, an intersection that screamed queer activism and suited him well.

Soon after, I was introduced to Michael Callen, one of the city's most outspoken AIDS activists and another cofounder of the People with AIDS Coalition, and Michael Hirsch, its executive director, who later founded Body Positive. Griff had lured me to PWAC's small office inside donated space at a local church. "We can meet there before lunch, and you can see where things *really* happen," he said.

With Gold, Callen, and Hirsch, I had found the beating heart of AIDS activism in New York: HIV-positive gay men who demanded to be heard and to live without stigma.

I was also hearing their anger. Anger at President Reagan for barely mentioning the crisis. Anger at Mayor Ed Koch for his timid response in this city with more AIDS deaths than any other. Anger at the press for rarely mentioning AIDS and, when they did, for calling them "victims" instead of people living with HIV.

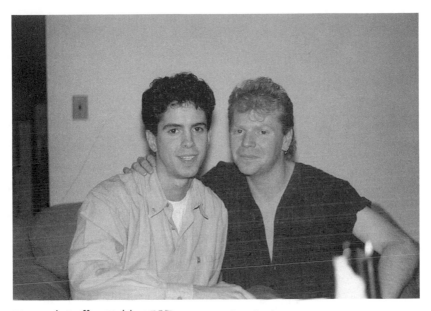

Me and Griffin Gold, 1987. *Courtesy of Michael Lesser*

Griffin introduced me to a small trove of literature to help people with AIDS learn about any and all possible research leads to fight the virus, including PWAC's *Newsline,* and *AIDS Treatment News,* published by John James in San Francisco. I read all the back issues in the coalition's possession.

As I climbed this learning curve, my anger began to match that of the activists I was meeting. We were almost six years into the epidemic, and our government didn't seem to care. Those in power were standing by, just letting us all die.

Back in 1976, I was living just outside Philadelphia when a new disease killed twenty-nine people attending an American Legion convention. Our government went into high alert to find the cause and stem the epidemic of what had been dubbed Legionnaires' disease. Within two months, the *New York Times* had run sixty-two stories about the outbreak—eleven of them on the front page. But the *Times* waited two years after the first reported AIDS cases to run a front-page story about what was already a far deadlier epidemic. There wasn't a single television network news story on AIDS until a full year had passed after the first deaths in 1981.

Along with my growing anger, I experienced my first taste of grief. Griff asked me to join him at a memorial for Michael Calvert, the first PWAC board member to die from AIDS. I had only met Calvert once, just before he returned home to Atlanta around Thanksgiving. He had looked perfectly healthy but was dead by January.

His memorial was in February. And in March 1987, I finally found a place to channel my anger and grief after I was handed a flyer on my way to work, a flyer announcing ACT UP's first demonstration, prodding me to attend my first ACT UP meeting.

I left Morgan's chandeliered headquarters in my suit and tie and starched white shirt, and fifteen minutes later walked into the linoleum-tiled, paint-peeling ground-floor meeting hall at the Lesbian and Gay Community Services Center on West Thirteenth Street. I felt like a closeted Clark Kent becoming a gay Superman, my true self, in an entirely new and surreal world.

The Center's hall was full. With every seat taken, folks stood along the sides and back, gay men from all walks of life but also a surprising number of women—the lesbians, who had far more experience with activist movements than most of the guys in the room. At twenty-six, I was one of the younger attendees, but not the youngest. A few looked fresh out of high school. If my age didn't stand out, my suit and tie did. You could count those of us in business drag on one hand.

The room crackled with raw emotion. Folks were desperate, but even the sickest among them were fit for a fight. With the huge press response from ACT UP's first Wall Street demonstration, no one seemed to doubt that history was being made. Alumni from the Stonewall riots were there too, and you could feel their relief as the community was coming alive again in the face of death, righteously angry and more than ready to take action. Youthful arrogance powered many of us in our teens and twenties. This was our moment—ACT UP could be our Stonewall.

Someone suggested using the federal tax filing deadline in two weeks as a launching point for the next demo, especially since we were demanding that some of our taxes go toward AIDS research. "Let's fill the front steps at the General Post Office Building as thousands of folks are rushing in before the deadline," someone else chimed in. It was communal brainstorming at its best.

And, holy fuck, look at that guy in the tight bicycle shorts who just walked in. The room was as cruisy as my first night in Heaven. The tightly packed bodies in the standing-room-only section listened intently but had plenty of time to look around, lock eyes, and get acquainted. Since my diagnosis a year and a half ago, I had only had sex once, with Griff, but now it seemed like I had a fighting chance of further breaking the drought.

While the cruising was fun, what smacked me in the face the hardest at that first, long meeting was a sense of community. Sure, I had been with throngs of gay men on dance floors, where I felt that beautiful bond of sexual freedom, but this was something entirely different. The stakes were enormous, because our fucking survival as a people was on the line. By now it was obvious that no one else would save us. We realized that our only chance to stop the slaughter was in this room.

At my first few meetings, I stood with others in the back, just taking it all in. Two facilitators ran each meeting with genial efficiency. After introducing themselves, they'd lay out the ground rules, from how motions were made to how debates were handled. Every decision our new movement made was put to a majority vote by all the members who showed up that week. It was the purest form of democracy I had ever witnessed, for better or worse, and I was fascinated by the ebb and flow of our debates. A proposal could become imperiled after a single impassioned objection from one member, then be saved five minutes later by an even more impassioned defense from someone else. The good debaters—confident speakers who could gauge how a discussion was going and time a pivotal interjection—could swing the room in their direction just as the facilitators pressed for a vote. I was drawn to those with this talent, and hoped to emulate them in the months ahead.

One in particular caught my eye. Michael Nesline was tall and slim, with a gorgeous head of light brown hair and a long, sharply sculpted face. His voice was confident and booming, and he raised his hand often in those early meetings, always making succinct points that would summarize and advance the discussion. By that summer, he was standing in the front, facilitating our semistructured chaos.

Like many of the gay struggling artists/actors in the room, Michael lived in the East Village, which had the cheapest rents in Lower Manhattan. He drove a cab to pay the rent.

He was also ACT UP's first treasurer, and that was my excuse to introduce myself. Since I was still closeted at work, I didn't want to take the risk of joining others on the front lines during demonstrations, getting arrested, and appearing on TV. But I could help in other ways, behind the scenes. After a meeting in late June, I walked up to Michael and handed him a check for a thousand bucks, payable to ACT UP.

"A bunch of us are going to grab some dinner at Woody's—want to join us?" he asked, after thanking me for the donation.

"Sure!" I replied.

I quickly learned two things. First, the bunch of folks Michael referred to were the unofficial leaders of ACT UP, the hard-core founding members who chaired its new working committees and spent almost every night planning our next demonstrations and discussing how to structure the organization. And second, Woody's was the restaurant a few blocks south of the Center where they kept working after our Monday-night meetings. Just add greasy food, gossip, and lots of alcohol.

This cabal of a dozen rowdy activists would push together a bunch of tables toward the back of the restaurant's windowless overflow room, which was downstairs past the bar. Woody's was typically dead late Monday night, so the ACT UPers usually had the overflow room to themselves.

There was Larry Kramer, the controversial writer who had been semi-banished from the gay community after publishing *Faggots*, a tell-all (and some say moralizing) novel about gay life on Fire Island in the 1970s. But by now, he was a community treasure. Kramer had cofounded GMHC, and he had recently delivered a powerful speech at the Center that sparked the formation of ACT UP.

And there was Maxine Wolfe, the wise older lesbian with war stories from prior movements, who would trash talk her gay male contemporaries, including Kramer. She was "one of the boys," just smarter and more mature than everyone else in the room.

Larry was fifty-two, and Maxine was forty-six, and both appeared to be the oldest in this budding ACT UP clique. Maria Maggenti, at twenty-five, was probably the youngest, and had an infectious energy and optimism that would carry us through some dark times ahead.

Others who stood out to me included Bradley Ball, only six months my senior but seemingly far older in campy-cynical-gay-humor years. He became ACT UP's first administrator, tirelessly doing the thankless work of keeping the group from collapsing into a bureaucratic sinkhole.

And Avram Finkelstein, the handsome intellectual artist and founding member of the Silence = Death Project, which had plastered its stark posters across Manhattan months earlier. I remember seeing them on every construction site I'd pass on my way to work, pink triangles on pitch-black canvases with a gut-punch warning:

SILENCE = DEATH. Those posters sparked our movement as much as any activist did.

In the weeks ahead, as Michael and I drew closer, I'd meet most of the other founders over pitchers of beer in the bowels of Woody's. Many were gorgeous young men like Avram's hunky boyfriend, Steven Webb. And Chris Lione, also with the Silence = Death Project, with his sexy pornstache. And Eric Sawyer, and Michael Savino, and Frank Jump, and Alan Klein, and Karl Soehnlein, and Bill Bahlman, and more, and more as we kept adding tables to our growing unofficial politburo.

Though Larry Kramer's reputation for angry outbursts and confrontation was often reinforced during our Monday-night meetings, he surprised us at Woody's, revealing a kind and loving Dr. Jekyll to his more public Mr. Hyde. For years he had been advocating for a more aggressive community response to AIDS, and now he was finally witnessing his dream come true.

Larry seemed most enthralled by the younger members of ACT UP. He understood that new blood was essential for a new movement's survival. If it had only been a reunion of the old guard from the post-Stonewall civil disobedience groups, most of which had self-destructed, then their old dramas and baggage would just get replayed. He drew so much hope from the energy and novel ideas these fresher faces brought to our meetings and social gatherings that he even started calling us his children. And on those late Monday nights, he seemed like the proudest Jewish mother in New York, grilling us about our backgrounds, our jobs, our sex lives, our loves, and our dreams. To this day, I never saw a happier and more alive Larry Kramer than the one sharing toasts with us at Woody's in the summer of 1987. If I was one of his children, then it is equally true that he was a father figure to me, one whose approval I would seek from that time forward.

At the Center and at Woody's, I was discovering the safety of a second family. With Larry and Maxine as the stand-in parents, and the plethora of brothers and sisters in arms, ACT UP became my church, my reason for being, and my source of hope.

Meanwhile, Michael and I were fucking like bunnies. Safe bunnies, of course. Michael had tested HIV negative, and we became early adopters of ACT UP's radical spin on the so-called condom code that gay men started living by in 1985, after the CDC announced that condoms effectively block HIV transmission.

ACT UP's spin on safe sex in the age of AIDS was its equal emphasis on *both* words—we know how to be safe, so we're going to have plenty of sex, and so can you! AIDS had reinforced America's homophobia, with a backlash against gay men specifically, about how and how often we had sex. Anal sex became the most offensive sin of its time, the reason we deserved to die.

ACT UP's great conceit was to refuse to tread lightly against this backlash. We were righteously sex positive and aggressively celebrated sex between men. We held kiss-ins—flash demonstrations where we'd all deep kiss each other, only coming up for air to switch partners—at some of the most popular straight bars in the city. We wheat-pasted hundreds of flyers around town showing a close-up of a fully erect penis with the instruction, MEN: USE CONDOMS OR BEAT IT.

If ACT UP was our church, then we certainly practiced what we preached. It was considered treasonous among ACT UP members to stigmatize an HIV-positive person in any way, including sexually. The science was clear that condoms worked; annual HIV infections quickly dropped after gay men started using them religiously in 1985. ACT UP was a living laboratory that proved the science again and again and again. Nightly. We proselytized less fear and more joy, countering the hatemongers and finger-waggers. Safe sex works! Enjoy safe sex!

Michael and I certainly did. I latched onto this new relationship for dear life, just as I had with Peter. Even if it didn't make sense with our mismatched personalities, I was desperate to have a partner by my side during my final months of life. Yet later that summer, the juggling act—with my new boyfriend, the trading job, the nightly activism, and a falling T cell count—started to shake.

The first ball I dropped, more than once, was my Wall Street job. I tried to compartmentalize my bond trading career from my diagnosis and fight to stay alive. I decided to keep the career going as long as my health allowed, as if I weren't sick at all. But in this case, compartmentalization led to some really stupid decisions.

A new trading firm, Chicago Research & Trading, had set up shop on Wall Street. CRT Securities started actively poaching bond traders from other firms. At Morgan Guaranty, I was still trading short-shorts, the quietest end of the bond market, and had yet to be promoted up the yield curve, where the stakes were higher. CRT offered to let me trade the high-volume two-year notes, along with a signing bonus and more than double the salary. Ignoring the added stress this might have on my health, I took the bait and left Morgan.

I immediately started losing money trading the two-year notes. The arbitrage bets I had placed in short-shorts took a while to set up and pay off, but with the two-year notes, I had to predict the market's direction in the minutes, days, or weeks ahead. I second-guessed myself constantly. At first, my losses were small, but they slowly kept growing.

Meanwhile, I blindly threw another ball into the air, saying yes when Michael asked if I'd take over as head of ACT UP's fundraising.

Less blindly, I had to risk another ball in the air for my compart-mentalized but increasingly scary HIV life: I started taking AZT, the first drug approved for AIDS. And it kicked my ass. The researchers behind the first studies decided that hitting the virus as hard as pos-sible offered the best chance of controlling it, so the initial dosing was high. A patient had to take the drug every four hours, day and night, including a dose while you were normally fast asleep. It caused anemia in about half the patients who tried it.

Unfortunately, I was in the unlucky half. I began to look ghostly pale and felt exhausted all day. When I wasn't losing money at CRT, I was nodding off at my trading desk, which should be impossible to do in such a noisy and stress-filled environment, not to mention being financially hazardous. By mid-October, I threw in the towel and stopped taking AZT. It felt like a crushing defeat. I was unable to handle the only drug approved to fight HIV.

Then came Black Monday.

On October 19, 1987, the Dow Jones Industrials dropped by almost 23 percent, one of the largest single-day drops in history. It wasn't a complete surprise; the markets had been acting spooked, with two big sell-offs the week before. I was concerned enough to protect my own savings, selling out of stocks four days earlier and parking it all in a money-market fund that was safe from the chaotic swings.

When stocks crash, big investors flock to US government bonds, a so-called flight to quality. As I sat at my trading desk that Monday, the sales force started barking at me with desperate orders from CRT's customers. A trickling of calls soon became a flood. All day long, I was furiously buying the notes from other Wall Street firms a few seconds before, or a few seconds after, selling those same notes to a customer, often taking losses on each flip. As each hour ticked by, the Dow kept plunging and my losses mounted. I was panicking, as if swimming as fast as possible so as not to drown. If I had loaded up on two-year notes before that fateful Monday, I would have made a small fortune for CRT. Instead, my losses were worse than ever.

On the bus ride home that evening, I decided to visualize a calming scene for myself at home, preplanning how I wanted to emotionally cope behind closed doors by smashing some dinner plates against a wall. As soon as I walked into my apartment, I grabbed the less-used pile of plates, as planned, from two unmatched sets, walked to my bedroom, and set the plates down on the floor. One at a time, I threw each plate at the exposed brick wall as tears rolled down my face. It was a methodical rage—at myself, at all the shit life had been throwing at me, and at how poorly I was handling it.

I desperately needed to let the rage out, and this exercise worked. Halfway through the pile of plates, I was sobbing. But before the last plate could hit the wall, Michael, who was living with me at that point, walked in. The meltdown scared him, and he tried to stop me, but I pushed him off, ignoring his pleas until I was done.

Finally, when I had no more plates to throw, Michael tentatively put his hand on my arm and again asked just what the hell was going on. I dropped to my knees, picking up the big pieces first as I tried to explain through tears my rage about missed profits, even comically detailing what "flight to quality" meant. Michael joined me on the floor, carefully picking up all the porcelain shards.

That's when I cut my thumb on a broken plate. Michael had been taking classes to become a nurse, and he leaped into Nurse Nesline mode. He led me to the bathroom to clean and bandage the small cut. In was then, during this awkward moment among the three of us—Michael, me, and the millions of HIV virions dripping from my thumb—that my nurse and boyfriend decided to prove how unafraid he was of the intruder between us.

He looked at the small drop of blood on my thumb and licked it off.

Now, without forethought, I truly snapped. "What the fuck, Michael!"

I yanked my hand away and launched into a tirade about not taking risks with the killer inside me. Michael was fully cowed: mouth agape but not able to speak. The pooling in his eyes was his only response.

Unable to keep juggling so many balls, I broke off our relationship two weeks later.

Usually with breakups, one person is the asshole and the other gets his heart broken. I usually got my heart broken during the breakups in my life. But this time, I was the asshole. I had latched on way too hard within weeks of the relationship starting, then abruptly ended it four months later as it dawned on me that we weren't the best match.

Even though the relationship had a less-than-Hallmark-movie ending, we've stayed in touch, and neither of us regrets our drama-filled fling during the first months of a new movement. He saw me hit an emotional bottom since my diagnosis almost two years earlier, and he didn't run away. Memories like that, and people like Michael, stick with you.

After the meltdown, I did what any unstable New Yorker with a savings account does: I found a good shrink. Dixie Beckham was a psychotherapist who had earned a reputation working with people with AIDS, another shining example of the lesbians who fought for and took care of gay men at death's door.

She quickly encouraged me to decompartmentalize my life, to face it all squarely and see what did and didn't make sense. In the months ahead, we would double down on what made sense and take a cleaver to what didn't.

So I doubled down on ACT UP. While my closeted Wall Street life still prevented me from getting arrested at our demos, I could safely throw myself into raising money to fund them. As head of fundraising, I also sat on ACT UP's Coordinating Committee, a group that was largely powerless but full of drama queens, where information from our various committees was theoretically shared and their work was theoretically coordinated.

My nights quickly filled up with meetings and fundraising projects. But my weekdays were filled with the soul-crushing job at CRT, where my bond trading losses slowly mounted. Something had to give.

That something was my T cell count, which dropped to 171 by February, four months after Black Monday. This was the first time it had dipped below 200, entering the danger zone where the odds of getting hit by an opportunistic infection rose sharply. This was the point when doctors, if pushed for a prognosis, would say, "You've got about two years left, Mr. Staley."

For weeks, Dixie had been preparing me for this moment, gently nudging me not to separate my career on Wall Street from my health care reality, hinting that I was holding on to a job that made less and less sense. It was probably costing me some T cells, and it was definitely fucking with my mental health.

She also pointed out that the only time I smiled or expressed any joy during our sessions was when I talked about my life in ACT UP. "You could go on disability and dedicate yourself to the activism work that really matters to you," she suggested at one point, further planting the seeds for a great leap into the unknown. All I needed was one last good push. And the lab results about the lower T cell count had sure shoved me hard.

The very next morning, I walked onto the trading floor at my usual time, but surprised my boss, John, the head of CRT's New York headquarters. First, I asked him for a private discussion in his office. Then I told him I was HIV positive.

"Today will be my last day here," I said.

I explained that my latest T cell count had fallen to a dangerous level, so I'd be going on disability. I told my boss that he could share my medical news with the other traders at tomorrow morning's staff meeting. "Feel free to tell them the truth . . . the whole shebang—including that I'm gay."

Although John was stunned, he acted professionally, expressing compassion and concern. Since there was nothing of personal value at my trading desk, I walked straight from his office to the elevators, never looking back. My short, topsy-turvy career on Wall Street had ended.

As soon as I got back to the apartment, I called Lou, who was at his broker's desk at Garban. "It's done," I said.

I had given Lou a heads-up the day before, just after the blood results came back. We both wondered aloud how our small world of bond traders and brokers would react. Lou agreed to arrive at work early the next morning so he could monitor the chatter over the direct phone lines that connected all the trading desks in New York, Tokyo, and London.

The traders in Tokyo would be winding down their day just as my former boss, John, broke the news. Lou's phone bank started to light up within minutes of that staff meeting.

"It's out," Lou told me on one line while he held a second phone to his other ear, fielding a flood of calls coming into his switchboard.

"That was fast," I said. But neither of us was surprised. The phones that connected our market were the most efficient news and gossip relay system on the planet. It's how I learned that Rock Hudson had AIDS hours before it appeared on TV. And now "Peter Staley has AIDS" was ricocheting around the bond market at a similar clip.

"They just heard in Tokyo," Lou said about fifteen seconds later.

In the days that followed, only three of my former colleagues from Morgan Guaranty called to ask how I was doing. Bill Schreiner was the first. And then Tommy Kalaris called. As always, he impressed me with his empathy and frankness, and even offered some levity.

"So I'm guessing that girl you almost moved to Amsterdam for was actually a guy," he said.

"Um, yeah—sorry about bending the truth on that," I said.

"It's all good," he said.

Less than a month later, I returned to Wall Street, not to trade but to protest. It was March 24, the first anniversary of ACT UP, and we decided to show the world our staying power by returning to the same intersection, where Wall Street ends on lower Broadway, only this time in far larger numbers than the year before.

My transition from bond trader to radical activist was almost complete. I had only to join my new family—the angriest queers in New York, if not the world—to lay down our bodies in wave after wave while cars honked and cameras rolled.

In the past year, I had avoided arrest. I would hold a protest sign close to my face, making sure not to be captured on film, not wanting to risk losing my pointless job. But here I was joining the first wave of many waves of activists who sat down on the hard pavement, becoming part of history's next great tide of civil disobedience.

"ACT UP! FIGHT BACK! FIGHT AIDS!" we chanted as the cops and cameras moved toward us. And when a beautiful young reporter with perfect makeup and a stylish winter coat thrust a microphone toward me, her TV cameraman close behind, I didn't shy away when she asked me, "Why are you here today?"

I tried my best to stick to the ACT UP script of practiced soundbites as the cops gave their warning, announced through a bullhorn, that we would soon be arrested if we didn't move from the street to the sidewalk.

Instead of following the law, one by one we went limp. It was just as we had practiced during the civil disobedience trainings conducted by some of our lesbian members who had experience in prior movements. Teams of officers were forced to drag us to waiting vans. As two cops pulled me toward the van, each tightly gripping one of my arms, I kept chanting our movement's slogan, adding to a cacophony—police sirens wailed, cars and trucks honked, and hundreds of my comrades chanted as one.

And those poor cops. Once the intersection was clear, another wave of activists would replace those dragged away, on and on, until 111 of us filled the holding cells at three downtown police precincts.

At the NYPD's First Precinct, an officer held my hands firmly as he pressed my fingertips and thumbs between an inkpad and fingerprint card. I was led to a holding cell that was already packed with other ACT UPers, and the few hours we spent there passed quickly, filled with gossip and camp humor. Cute cops would pass by and we'd all whistle and taunt them—"What a big billy club you have, officer!"—triggering our own endless giggling fits.

With a heady mix of exhilaration and exhaustion, I got home just in time to catch our coverage on the local news. Flipping through the stations, I stopped when I saw the reporter who had asked me what I was doing there. As I answered, a caption appeared below my face: PETER STALEY, AIDS VICTIM.

6

FUNDRAISING AND FUCKING

RACKING UP ARRESTS was one way to leave your mark in ACT UP. Organizing actions was another. In the months that followed, I'd burnish my activist bona fides by doing both. But well before that, I had gained a reputation in the group via other means, one of which was unique and the other, which I'll get to later, most definitely not.

Leading ACT UP's fundraising efforts was a singular, geeky challenge I energetically pursued. It moved me from the back-row, standing-room-only section at our meetings to a seat behind the T-shirt table near the front. Some of the fundraising projects had to be pitched to the floor for a vote, which placed me where I loved, front and center. But I'd need some help, so the first thing I did was launch a Fundraising Committee.

ACT UP's other committees had already filled out our nightly calendars, so we started meeting on Friday nights at 8:00 PM. Even with that less-than-desirable scheduling, an eager group of regulars started showing up, and once the committee was in full swing, I pushed to diversify how we raised funds. Up until then, we had covered the expenses of our demonstrations by selling SILENCE = DEATH buttons and T-shirts, supplemented by a few artsy benefits at small venues downtown.

So I formed an informal partnership with Chip Duckett, a rising star among New York's gay nightclub promoters. He created increasingly spectacular benefits for us at larger clubs, convincing the venues to give us the entire amount collected from entrance fees. With the draw of an ACT UP benefit, a club would get a much larger crowd and sell many more drinks. And while Chip did it all pro bono, his reputation as a skilled promoter deservedly grew.

Initially, to test ACT UP's appeal among club-goers, Chip partnered with Deb Parker, a fellow promoter and nightlife fixture who sidelined as a dominatrix. They decided to go really big and try to fill the largest club in the East Village, an old converted theater renamed the World. As the night approached, I had my doubts that the city's queer youth would turn out in force to support ACT UP, which spotlighted the deadly epidemic that most partiers partied to forget about.

I shouldn't have worried. By opening time, a line stretched a full city block, down East Second Street and up Avenue B. For the first hour, I manned the ticket booth, thanking each potential new ACT UP member as I gave them their change with a smile and a friendly wink.

Chip had ringed the dance floor with gorgeous go-go boys in white underwear briefs. Michael Musto from the *Village Voice* dubbed them the BVD Boys. The DJ played "Let the Sunshine In" as the sweaty, horny, dancing crowd peaked, thanks in part to a new party drug making the rounds called ecstasy. The club nearly levitated with joyful cheers and loving embraces.

Four months later, Chip pulled off an even bigger ACT UP benefit at the World, headlining Robin Byrd, the porn star host of the most popular public access show on Manhattan Cable TV. Byrd would interview strippers and porn stars who would then end each show with

a full-monty striptease. Most every adult and teenage New Yorker with
a TV remote and a pulse would masturbate to her late-night offerings.

Byrd brought sixty of her best performers to our second benefit
at the World for a massive performance of swinging dicks, wiggling
tits, and jiggling bubble butts. I'm certain that multiple fire codes, city
ordinances, and vows of celibacy were broken that night. The World
is long gone, demolished for condos, but many today still remember
how a community gathered there to enjoy cathartic breaks from its
grief and activism, released through mind-altered dancing and the
merging of sweaty bodies, HIV be damned.

Besides nightclubs, our Fundraising Committee tapped other venues and groups for benefits. By early 1988, we averaged one benefit
a month, each raising a few thousand bucks to fund an increasingly
ambitious schedule of demonstrations—usually one a week—covering
poster supplies, thousands of fliers, chartered buses, packed motel
rooms, and an often-tapped bail fund for our mounting arrests.

With benefits and merchandise sales bringing in cash, sometimes
in four-figure takes, I pushed for a third leg for our fundraising stool,
one that could bring in five figures in one pop. With high up-front
costs, direct mail was a controversial but standard fundraising tool for
not-for-profits back then. Since ACT UP was making national news,
I proposed that we should build a national list of donors. Before the
Internet, direct mail was the only way to do this.

I heard about a direct mail firm that worked with GMHC and
other AIDS groups, and set up a meeting with its owner, Sean Strub.
With his entrepreneurial spirit and my Wall Street business sense, we
instantly clicked. It also didn't hurt that we were both gay men who
had been diagnosed with AIDS-related complex.

Sean explained how direct mail worked. You first had to build a
list of donors by doing expensive acquisition mailings—tens of thousands of letters to rented lists of prospective donors—hoping that
about 1 percent will bite and send back a check. These first mailings

rarely made money, but they did find new donors. And once you've found them, the renewal mailings sent to just that list could potentially raise substantial sums for years to come.

Sean offered ACT UP what I viewed as an amazing start-up deal: we'd only have to pay for the $3,500 postage on our first acquisition mailing. All his other expenses would be paid back as donations came in, and if the donations didn't cover them all, we'd owe nothing further—he assumed almost all of the up-front risk.

Even so, it was still going to be a hard sell to ACT UP's membership. A vocal minority just couldn't stomach the idea that a for-profit business might make money off our fundraising efforts. And like almost all private businesses, Sean's profit margin was largely hidden and could only be estimated based on industry standards. The first $22,500 sent in by donors would go to Sean's firm for its expenses, followed by reimbursing our $3,500 postage bill. ACT UP had yet to spend that much on anything.

Another problem I faced was explaining the mystery of direct mail to ACT UP's membership. It was an industry shrouded in complexity, with its own language and acronyms, many of which sounded like covert sex acts, like nixies, dupes, CPM, white mail, buckslips, and "the package." It was a tall learning curve to climb.

Though HIV had dashed my teenage hopes of being a congressman or senator, here was a chance to see if I had the innate skills of a politician. As I looked at it, ACT UP was a little country, and I had to convince a majority of its parliament to approve a complex new tax program to raise much-needed revenue.

First, I had to get it approved at the committee level, which ended up being the easiest step. Being the Fundraising Committee's founder probably helped, as did the fact that we were all members of the same party—the Let's Try Anything to Raise Money Before We Die Party.

The next step was to introduce the bill on the floor. I got on the agenda for a Monday-night general membership meeting and broadly outlined what the Fundraising Committee wanted our little country to try. In my pitch, I acknowledged that members would have plenty of questions and concerns, so we wouldn't be voting on this proposal right away. Meanwhile, in the weeks ahead, I told them I would visit each ACT UP committee for more in-depth briefings. This was akin to a politician pledging to visit every district in her state, and it really helped seal the deal.

When I returned to the floor to make my final pitch, there were no surprises. The vote was lopsided in favor of proceeding. ACT UP would launch a national direct mail fundraising campaign, with a cover letter signed by actor/playwright Harvey Fierstein. Fifty thousand letters went out. And close to $70,000 came back in, stunning us all.

Understandably, the floor easily approved our next proposal to mail out the same letter to another 150,000 prospective donors. In total, our Harvey Fierstein direct mail campaign grossed around $300,000. We followed that up with a letter signed by pop art legend Keith Haring, which raised even more. Direct mail would become a stable source of funding for ACT UP in the years ahead.

―――――――――――

But enough about money. Let's talk about sex.

At around the same time all this fundraising raised my profile within ACT UP, I also gained a reputation for being a bit of a slut. Not that there's anything wrong with that. In fact, it was practically a badge of honor within the movement, and one of the badges most commonly earned by our members. The sluts were our largest fraternity. And it wasn't just the boys. ACT UP's lesbians had their own like-minded sorority. There was even some intermingling between the two shameless houses.

Robert Hilferty helped me earn my badge. He was about my age but almost nine inches taller, with a strong jawline, huge smile, and curious sense of humor, as if he always had a secret you'd never find out. Having studied film at New York University, he became one of ACT UP's dedicated videographers, always carrying a camcorder to capture our history. He was also armed with a music degree from Princeton and loved the performing arts.

Robert was probably first in line for an ACT UP benefit at Performance Space 122 in the East Village. The program included the most talked-about downtown performers of the late eighties: David Wojnarowicz, Diamanda Galás, and the alt rock, all-female group BETTY. Once the doors opened, the room filled up quickly, and as I set up our merchandise and literature table along one of the side walls, Robert wandered over.

Robert Hilferty and me, 1989.
Courtesy of Philip Hannan

"Can I sit with you?" he asked before the show started.

"Sure!"

We sat close together in two folding chairs pulled tight against the T-shirt table, which was covered in a large black cloth. The standing-room-only crowd pressed into us on both sides. As the house lights went down and the performances began, Robert made his move, resting one hand on my thigh.

Would he dare? I wondered. His fingers started to massage my inner thigh. I reached down, grabbed his hand, and pulled it toward my crotch.

"Hmm," he whispered.

Then I brought my arm back up and folded my hands on the table in front of me. He very slowly released me from my jeans and underwear. We both kept our eyes forward, pretending to watch the actual show, as he slowly brought ours to a close by making me climax in his hand. I was convinced we hadn't fooled most of the guys standing next to us, but who the fuck cared? Our fraternity would approve, and probably present us with badges of honor at the next meeting.

Beyond our fundraisers, ACT UP's social calendar was highlighted by parties in cramped apartments or large lofts, and nights of dancing at our favorite clubs—the World, the Palladium, the Pyramid Club, and the five floors and roof deck at Mars, at the far edge of the Meatpacking District.

Those of us who attended Maria Maggenti's ACT UP parties still glow when we recall one night at her place in particular. Maria lived in a third-floor East Village walk-up overlooking Tompkins Square Park, within a coin-toss of Life Cafe, later immortalized in the Broadway musical *Rent*. Protests against a new park curfew had racked the neighborhood the previous weekend. Police had charged demonstrators, and a night of rioting became national news. The spirit of that rebelliousness was still in the air when we gathered at Maria's.

It was one of the hottest nights of the year, and her un-air-conditioned living room became our dance floor. A few of the younger boys took off their sweaty T-shirts, and we all smiled, just like we did earlier that year when the dozen or so barely twenty-year-olds from the East Village had started showing up at our Monday-night meetings. ACT UP's Ken Woodard dubbed them the Boys in Black, and they looked like Marlon Brando's reincarnated biker gang from *The Wild One*, with black leather motorcycle jackets, black Doc Martens, and dark blue jeans, neatly cuffed.

They were gorgeous and boldly sexual—the first generation of young gay men coming of age during the most fearful years of the AIDS crisis, and they outwardly refused to be cowed. The Boys in Black were going to have safe gay sex, and plenty of it, so when they peeled off their shirts at Maria's party, everyone took notice.

But then, minutes later, they all disappeared. I wasn't sure where or why they had gone, but I sure missed them. Thankfully, they soon made their triumphant return, cheering and mostly naked—just boots, socks, and soaking wet white briefs. They raised their arms in victory as our eyes widened, our libidos teased by the wet cotton around their asses and cocks. They'd gone to cool off in Tompkins Square Park. The boys scaled a high fence, stripped down, and splashed each other in a small city pool marked FOR KIDS ONLY.

We quickly joined their cheers, savoring their sexy rebelliousness, embracing it as our own. Someone cranked up our new favorite song—Patti Smith's "People Have the Power"—and our cheers turned to chants.

"Shirts off! Shirts off! Shirts off!" Men started to strip off their tees, and the chanting pivoted: "Dykes too! Dykes too!"

Maria, already braless, started to tease her shirt off, then insisted *all* the men strip theirs first. She was the host, after all. So we immediately complied before she finished her strip to thunderous applause. Most of the women gleefully followed her lead.

We were one happy, naked tribe, bonding by overcoming our shared vulnerabilities, lost completely in dance as the world outside slipped away.

Patti Smith's anthem lifted us higher.

> *I believe everything we dream can come to pass through*
> *our union*
> *We can turn the world around; we can turn the earth's*
> *revolution*
> *We have the power*
> *People have the power*

When Matt Ebert got home that night, still drunk, he sketched an outline of his hand on a page in his journal and wrote fragmented memories of the party around each finger. Matt, the ringleader of the swimming pool cool-off, with his Hollywood bad-boy looks, was my favorite among the Boys in Black. Or maybe Todd Marsh was my favorite. Or Adam Smith. Each ACT UP memory can change my mind.

Matt wrote about the men he lusted for at Maria's party and her shrewd bargaining with the boys and their shirts . . . about reaching for guys' crotches with the hand he had just sketched. He wrote the first lines from Patti's song, "I was dreaming in my dreaming of an aspect bright and fair." He also wrote about his urge to swim.

Inspired, Ken Woodard, who'd christened Matt and his hunky friends the Boys in Black, came up with a more fitting nickname for our beloved East Village boys. Like the wet underwear stretched over their ass cheeks on that night, the new name really stuck: the Swim Team.

Some might ask how we could do all this partying and hooking up when our friends were dying.

Well, how could we not?

By its first anniversary, ACT UP had already lost some founding members to AIDS. And at any given time, some in our group were caring for dying friends or lovers, or were sick themselves, bedridden or in hospitals. We'd start our meetings with a moment of silence for someone who had died that week. It was becoming a sea of misery. Some, understandably, couldn't avoid being swallowed up by it.

But our movement kept growing, built by those who somehow, against the ominous odds, refused to be overwhelmed. We were determined to cram as much life into whatever time we had left, with a burning need to find joy and comradery as respite from the grief and pain. Our very sanity depended on it. Our activism depended on it.

Show me an activist who is so overwhelmed by darkness that they can't feel joy, and I'll show you a useless activist. Grief and anger are powerful motivators. In our case, they sparked a movement and helped it grow. But it was sustained by a desperate need for community, happiness, and love.

It was all very surreal. We were under siege, even terrorized by the threat of death. But somehow, in response, we thrived.

7

UNLEASHED

AFTER MY FIRST ARREST, I was hooked. Doing civil disobedience for the first time can be scary for some, but I loved it. Having been a bit of a showman and prankster growing up, I thrived on this new stage. I could break little laws with little consequence, and even be hailed as heroic in the process. Depending on the demo, various versions of my younger self could not only shine but do so on national TV, no less! My inner child was really having a blast.

It certainly helped that I didn't have a job to worry about, much less a future career. And even though I was slightly manhandled during two of my arrests, it's worth acknowledging that my Whiteness had a lot to do with my relatively gentle handling. And compared to other movements, ACT UP had an easier ride as well, and was treated gingerly by both the police and the courts.

The police were often scared of us because of their unwarranted fears of HIV. No one got punched by a cop, even off-camera. Often they'd wear yellow rubber kitchen gloves during some of our demonstrations, which only bolstered our main storyline with the media and the public—we were highly stigmatized by those in power. The kitchen gloves prompted one of ACT UP's campiest taunts: "Your gloves don't match your shoes! You'll see it on the news!"

After we were arrested, the courts had little interest in giving us jail time. Prosecutors and judges didn't want to look like they were throwing sick and dying patients into prisons. For those taken in, there was no financial cost involved, because ACT UP maintained a bail fund to get us released quickly. We also had a small corps of dedicated, progressive lawyers who offered their services to the movement, pro bono.

Most of our larger demonstrations were highly organized shows, like opening night on Broadway. Everyone had their roles to play. The cops knew their roles. We knew ours. And both sides knew the press would be there in force to record everything. Beyond the drama, I was fascinated by our demonstrations' power, along with the kinds of change they could bring. They weren't only about achieving specific policy goals, although when an action did this, it felt exceptionally glorious. Harder to measure, but often of more importance, were actions that slowly changed public opinion.

And sometimes actions didn't do either of these things yet still built the movement. ACT UP's large and militant contingent at the 1987 National March on Washington for Lesbian and Gay Rights probably went unnoticed by President Reagan, even as we marched past the White House. But over a dozen ACT UP chapters—Boston, Los Angeles, Chicago, San Francisco, Philadelphia, and more—were formed around the country in the weeks that followed.

I was fascinated by the intricate mix of factors that made us stand out that day and at all our demonstrations prior to that. What were our targets? What were our goals? Which visuals and tactics worked best?

With a healthy dose of youthful arrogance, I often thought I could answer those questions. But one thing is for sure: I was eager to test my instincts. It was time to get my hands dirty and plan some actions myself.

Ever since I had visited most of ACT UP's committees during my lobbying efforts around direct mail fundraising, I had been itching to join the Issues Committee. It appeared to have the highest quotient of nerds and the lowest quotient of emotional loudmouths who often slowed other committees down.

In other words, they were all business, determined to get shit done. And they were already focused on finding and clearing a regulatory path for treatments that would extend the lives of people living with HIV. For folks like me who had been handed a death sentence with our diagnoses, this was our focus, too.

By the time I joined the Issues Committee in April 1988, they had a new subcommittee called Treatment and Data. It was even geekier and more focused than the larger committee, so naturally, I shifted my energies there.

They were an intimidating group. The meetings sometimes felt like an advanced placement course, where each student would try to out-geek the others. The latest science or treatment would be discussed literally down to its molecular level, and if you couldn't keep up, they rarely paused to reteach things. Like many in the room, I faked it for a while until eventually the repetition made things click, and I could actually follow a conversation. And by then, I decided it wasn't necessary to compete with the subset of geniuses there. All of us brought unique skills to the table, and mine could be different from the whiz kids. Maybe my political instincts could help. Maybe, with my corporate experience, I wouldn't be intimidated if we negotiated with pharma executives or senior public health officials. And maybe I could design and carry out actions against targets the group identified.

T&D, as the subcommittee became known within the movement, had a growing list of possible targets, starting with the Food and Drug Administration and its historically glacial drug approval process. With so many new ACT UP chapters forming around the country, there was talk of attempting a massive national demonstration that would target the FDA's headquarters in Rockville, Maryland.

In the meantime, I looked for a more bite-sized target on which to test my planning skills. Kowa Pharmaceuticals seemed like a good fit. Kowa was a division of a larger Japanese conglomerate that had unwittingly become important to desperate AIDS patients. In 1987, a small test-tube study was published in the *Lancet* saying a drug called dextran sulfate might have antiviral effects against HIV. Kowa had been selling the drug for more than twenty-five years in Japan, where it was approved for over-the-counter use to lower cholesterol.

Within weeks, the underground buyers clubs launched by AIDS activists had sprung into action. These clubs had been set up to distribute experimental treatments that the FDA had not yet approved. Staff members would fly to Tokyo, snap up all the dextran sulfate at a bunch of pharmacies, and then resell it at cost to people living with HIV back in the United States.

In late May 1988, T&D was hearing reports from the buyers clubs of a disruption in access to dextran sulfate. Pharmacies in Tokyo were refusing to sell the drug to Americans. One of them finally admitted that Kowa had ordered them to do this. AIDS was still pretty rare in Japan, but the stigma around it was extreme. The buyers clubs assumed that Kowa got spooked when one of its products became associated with AIDS. It was also possible that the Japanese government asked the company to clamp down on the possibly infected Americans flying to Toyko each month.

I wondered if the company had an office in the United States. My Manhattan phonebook had a promising clue: Kowa Limited at 1140 Avenue of the Americas, in Midtown. Curious to see if there was a connection, I called them. "Is this Kowa Pharmaceuticals?"

"No, we're with Kowa, but we import ladies' shoes."

As long as it was the same parent company, I figured this wouldn't be a deal breaker. It was time to investigate further. Like many multitenant office buildings in the 1980s, security was almost non-existent—just walk past the front desk like you know where you're going and hop on the next elevator. Kowa's glass front door was unlocked, and I could clearly see the Kowa logo in their small front office—the same logo as the one on boxes of dextran sulfate. As long as the logos matched, we could laugh about the ladies' shoes later.

Our action would involve a simple sit-in. I'd only need about fifteen volunteers to fill Kowa Limited's reception space. We'd punch up the visuals by handcuffing ourselves to a long chain. Since our ultimate targets were executives in Japan, I thought our best hope of pressuring them was through the Japanese media. Like the United States at the time, Japan had three major television news networks, and all of them had branch offices in New York City.

I cold-called each of them, asking for an assignments editor. My pitch was simple: if American AIDS activists demonstrated at a Japanese pharmaceutical company, accusing it of withholding a treatment that could save our lives, would they want to film that?

I could practically hear each of them drooling during the pitch. The Japanese press was fascinated by this new plague but had found few domestic angles to base their stories on. From their perspective, this story was juicy. Without mentioning the company, I told them to bring their film crews to the sidewalk outside 1140 Avenue of the Americas at exactly 9:00 AM, or they'd miss the action.

On a late June morning, fifteen activists disguised in business drag walked into Kowa's front office just a few minutes before 9:00. As we started to pull out handcuffs and a long chain, I said to the receptionist, "We're with ACT UP, and we are doing an act of civil disobedience. Please remain calm."

Once we were settled in, I went back to the building's lobby and told the security guard I was with Kowa and that we'd be holding a press conference in a few minutes. I met the film crews outside and walked them past security. As I rejoined my comrades in a chain-gang circle on the floor, handcuffing myself in, our press pool barely fit into the cramped space between us and the elevators. The receptionist kept her cool and never left her desk. One Kowa executive, an American, peeked his head out of the door leading to all their offices, then just as quickly retreated. Minutes later, he summoned the courage to engage with us and the press.

"Why are you here?" he asked. We handed him our detailed press release and took turns delivering all our prepared soundbites.

"But we just sell shoes," he replied.

"We know what you do here, but it's the company you work for that's threatening our lives," I said. Once the cops arrived, the conversation ended. We were arrested, processed, and released in time for a celebratory lunch.

We were the lead story on all three networks in Japan the next morning. For good measure, pictures of our sit-in ran in *Newsweek* magazine and the *New York Times*.

Kowa raised a white flag almost immediately. Within weeks, Japan's Ministry of Health and Welfare announced an agreement with the company authorizing three designated pharmacies in Tokyo to sell dextran sulfate to foreigners, creating a government-sanctioned supply chain for the US buyers clubs.

I was now totally hooked on the power of activism. And not just activism in the streets. T&D decided early on to play a dual-track, inside-outside game. We were always willing to meet with government officials and pharmaceutical executives to push our demands. If they refused to meet or ignored our demands, we'd take to the streets—the outside game. And often, after a demonstration, we'd return to a negotiating table and continue the inside game with some added leverage.

This wasn't a novel approach. Instead, it was the mark of most successful movements. Martin Luther King Jr. never stopped meeting American presidents while planning large demonstrations and campaigns. Greenpeace snuck inside Exxon's headquarters to demonstrate in their executive boardroom yet still negotiated with the company many times, both before and after their trespass. Not that we made these connections at the time. Our inside-outside strategy was born of desperation. We felt the clock ticking and latched onto any and all tactics that might work.

Luckily for me, I loved doing both kinds of activism—the hard-nosed lobbying and the adrenaline-primed lawbreaking. And doing both together as a one-two punch seemed to have the greatest effect.

So it was with T&D's next target, the FDA. We set up the one-two punch: we announced a huge demonstration at their national head-quarters for October 11, 1988, and requested a meeting in advance with the FDA to press our demands. We also dangled the option of canceling the demo if the meeting went well.

It didn't. Frank Young, the FDA commissioner, assembled most of his senior staff for our meeting at their headquarters in early September. A handful of T&D members sat across from them in a large boardroom. Each of us was tasked with presenting one or two of our demands.

Since I already had a reputation defending the buyers clubs after the Kowa action, I was tasked with demanding that the FDA not shut them down. Frankly, it was probably our easiest ask. The FDA had already taken a largely hands-off approach to these technically illegal drug distribution clubs. They were rightly afraid that closing them would lead to a public relations fiasco—big government cutting off dying AIDS patients from their last-hope treatments.

Regardless, I presented this demand in full mobster style. "Don't even think of closing our buyers clubs," I said. "Next month's demonstration will look like a cakewalk if you do. We'll come back and burn this place down."

Because ACT UP already had a very in-your-face reputation, Young didn't blink. He calmly outlined the agency's gentle approach to the clubs, and said there were no plans to shut them down. But most of our other demands on how to speed up the drug approval process were met with stiff resistance from Young's senior staff. After a full airing of both sides' views, they conceded little but agreed to an ongoing dialogue.

Our demonstration would proceed as scheduled.

As we smoked cigarettes outside the FDA's Rockville office building, I imagined the scene that would unfold five weeks later. Dozens of cops would be defending the front doors we had just exited. But what about that huge awning above? I could feel the creative gears spinning in my head, the same magic that had illuminated my family's living room with controlled pyrotechnics during my high school party years.

Over one thousand activists converged on the building that day. Our flyers proclaimed SEIZE CONTROL OF THE FDA. Close to a dozen affinity groups—smaller groups of activists who planned specific tactics or visuals during the larger demonstration—would create a twelve-ring circus of powerful made-for-TV moments throughout the day.

I wanted to pounce early, hoping to give everyone a fist-pump moment to help launch our empowered spectacle. As expected, dozens of cops were guarding the main entrance. They stood in formation, three rows deep, wearing medical gloves and riot helmets. Clumps of thick nylon zip ties were attached to their belts, ready to bind our wrists. They had correctly predicted that waves of activists would try to push through their lines for dramatic, camera-ready arrests.

As I had hoped, all the cops were under the building's large awning, with their front-line formation about three feet behind the awning's outer lip. They had trained and were mentally prepared for horizontal engagements—activists moving toward them—but my hope was that they were unprepared for vertical engagements, like an activist leaping over them.

My plan required a helping hand, so I recruited my newest and closest friend in ACT UP. Charlie Franchino had joined T&D at about the same time I did. He was a thirty-year-old Italian with the sexiest self-confidence I had ever witnessed, and as ACT UP's Don Juan, he could quickly snag men with breathtaking efficacy. We once walked into one of ACT UP's favorite watering holes in the East Village, the Bar, and after a quick scan of the room, Charlie made his move.

"I'm going home with that one," he told me, pointing to the hottest guy there, who barely looked old enough to drink. Sure enough, he walked right up to the kid, whispered a few lines in his ear, and then received a nod in return. As they walked past me on the way out, Charlie cracked a smile and said, simply, "Told ya."

Charlie's jaw-dropping bar etiquette aside, he also had a wickedly vicious sense of humor. He'd do long riffs on his friends and their endearing and/or annoying reputational soft spots, keeping everyone's egos in check. He ruthlessly teased me about my growing celebrity within the movement, and . . . well, I loved him even more for it.

As I described my FDA demo plan to him, Charlie offered to recruit his most recent flirtation. Bill was young and beautiful (of course) and strong, which this mission required. With his additional and capable hands, we had our team.

With a small knapsack on my back, the three of us walked at a nonthreatening pace toward the formation of cops below the awning, as if we wanted to discuss something important with them.

"Here," I said quietly.

Charlie and Bill swiftly locked their hands in front of me as we had practiced, bending down just enough so I could put my right foot in their palms. The cops lurched forward, but they were too late. I had already been catapulted to the awning above their heads, out of reach. Charlie and Bill ran, and the flummoxed cops, not wanting to break formation, let them get away. We had been so quick and quiet that few in the crowd even noticed our effort at first. But once I started unfurling a twenty-foot SILENCE = DEATH banner from the knapsack, the cheering and fist-pumping started.

I had on a white headband, given to me by a Chicago-based affinity group earlier that morning. Their acronym, PISD, for People with Immune System Disorders, was written across the front. I looked like the *Karate Kid*'s Ralph Macchio, having just outmaneuvered dozens of cops.

When I finished hanging ACT UP's call to action under the noses of startled FDA employees, who were pressed up against the building's second-floor windows, I strutted back to the edge of the steel-and-asphalt awning and raised my arms in victory. Various ACT UP chapters had surged toward the entrance, letting out an empowered roar. I was hamming it up, but the sense of victory felt genuine. We were seizing control not only of a building or a government agency but of a nation's attention.

Atop the FDA awning, October 11, 1988. *Rick Reinhard*

The police ignored my antics because I wasn't threatening their primary goal—preventing activists from entering the building. And they didn't seem to care when my comrades tossed me protest signs that I plastered on the building above and around the banner. After my agitprop mural was as large as my arms could reach, some shouting down below got my attention.

It was Mike Signorile, who was in charge of coordinating ACT UP's media coverage that day. "Peter, don't get arrested!" he implored. "I just booked you on CNN's *Crossfire* with Pat Buchanan tonight!"

"WHAT?" I blurted out, incredulously.

"They want you in the hot seat on *Crossfire*, which you can't do from a jail cell," he said, laughing.

Luckily, the police had employed a don't-arrest-them-unless-you-have-to attitude thus far. I yelled to one of the cops in charge below, asking if they would let me go free if I climbed down from the awning. "Sure," the guy said, and kept his word after a few officers helped me down as I dangled precariously off the edge, thankful to avoid injury.

Being a spokesperson for a movement is a tricky thing. Being one for a movement that bills itself as leaderless is even trickier. Do it badly, and you'll squander a major opportunity for the movement, and get skewered within the group. Do it well, and you'll be asked to do it again and again, and then resented for it, especially if you enjoyed it like I did. And you will deserve that resentment when, like me, you were young and cocky and still lacking the political maturity to share the limelight with less-represented members of your AIDS community.

But this was well before I had reached that understanding. This was my first real test as a spokesperson, and it was a doozy. I hadn't done an interview for a national press outlet before. I hadn't done a live television interview with *anyone*, much less with Pat Fucking Buchanan, the most rabid right-wing ideologue on TV at the time.

As I sat down in the so-called hot seat on the *Crossfire* set in downtown Washington, DC, less than an hour after the final arrests in Rockville, the show's unseen producer started talking to me through my earpiece. "Have you seen the show before?" he asked.

"Only a few times," I responded. "To be honest, I'm not a fan of Pat Buchanan."

"Oh really?" a voice from behind me interrupted.

It was Buchanan—we were off to a great start.

"Well, you've said some pretty terrible stuff about my community," I replied, as we shook hands, firmly.

"Let's save it for the show," he said.

We sat in our seats quietly as Tom Braden, Buchanan's cohost— the left-winger to his right-winger—slipped into his seat just before the producer's countdown.

As ACT UP's media guy, Mike had prepared me well. The producer had told him that Buchanan would actually take my side on the FDA debate. ACT UP's demands for quicker drug approvals inconveniently aligned with the right's desire for less regulation and less government. But the producer also warned Mike that Buchanan would pivot at some point to attack homosexuality as it related to AIDS.

I was as ready as I could be. My veins were still surging with adrenaline after witnessing the arrests of close to two hundred comrades. It felt like we had bled and won on the battlefield that day, with a collective emotional venting that released years of suppressed rage and grief.

The militaristic theme music swelled as some offscreen master of ceremonies announced the fighters: "Tonight, from Washington— *Crossfire*, against all odds. On the left, Tom Braden. On the right, Pat Buchanan. In the crossfire, Peter Staley of the New York AIDS Coalition To Unleash Power."

They started with ACT UP's focus on the FDA. Braden seemed unprepared for the debate, even calling the FDA the *Federal* Drug Administration, forgetting its food mandate. As he fumbled, I got my best soundbite in, saying, "The problem here is that the FDA is using the same process to test a nasal spray as it is to test AIDS drugs, and it's a seven- to ten-year process."

Thanks to Mike's prep, Buchanan didn't astonish me at all when he started by saying, "Mr. Staley, this is going to astonish you, but I agree with you one hundred percent." It didn't hurt that Braden seemed to be almost apologetically defending the FDA, and was probably on my side too, but couldn't say so, given the show's format.

But then Buchanan pivoted to his comfort zone: bashing gays instead of agreeing with them. "You've got the pink triangle on your shirt, Silence Equals Death," he began.

"That's correct," I replied.

"I gather that means you're a homosexual," he continued.

"Yes," I said, waiting for the attack.

"Looking in the camera, what would you tell some kid, say you had a younger brother who also, uh, might have homosexual tendencies, what would you tell him if you wanted him to live a long life?"

"I would tell him to use a condom," I replied quickly. "And also to use a lubricant, by the way . . ."

"But aren't you—this is Russian roulette!" he shot back.

"It is *not* Russian roulette. It is Russian roulette to not give people this information when human nature dictates that they're gonna go out there, and they're gonna have sex."

"You mean celibacy is impossible?" he pressed.

"It's just not going to work. People aren't going to do it, and lots of people are going to die. Now, would you rather have a lot of people cheating on their celibacy with thousands of people dying, or would you rather save those lives and let them have sex?"

And with that, he seemed to give up, cutting to a commercial.

Mike told me later that I had solidly won the showdown with Buchanan. But I wasn't sure. I worried that the mention of using lube was a bridge too far for most of the viewing audience in 1988. I had pivoted to the specifics of safe anal sex for gay men—standard rhetoric within the movement but rarely heard on prime time television. Just after saying it, I imagined tens of thousands of TV remotes changing the channel.

But my doubts about my appearance were removed when Mike and the Media Committee started using me again and again after the success on *Crossfire*. And within a year, I was considered one of the most prominent ACT UP poster boys, for better or worse.

8

AZT

———

T0 THIS DAY, I remain gobsmacked at the pace of change we forced on the FDA in the months after ACT UP's high-profile shaming of the agency. Its bureaucracy had been considered one of the most entrenched in the US government, immune to public pressure and convinced of its old-school ways in regulating drug approvals. Our daylong siege of its headquarters marked ACT UP's big, national coming out, and firmly planted us as the country's civil disobedience movement du jour. Within just nine months, the FDA caved to many of our demands.

Surprisingly, we got a hugely helpful assist from a leading government scientist outside the FDA—a dashing, if a little short, smooth-talking Brooklyn native who had nabbed the top job at the National Institute of Allergy and Infectious Diseases (NIAID), just three years into the AIDS crisis. At forty-three, he was the youngest person ever to hold the position: Dr. Anthony S. Fauci.

Yes, *that* Tony Fauci. He was the de facto AIDS research czar for the US government. As such, he had been meeting with various AIDS activists, including ACT UP's finest, since early 1987. So Fauci wasn't alarmed when a bunch of our members showed up at NIAID, unannounced, demanding a meeting with him.

Already riled up, the activists had just left an ACT UP demo at a public hearing about an experimental drug—ganciclovir—that prevented blindness caused by a common viral infection in people with AIDS. Fauci calmly agreed to meet with three of the activists in his office, where they pressed him hard to intervene with the FDA to help speed up the drug's approval. He could only promise them he would try.

Five days later, the *New York Times* reported "an unusual move" by the FDA. They were reevaluating how much data they needed for ganciclovir's approval. An anonymous source within the FDA leaked the news, crediting pressure from Fauci on FDA commissioner Frank Young. Fauci not only made true on his word, he credited ACT UP, fully describing the unscheduled meeting with our activists.

It wasn't lost on us that Fauci came off as a rescuing hero in the *Times* story. Was he using us as much as we were trying to use him? Or were we simply on the same page by this point?

Fauci was treating dozens of patients with AIDS, many of whom were enrolled in NIAID trials at the NIH hospital. He was unable to save their lives. Doctors, at least the good ones, become advocates for their patients—every member of ACT UP took on that same responsibility. Regardless of motives, we decided to fully leverage our new relationship with the good doctor.

So for the next few months, T&D relentlessly pushed Fauci to endorse our most ambitious demand of the FDA: to provide widespread access to experimental AIDS drugs before they were approved. We had formulated a detailed proposal called Parallel Track, whereby people with HIV who weren't able to get into a drug's late-stage clinical trials could be enrolled in a large, parallel observational trial. Patients' doctors could use a toll-free number to enroll them. Basic data would be collected and used by the FDA during the approval process.

Our final push came during another meeting in Fauci's office, this one planned, in June 1989. I was in the room for this one, joined by Mark Harrington, T&D's boy genius, and Jim Eigo, the primary architect of our Parallel Track proposal. By this point, Fauci was on board. We just needed to hammer out all the details.

The *New York Times* got the scoop. But this time, it was on the *front* page, above the fold. The headline screamed, AIDS RESEARCHER SEEKS WIDE ACCESS TO DRUGS IN TESTS. Fauci was once again the central hero of the story, quoted saying, "I call this a parallel-track approach to clinical trials." Even Frank Young tried to take some credit, saying, "I've been pushing it as much as Tony has." As the story continued on an inside page, Mark was finally quoted at length, well after the officials had their say.

But we didn't care. Credit is secondary when change happens, and we had just caused a whole lot of change. Before the year was

Dr. Fauci meets with T&D, October 19, 1989. Left to right: me, Jay Funk, Mark Harrington, Simon Watney, Peggy Hamburg (assistant director of NIAID), Tony Fauci, Richard Elovich, and Charlie Franchino. *Tracey Litt*

out, the second experimental AIDS drug, ddI, was being shipped to over thirty-five thousand people with AIDS through the first FDA-sanctioned parallel track trial.

With each victory, T&D expanded its range of targets and goals, or just revisited targets that gnawed at us. In this latter category, one stood above the rest: the outrageously high price of AZT.

The first AIDS drug and ACT UP were born just days apart. AZT was approved for sale by the FDA on March 20, 1987, and ACT UP's first demonstration was four days later.

In one of history's greatest examples of corporate chutzpah, Burroughs Wellcome, the manufacturer of AZT, announced that it would cost more than any drug in history. Though it sounds quaint compared to today's pharma pricing, AZT's initial $10,000-a-year price tag shocked everyone, including activists, members of Congress, and editorial boards at leading newspapers. Activists were particularly enraged by the free ride Burroughs Wellcome had been given while bringing the drug to market. AZT was synthesized in 1964 by an academic researcher in Chicago. A possible anticancer agent, it was developed with funding from the NCI, our government's National Cancer Institute, but when it didn't pan out, the researcher never bothered to patent it.

Twenty years later, the NCI put out a call to researchers and companies for compounds it could test against the newly discovered AIDS virus. Burroughs Wellcome sent them almost a dozen candidates, including AZT, which had shown antiviral activity against other retroviruses. BW's legal department hedged its bets by filing patent claims on all of them as possible anti-HIV drugs.

It was an NCI lab that in early 1985 discovered AZT blocked HIV in a test tube. And it was the NCI that conducted the first clinical trial in people with AIDS. Burroughs Wellcome paid for the phase 2 trial, but it only enrolled 282 patients and was cut short after showing early results.

Basically, Burroughs Wellcome paid a fraction of what most companies spent to bring a drug to market, then slapped on the highest drug price in history. Even though taxpayers had funded much of the research, they'd still get stuck with huge bills going forward, since most people with AIDS were on Medicare or Medicaid.

The public outcry was immediate and still percolated many months later. In December 1987, the New York State Consumer Protection Board scheduled a hearing to look at AZT's price. Two days before the hearing, Burroughs Wellcome cut the price to $8,000 a year. That was enough to dampen the backlash, at least temporarily, but AIDS activists still fumed.

One month later, in what the *New York Times* called "one of the first civil disobedience protests against a drug price," nineteen activists with AIDS Action Pledge, a precursor to ACT UP San Francisco, were arrested outside a Burroughs Wellcome distribution center about fifteen miles south of San Francisco. They scaled the building and hung a banner that demanded END AIDS PROFITEERING. These ballsy activists did this *after* Burroughs Wellcome lowered the price, basically saying, "Sorry, that's not good enough."

Reading about it in the *Times*, my head swam with incitement. With two other drugs similar to AZT in development, I feared that AZT's price would set a benchmark that could affect AIDS treatment access for years to come. The San Francisco activists were right not to let this go, and ACT UP New York could turn this into a full-fledged campaign. If we succeeded, we could lower the prices on all future AIDS drugs, while sending an unmistakable message to big pharma: listen to AIDS activists; ignore us at your peril.

When I saw a magazine photo of Burroughs Wellcome's headquarters in Research Triangle Park, North Carolina, just outside

Raleigh, I almost drooled—it was the perfect backdrop for a demonstration. The futuristic honeycomb building, nestled within a hillside pine forest, was designed in 1969 by the modernist architect Paul Rudolph. While the San Francisco activists had to settle for climbing onto a warehouse, with a little travel, we could invade what looked like the Big Pharma Death Star.

I'd need a young Jedi for the scouting mission. So, in late '88, I pitched the idea to Mark Harrington. A year older than me but seemingly worlds apart, Mark had an intriguing combination of skinny punk-rocker looks and a stratospheric IQ. After tackling history, literature, and art at Harvard, he was now mastering immunology and virology within T&D's study groups. On a committee full of polymaths, Mark was in a class by himself.

If Burroughs Wellcome's research executives agreed to meet with us to discuss AZT's pricing and the company's continuing antiviral research, I could handle the financial issues we'd raise, and Mark could handle the science.

The company, wanting to make a good first impression, invited us down for talks and a tour of their headquarters, just as I had hoped. On January 23, 1989, Mark and I flew down to Raleigh-Durham. Lisa Behrens, the tightly wound Burroughs Wellcome public affairs officer, greeted us at the airport and drove us to Research Triangle Park, playing local tour guide along the route.

We were given the full red carpet treatment, wrapped around a discussion with the man Mark and I most wanted to engage: Dr. David Barry. He was the company's head of virology and had overseen AZT's development, including the setting of its price. The press had dubbed him Mr. AZT. Equal parts arrogant and brilliant, Dr. Barry seemed eager to spar with a couple of outsiders, as if he had no one left to argue with within the company. The discussion started during a fancy lunch inside a private atrium next to their dining hall, and continued for about ninety minutes in a conference room upstairs, near their executive suites.

Mark asked if he could tape the discussion, and Dr. Barry agreed. This being North Carolina, Mark and Dr. Barry both lit up cigarettes as the discussion became heated. They were chain smokers, so the ashtray was kept busy.

Dr. Barry laid out a pompous defense of AZT's price: The company deserved every penny because his virology team was one of the best in the world. If people with AIDS wanted a cure, giving money to Burroughs Wellcome was their best bet. "We're egotistical enough to think we can do it better than anyone else," he said, in his baritone voice. Then, playing to our critiques of the FDA, he piled on. "*We're* the experts in drug regulation and getting drugs through. *We* have to show the FDA how to get drugs through rapidly."

Using what I had learned during Morgan's commercial bank training program, I pulled out an analysis of their annual financial statements that I had prepared in advance. "We're hearing a profit margin in December '87 of about 60 percent," I said.

"I don't know what you mean by profit. Is that gross revenues minus what the sales cost?" Barry asked.

Tom Kennedy, one of the two corporate vice presidents sitting in on the meeting, jumped in. "Classic GP," he agreed. "That's right."

"And this is what we're hearing from a lot of analysts, that it's increased over time to 80 percent," I continued. "There is this vague concept of excess profit here, and it's very hard to define, but you went point by point by point to try to refute that the world doesn't need that money as much as you. I think you can stand a price reduction without any problem. That's what I'm trying to say."

"I've got to have an income," Dr. Barry complained. "We have all kinds of very, very sophisticated accountants working out how much is available for research, how much each product within our whole panoply has to cost. If you decrease the amount of money that comes in from any product, be it Neosporin, AZT, acyclovir, Septra, you name it, it's going to be that much of a decrease for the amount we have on research."

I referred to my analysis again, pointing out that their research budget was barely larger than their marketing budget, and their profit dwarfed both, often returned to stockholders as dividends.

Dr. Barry pivoted to another defense. "Well, I must say, that as egotistical as we are, we want to encourage lots of other companies to get involved in this area. You know as well as I that once we got involved with AIDS, there were lots of companies that said *you're crazy, and we're sure as hell not going to do it*. Now there are lots of drug companies involved, OK? If we had taken a bath on this, or take a bath in the future, do you think drug companies would have been involved or will be as involved?"

"I mean, with your argument, you may as well price it at $20,000 a year," I replied. "You have to pick a point somewhere. You've got to judge what's too much. And don't point to Hoffmann–La Roche and Schering-Plough and their prices, because they're too high too, and we're going to talk to them about it. It's just that the companies that are involved in this are making it one of the most expensive diseases ever, and we're getting squeezed because of it."

Mark pointed out a recent study from the New York City Department of Health that was showing a huge undercounting of AIDS deaths among IV drug users. Thousands of them hadn't been offered AZT. They hadn't even been diagnosed with AIDS. "Although you don't realize it, because you're far from the scene of the actual battles, people are dying all the time," Mark said, growing visibly angry. "People are dying because they do not have access to the drug which is priced beyond the range of most of them, and which in many states is not available. And you're totally washing your hands of responsibility for it."

"I think it's really casting aspersions on our morality, which I don't think are appropriate, to say we're washing our hands of it," Dr. Barry shot back. "We're doing lots of things. Now, maybe we're not effective enough in those areas. Maybe we need to do more and will be doing more, but believe me, we feel the burden of that illness and death every day. I do think we need to talk to each other because I don't think our goals are that much different."

"Well, if we don't get any price reduction, we're not going to get closer," I said, circling back to our central demand.

"Tell us what we can do."

"Lower the price."

Kennedy jumped in, trying to cut the tension. "I think the statement has been made that we'll reassess our position periodically. We've always taken the position that it's not a closed book."

"The price?" I asked.

"The situation is dynamic. It's always being viewed and reviewed. Who knows what tomorrow will be?" Kennedy replied, as Dr. Barry raised an eyebrow. "But I don't think that can be construed as an official quote or anything of that nature," he quickly added.

The ashtray was now full. Lisa Behrens, who had been nervously looking at her watch, stood up, reminding us of our return flight to New York. "I've got a cab waiting downstairs," she said.

We said our good-byes to Dr. Barry at the elevators. Behrens, Kennedy, and Thack Brown, the other corporate affairs officer, walked us out. I was making mental notes of the floor plans and modest security along the way, figuring we might need to return on our own terms for an unscheduled affair.

Once outside, the five of us passed the calming waters of a large reflecting pool that mirrored the blue sky next to the building's concrete almost-white trapezoids.

I pointed to the pool. "This would make a great backdrop for a demonstration," I said, grinning. "We could dye it red."

Behrens grabbed my shoulder, laughing nervously.

"Just think," Brown interjected, "in a few years, we'll all look back on this and—"

"Not all of us will be around to look back," Mark snapped.

———————

Three months later, I pulled into the same parking lot in a Budget rental van filled with seven other activists. After three weeks of intricate planning, we had driven nine hours from New York, and this time we weren't there to talk.

To no one's surprise, Burroughs Wellcome had not lowered the price of AZT in response to our impassioned ethical and financial arguments. It was time to let the company know we wouldn't let this go.

My recruited comrades hadn't seen the building yet, so we parked near the back of the parking lot. I rehashed the action plan, pointing to where things would happen the next morning.

But we still had a busy night ahead. We drove to the airport to pick up a second, less conspicuous rental vehicle, a black, midsized Ford Tempo—exactly what traveling salesmen would use. Then we drove both vehicles to our temporary home base, the Heart of Durham Hotel. At thirty-seven dollars a night, it was the cheapest hotel I could find, and they didn't care if we packed four to a room. Jay Blotcher and Steve Rosenbush, known for their relentless work on ACT UP's Media Committee, started setting up a fax machine and rearranging furniture to create a media center in one of the rooms.

As this was going on, four of us started packing the briefcases we'd use to bring all our gear into the building. James McGrath, our butch, six-foot-two part-time carpenter, suggested equipment for our mission: battery-operated drills and enough steel mending plates, corner braces, and self-drilling Tek screws to build a one-room extension on a house.

I packed up all the tech gear we'd need for media interviews, including a rented first-generation cellular phone that looked like a gray brick, and a dinky portable TV, along with a backup battery in case they cut the power to our location. I also squeezed in a glass-cutter and two suction cups for grabbing glass panes.

Blane Mosley, a twenty-six-year-old interior designer, packed our walkie-talkies, a huge banner that said, AZT: PAY OR DIE!, four handcuffs, a padlock, and a long chain.

Lee Arsenault, a forty-one-year-old clothing importer who had been diagnosed with AIDS the year before, stuffed his briefcase with Snickers bars, bottled water, a first aid kit, a roll of toilet paper, and some industrial-strength garbage bags that could double as a portable toilet.

"Shit," whispered Lee. With all four briefcases still open, someone was knocking on our hotel door.

My heart skipped a beat before I quickly remembered our local pro bono lawyer had come to brief us. I had found Stewart Fisher through recommendations from local gay rights activists. One tenet in American civil disobedience: if you plan to get arrested for a good cause, find a pro bono lawyer to represent you in the county where it will happen. Just like gay folk, lefty lawyers are everywhere.

Stewart gave us all the same briefing he had given me a couple of weeks earlier. Based on the action I had described, the four activists involved would likely face a charge of misdemeanor trespass, and felony charges for breaking and entering and damage to property. The local prosecutor could also get creative with a charge of misdemeanor assault, even though we had no plans to assault anyone. Just one of these charges—felony breaking and entering—carried a possible ten-year jail sentence.

It's a lawyer's job to spell out the worst-case scenario, but also provide you with a best guess on what a final plea bargain might look like. The difference between these two scenarios is always vast.

Finding activists who aren't scared off by the worst-case scenario is often the most challenging pre-action task, but far less so in ACT UP. Our activists did not suffer from a lack of courage.

When Stewart asked James, Lee, Blane, and me if we understood the risks we faced, we all answered quickly: "Yup, we're ready." Rounding out our team of eight, Dan Baker and Deborah Gavito would provide us with on-site support and could face arrest as accomplices. They didn't bat an eye either.

I barely slept that night. This action involved getting past security in the main lobby, and I hadn't nailed down exactly how we'd do this. I brought everyone down to North Carolina based on an untested hunch, and it felt like a total crapshoot. Lying in bed, my head kept spinning. Was there a way to test things first before leading the four of us into an embarrassing fiasco?

At around 2:00 AM, it hit me. If Dan Baker was up to it, he'd be pressed into service the next morning, but at the moment, he was fast asleep. With my mind calmed by this new plan, I finally dozed off.

The alarm clock buzzed loudly at 7:00 AM. With Jay and Steve staying at the hotel to run a hopefully busy media center later that morning, the six of us heading to Research Triangle Park needed to look the part. As we had on earlier actions, we donned our best corporate drag: coats and ties for the guys, a nice blouse and skirt for Deborah. Evidence of our queer city roots was removed, including multiple earrings on Blane and a single diamond stud from my right earlobe. Deborah actually had to *add* earrings.

I briefed Dan on my new plan, and he was game. After a high-protein breakfast, the six of us hit the road in our two rented vehicles for the short drive to Research Triangle Park. We parked the van in a lot across the street from the headquarters at 9:45 AM and did final checks of our cell phones and walkie-talkies. Dan and the four infiltrators piled into the Ford sedan and drove to our target.

At 9:55 AM, Dan confidently walked into the lobby of Burroughs Wellcome. He asked the guards behind the reception desk for directions to the B. W. Fund, which we already knew was across the street. They pointed the way for him and described the short drive.

"Thanks, guys. We've been on the road a while. Is there a bathroom I can use?" Dan asked in his Dan Rather voice, the perfect spokesman voice during interviews, making ACT UP sound calm, determined, and reasonable.

Five minutes later, Dan was back in the car with a full description of his just-completed test run of our infiltration plan. First, the bad news: there were three guards behind the reception desk, not the single guard that had been there during my visit in January. Then, some good news: the lobby's bathroom was just around the corner from the elevator, which was about twenty feet from the reception desk.

At 10:15 AM, all five of us entered the lobby, briefcases in hand. Dan led, and played it casual and cool.

"Hey guys, we're back," he told the guards with a chuckle. "The folks at the B. W. Fund couldn't find the person we have a meeting scheduled with in their directory, and suggested we try here."

"What's the employee's name?" one of the guards asked.

"Peter McGrath," Dan replied, using a mash-up of James and my names.

"Excuse me," I interrupted. "Can the rest of us use the bathroom while you try to find this guy?"

"Sure," the guard said, pointing. "It's just around that corner."

As Dan stayed behind, we walked toward the bathrooms. Luck was with us. A female employee was entering the elevator as we approached, and we slipped in behind her.

"Hey, that's the wrong way!" a guard yelled out.

Our hearts were pounding. The female employee, hearing the guard, began to reach across me for the door open button.

"It's OK," I told her as I put my hand gently on her arm, while the elevator door started to close. We heard the guards' hard leather-soled shoes hitting the lobby's marble floor in a sprint. Thankfully, they were too late. In the confusion now below us, Dan quietly walked out of the lobby to the safety of our car. Our elevator guest, with her slightly concerned expression, got off on the second floor.

We exited on the third floor and made our way to a row of offices facing the nearby highway, where TV trucks could get a good look at us. Along the way, I snapped open my briefcase and pulled out the cell phone and walkie-talkie, handing the latter to Lee. I pointed to the first office with a good highway view, holding the cell phone to my ear. A woman was sitting at the only desk in the small, ten-foot-by-ten-foot space, talking on her phone.

"Excuse me, ma'am," Lee said with authority, pointing with his walkie-talkie with the demeanor of a security guard. "There's a situation on this floor. Please walk calmly to the lobby until further notice."

"Joyce, I gotta go," she said into the phone, then quickly hung up and walked out. As soon as she rounded the corner, the four of us squeezed into her office and shut the door.

I immediately called Jay and Steve at the hotel. "We're in," I said. "Do your magic." Using two phones, a fax machine, and a well-researched contact list of local and national media, they started alerting TV stations and newspapers, faxing out our prewritten press release:

> At 10 AM this morning, four AIDS activists seized an office at the headquarters of Burroughs Wellcome Co., demanding that Burroughs lower the retail price of its antiviral drug Retrovir, or AZT, by at least 25% from the current level of $8,000 a year.

After explaining the issues involved, it went on to say:

The activists, who include both people with AIDS and people with AIDS-Related Complex (ARC), say they plan to stay inside the premises until Burroughs agrees to their demands or until they are evicted. . . . The sit-in is the first time that a group of people dependent on a drug have taken action against the manufacturer's headquarters site. They have set aside $5,000 to reimburse the company for any property damage incurred during the action.

Before I had even ended the call to our media team, that property damage had begun. James wielded his battery-operated drill like a surgeon, while Blane played nurse, quickly handing him a steady flow of steel mending plates and screws. In less than a minute, James had secured all three edges of the metal door to its frame using more than a dozen plates. Even a battering ram couldn't open it now.

But we had a problem. The dinky office had a second door on the wall to the right of the exterior windows. Worse still, this one opened outward. Luckily, James had packed for multiple contingencies and grabbed a bunch of steel corner braces from his briefcase.

"Feed me these," he told Blane as they moved their operation to the second door, which was soon sealed.

The cell phone rang. It was a reporter with the Associated Press. Our media team was feeding us press interviews one at a time, each limited to five minutes, with James's busy drill providing a dramatic soundtrack for the curious reporters.

We also had another problem. Both doors had rectangular Plexiglas transom windows above them, which could be broken through pretty easily. We improvised; Blane emptied a small metal bookcase behind the desk and, with Lee's help, ripped it apart. Two of its disassembled panels fit perfectly over the windows, and James drilled them into place.

We were entombed. An AP wire story about our invasion had already gone out, and a few national radio stations began running it.

Someone started pounding on the office door, asking who we were and why we were there. "We're from ACT UP," I yelled back. "We're demanding that Burroughs Wellcome lower the price of AZT. We are nonviolent and unarmed. But we won't be coming out until the company responds to our demands."

Silence.

We returned to work. While others continued doing cell phone interviews, I unpacked the suction cups and glass-cutter, placing the cups on the huge, slanted wall of glass facing the highway. The plan was to hang our banner outside the window for a dramatic photo of the action. I tried cutting out a large square piece, but the cutter did nothing more than scratch the surface. The windows were almost an inch thick. I tried using James's drill, but none of the bits could penetrate the glass.

By this time, I had worked up a sweat. "Let's try the chair," I said. "Stand in the far corner and face away from the glass."

I closed my eyes and heaved the heavy leather chair against the glass. The smack was loud and scary but did nothing to the glass. I tried again. Nothing. Even studly James tried a couple of times, and still nothing. By this point, the chair wasn't doing so well, with its casters flying off and the armrests bent in.

I radioed Dan and Deborah on their walkie-talkie and told them we'd have to use plan B for the arriving press. We wouldn't be hanging a banner, and the tinted glass prevented cameras from getting a good view of us inside. The TV crews and newspaper photographers were told to congregate near the front entrance of the building.

Then came another knock on the door. "This is the Durham police. You are trespassing on these premises. Open this door, or we'll have to enter forcibly. You have ten minutes to decide."

"Drama queen," Blane muttered.

We waited in silence. Ten minutes later, the door rocked from a hard thud—they were trying to body-slam it open. James's handiwork was holding strong. They slammed harder, with no luck. We heard someone say, "Let me try." As the thuds continued, we all smiled and gave the thumbs up sign to James. Several minutes passed. We heard a muffled conversation down the hall, but couldn't make it out.

And then, *Boom!*

The room shook, and dust fell from the ceiling—they were body-slamming the damn wall instead of the door. Unlike older, hardened office walls, there was apparently nothing between us and the police except two layers of Sheetrock and some steel studwork. With another blow, the room shook again as the entire wall warped inward. A couple ceiling tiles crashed to the floor, as did our hopes of holding our space much longer. The air in the office became cloudy with dust.

"Handcuffs," I said. The others grabbed their handcuffs while I pulled out the long chain and padlock. I wrapped the chain around a radiator cover and locked it into a loop, then we handcuffed ourselves to the chain.

I radioed a last message to Dan and Deborah. "The jig is up. They're breaking through the wall. Tell the press we'll be outside soon."

Amazingly, though, the wall stood. The cops decided to kick a hole through it, then widen it. After three or four kicks, we saw a boot burst through the wall about two feet above the floor. The boot kept kicking until the hole was about two feet wide.

A cop on all fours peeked through, spotting us across the room. He crawled through, immediately followed by another cop, and then another. The three of them rushed toward us, sweating and angry.

"We won't resist," I said. "It's OK—we won't resist."

As they assessed the situation, they soon calmed down.

"What's this?" one of them asked, grabbing the chain.

"A chain," I replied.

The cops started ripping apart the radiator cover to release the chain. One of them used James's drill to remove all the mending plates from the door.

"Guess we don't have to handcuff you," a cop laughed. "Let's just lead them out with the chain."

Ooh, I thought to myself, *that'll make for a great picture.*

They grabbed our briefcases and unused banner and led us back to the elevator, then down to the lobby. Dozens of employees had gathered there, standing back, silent, but with all eyes observing us as we passed.

We had been inside for just fifty-five minutes. I was pissed off they got us out that quickly, but it didn't matter. We had given the press plenty of time to gather outside. They swarmed us as we approached the parking lot. One of the TV reporters yelled a question, asking us why we had sealed ourselves inside the headquarters.

"Burroughs Wellcome is profiting off of our lives," I said. "That's why we did today what we did. And if they don't see to start listening to my community—to our community, the AIDS community—then we're going to be back."

A photographer with the *Raleigh News & Observer*, the leading local paper, snapped the perfect picture: two sheriff's deputies from Durham leading us to their car. One is wearing a classic four-dent, flat-brim sheriff's hat with a large shield on the front. Blane is in the foreground, midstride, taking a confident step forward. James and I have our suit coats off, slung casually over our shoulders as if strolling on a lunch break on a warm summer day. The deputy in front is leading us all by a long looped chain. Perfectly framed, the headquarters of Burroughs Wellcome towers behind us. The picture filled almost a quarter of the *Raleigh News & Observer*'s front page the next morning. Another newspaper dubbed us "the chain-gang."

Getting arrested at Burroughs Wellcome headquarters,
(left to right) Blane Mosley, James McGrath, Lee Arsenault,
and me, April 21, 1989. *Raleigh News & Observer*

During the drive to the Durham police station, the four of us were crammed in the back of a sheriff's cruiser. One of the deputies asked us to explain the issue we were protesting about.

"Have you heard of AZT?" I asked.

"I think so," one of them replied. "That's that AIDS drug, right?"

"Yup," I said. "We're trying to get them to lower the price. They originally priced it at $10,000 a year, the most expensive drug in history."

"Ten thousand dollars?" the deputy asked, incredulously. "That's crazy!"

That was our first sign we might get some very sympathetic press coverage that day.

But not everyone would be so friendly. In Durham County, a magistrate sets release conditions and bail after your arrest. Our lawyer had warned us that the magistrate on duty that day had a reputation for being very tough. She would likely look unkindly on radical young activists from New York City flagrantly breaking laws in her tough-on-crime southern county. It probably didn't help that all three local TV stations were parked outside, each running live reports on their noon broadcasts. We were the lead story on all three.

After they booked and fingerprinted us, we sat in a holding cell for about two hours while charges were being decided. The police continued their kindness, only charging us with two misdemeanors: first-degree trespass and willful damage to property. The maximum sentence we faced was two and a half years in jail.

With the TV crews still waiting outside, we were brought before the magistrate. She was behind a high counter in a small room with no chairs, not far from the holding cells. "Gentlemen," she began, "I'm sure you were looking forward to some television interviews before getting home to New York, but these are still serious charges. I'm setting your bail at $5,000 each."

"So, twenty thousand total?" I asked.

"That's right," she replied smugly.

"Do you take traveler's checks?" I asked, breaking a smile, knowing full well they were acceptable. I reached into my inside coat pocket and whipped out a thick stack of $100 American Express traveler's checks.

Her eyes widened.

"Do you have a pen?" I asked. I had brought exactly $20,000, having withdrawn the amount from my brokerage account before the trip. Our lawyer nailed it: he predicted we might need that much if the magistrate got tough with us.

Outside, the press swarmed us again, and we answered all their questions. Jay and Steve also had two of us lined up for live studio interviews at the top of the 5:30 and 6:00 PM local news broadcasts. CNN had us on their hourly loop, running the footage of us being brought out of the building.

Our stated commitment to pay for any property damage not only helped with getting sympathetic press coverage but also kept us out of jail *and* out of court. Within seventy-two hours, Burroughs Wellcome struck a deal with our lawyer dropping all charges if we reimbursed them for the damage. Rebuilding the wrecked office and replacing the heavily scratched window would cost $9,180. It would make our demo an expensive one, but ACT UP made good on our press release promise to pay. Durham County sent a check to return the $20,000 I spent on bail.

The motel, rentals, and hardware had cost less than a thousand dollars, bringing the total spent to just over $10,000. Not bad for an action that created a local and national news story focused on the high price of AZT.

We had struck a blow, hurting the company's reputation in its own backyard. But I was under no illusion that it would be enough. On rare occasions, civil disobedience can have an immediate pay-off, like the zap against Kowa Pharmaceuticals. But more often, it takes months if not years of doggedness—a campaign of constant pressure, and if you can ratchet up the pressure, all the better.

Five months after our North Carolina action, we did just that, drowning out the opening bell and disrupting trading on the floor of the New York Stock Exchange. Burroughs Wellcome threw in the towel four days later, lowering the price of AZT by 20 percent—nearly what we had demanded. Four months later, the FDA cut the recommended dose of AZT in half, since studies were showing this was just as effective and far less toxic than the original dose. This brought the annual cost down to $3,200.

When the second drug against HIV was approved in 1991, Bristol Myers priced it 20 percent less than AZT, or around $2,600. Hoffmann–La Roche priced the third drug against HIV even lower. For a decade after AZT's approval, all of the pharmaceutical companies that brought AIDS drugs to market avoided Burroughs Wellcome's self-inflicted wound. Every new drug stayed well below $10,000—the original benchmark Wellcome had tried to set. Even when the first protease inhibitors, a new class of antivirals, were approved nine years after AZT came to market, they were priced at around $6,000 a year.

The cascading effect of a far lower benchmark ultimately saved Medicaid and Medicare—and thus taxpayers—billions of dollars.

Not a bad return on a $10,000 investment.

"AZT killed all my friends." I've heard this hundreds of times from survivors of the first fifteen years of the AIDS crisis. It has been said so often and by so many that it has taken on an aura of fact. The drug's early toxicity and inability to save lives, when used alone, forever branded it as a killer.

At the risk of angering many who propagate this legacy, this narrative is largely false. Yes, at the original high dose of 1,200 to 1,500 mg a day, AZT caused well-known toxicities in about half the people who took it. There were gastrointestinal effects, including nausea and diarrhea, though the most common side effect was anemia, a reduction in red blood cells. A modest drop in these cells could cause fatigue and make you look pale. About one in ten patients was hit with severe anemia, which was treated with frequent blood transfusions when AZT was approved in 1987.

Thankfully, a new biologic drug that reversed anemia, called EPO, was approved in 1989, and transfusions were no longer needed.

However, the biggest change came when the FDA cut the recommended AZT dose in half. At the lower dose, far fewer patients became anemic, and none required transfusions or EPO. But by this point, the damage had been done. A vocal minority of AIDS activists were declaring that AZT was toxic, and now the advice commonly shared among people living with HIV was to hold out as long as you could before trying the drug.

Even with the new dosage, AZT wasn't able to fulfill its promise and save lives. Sure, there were plenty of stories of patients starting it and having their health bounce back enough to return home from the hospital. But the effect was always short lived; almost everyone got sick again and eventually died. Only in hindsight do we know that this had nothing to do with AZT per se. It's what happened with *all* the AIDS drugs, even the first protease inhibitors. The virus developed resistance to all of the early antivirals when they were used as monotherapy—that is, alone.

In the early '90s, a self-fulfilling feedback loop reinforced AZT's bad reputation. Those with higher CD4 counts would hold off on starting the drug, while those closer to death would try it. The latter group might get a short-term benefit but still died within a year or two. This fed community perceptions that those who avoided AZT did better than those who tried it. While unintended, doesn't this noxious legacy challenge the hard but very rational choices our friends made before they died?

And this wasn't even the whole story. By 1995, about a third of those who knew they were HIV positive were taking an antiviral. Though most of them were taking only one drug, about 40 percent were trying two-drug combinations, using some combination of AZT, ddI, ddC, d4T, or 3TC. I was among them, and many of us lived long enough to add a protease inhibitor when they came out the following year.

So, in actuality, AZT wasn't killing us. It was saving us.

The kicker here is that few of those who still claim that AZT killed all their friends are aware of what happened to the drug after the protease inhibitors came out. Burroughs Wellcome released a new pill called Combivir that combined two of its older drugs. The new protease inhibitors were most often used with Combivir in the three-drug regimens that in just two years dropped the death rate in the United States by two-thirds.

Combivir soon became the biggest-selling AIDS drug, and the first to top $1 billion in sales. It remained the number-one-selling AIDS drug for the next ten years, until Truvada, another two-drug combo pill, passed it.

Combivir contains AZT, so when used in combination, AZT saved millions of lives. It also prevented hundreds of thousands of infections between HIV-positive mothers and their newborn babies.

How does all of this square with "AZT killed all my friends?" It doesn't. And it shouldn't.

I've talked with dozens of leading AIDS researchers over the years, and none of them know of a patient who died from AZT's well-known toxicities. I've never heard about a death certificate that included AZT-induced anemia as a contributing cause of death. The *actual* history of AIDS is important, both to the memory of millions who have died and the millions who live with HIV now, and this is one part of the story we've been getting wrong.

Which brings me full circle to our January 1989 meeting with David Barry, Burroughs Wellcome's Mr. AZT. His predictions of the future were far more accurate than some of our reflections today. After Mark Harrington pressed Dr. Barry on how much Burroughs Wellcome was cooperating with the National Institutes of Health on trials looking at experimental drugs similar to AZT, he looked beyond those trials.

"My prejudice, if you want to call it prejudice, is that a final real management of this disease is going to depend on multiple drug therapies, period," he said, leaning into the table. "And I think that's been true with other chronic infectious or transformational diseases for years. That was true for tuberculosis. It's true for leprosy. It's true for leukemias and lymphomas. Wherever you have prolonged infection and patient immunosuppression, your best management is going to be with multidrug therapy."

"And for $100,000 a year, you'll be able to keep 'em alive for the rest of their lives," I replied.

We both made some solid predictions then, with Dr. Barry's being the far more profound. Remember, this was early 1989. He nailed what would happen seven years later, when adding a protease inhibitor to two of the older drugs proved to be HIV's Achilles' heel.

If AZT and the next few drugs had been priced around $8,000 instead of $3,000 a year, then I would have been right, too. Today, after three decades of inflation, the cost of three-drug regimens for HIV is around $40,000. Their prices are ridiculous, but if we hadn't dramatically lowered the baseline drug prices of the first few antivirals, it would have been so much worse.

David Barry's predictive skills weren't perfect. For instance, he told us bluntly that a price cut for AZT would never help with access in Africa.

I pushed back. "A lower price may make it affordable for the World Health Organization or some other international agency to set up, to start distributing to Africa," I said.

"Peter, have you been to Africa?" Dr. Barry asked dismissively.

I had not, but the United Nations helped establish the Global Fund to Fight AIDS, Tuberculosis and Malaria thirteen years later. Activists successfully pushed all the pharma companies to allow generic antivirals into Africa and other parts of the world needing access. Millions were offered free treatment.

Regardless of Dr. Barry's lack of imagination on future access issues, he had provided Mark and me with a roadmap for the future of AIDS research, even if we didn't realize it right away. At the time, we viewed him as an evil genius. While we pushed back against the evil bits, we also tried to absorb his steady flow of genius. In the years that followed, we all grew and continued learning from each other. Dr. Barry became the CEO of Burroughs Wellcome USA and helped create a model for community engagement that other companies still try to emulate.

In the late '90s, Dr. Barry and I got invited up to Harvard Business School each year to help the students debate a case study about ACT UP's stock exchange action and Burroughs Wellcome's response. Over dinners and drinks, our shared history and mutual respect shifted toward friendship. No one could have foreseen that on the day when we first met.

While on a business trip to California in 2002, David died suddenly from a heart attack. He was only fifty-eight. That prediction he made about a multidrug solution came true, and it is the only reason I outlived him. Those of us fighting AIDS lost an imperfect colleague the day that he passed.

9

"YOU CAN ALL NOW CONSIDER YOURSELVES MEMBERS OF ACT UP"

A S I STEPPED ONTO THE STAGE inside the Moscone Center's cavernous main hall for a microphone and podium check, the space was already buzzing with tension. It was a half hour before the opening ceremony of the Sixth International AIDS Conference on June 20, 1990, and eleven thousand attendees would soon be pouring in. A few dozen ACT UP New Yorkers had already grabbed seats near the stage and were milling around, making the conference organizers very nervous.

Outside, the protests had already started. Hundreds of officers in full riot gear from the San Francisco Police Department were squaring off against about five hundred activists from ACT UP's West Coast chapters—a ridiculous ratio of one cop for every two protesters, which exemplified the city's fear after weeks of mainstream media reports had predicted a violent showdown.

Everything was coming to a head. ACT UP was at its peak as a national movement, frequently grabbing headlines. Just four weeks earlier, we had reminded the country of our first national demonstration at the FDA, this time converging on the beautifully manicured campus of the National Institutes of Health. My affinity group from the Burroughs Wellcome invasion, suggestively named the Power Tools, had plenty of new members. We symbolically stormed Building One, the NIH's main headquarters, marching toward it through two thousand demonstrators with surplus military smoke grenades atop twenty-foot poles, creating a majestic rainbow of battlefield fog above our heads.

Five months before that, ACT UP had stunned the nation with a demonstration inside St. Patrick's Cathedral, protesting the Catholic church's anti-condom, gay-bashing, AIDS-spreading policies. What was supposed to be a silent die in during the homily devolved into a handful of screaming hecklers, followed by what the church called a desecration of the Host when a wafer was thrown to the ground during Communion. People dying unnecessarily? That's OK. A wafer being crumbled? Blasphemy!

The AIDS research effort was finally in high gear, too, with the NIH's AIDS budget tripling since ACT UP's launch. The annual international AIDS conferences had become newsworthy events, with researchers announcing results from the latest studies inside large media centers packed with journalists.

Activists had stormed the stage during the previous year's gathering in Montreal, pushing past security after organizers refused to allow patients and their advocates to attend. Now the San Francisco organizers tried their best to play nice. Activists would be allowed to register and attend all the meetings. And in a major peace offering, ACT UP New York was given a speaking slot during the opening ceremony.

The 1990 conference would soon get more media coverage than any AIDS conference before or since. History can thank Larry Kramer for that. For many months leading up to the conference, Larry had been lobbying the organizers for a speaking gig. By any measure, he deserved the platform. His speech three years earlier at the Lesbian and Gay Community Services Center had sparked our movement and changed the course of AIDS history. He had a proven knack for seizing the moment.

But another member of ACT UP had recently galvanized the group with a speech titled "Why We Fight." Vito Russo, the author of the seminal book *The Celluloid Closet*, was a prominent AIDS activist in his own right, and unlike Larry, he was widely beloved.

ACT UP's conference planning committee sent the organizers a ranked list of three names, with Vito's at the top. Larry was listed third, after Michael Callen. Larry relentlessly lobbied the organizers, punctuating his efforts with a threatening letter. "I think you will find it to prove a big mistake not to have honored my fervent solicitations," he wrote, ending with "If you wish to view this letter as a threat, please do so."

Conference organizers, unbowed, picked Vito Russo.

Pissed, Larry made good on his threat, lashing out in a column for *OutWeek* magazine. "The same Doctor Strangeloves who control the ACTG system," he wrote, referring to the NIH's AIDS Clinical Trials Group, "are the same Doctor Strangeloves who are controlling the agenda of, and shutting out any dissident voices from, the Sixth International Conference on AIDS. . . . WE MUST RIOT! I AM CALLING FOR A FUCKING RIOT!"

Larry was besieged with interview requests and seemed to up the ante with each one he granted. Appearing on *The MacNeil/Lehrer NewsHour*, he dropped the *t*-word, saying, "We are up against a wall. There is no avenue left to us except terrorism." Most of ACT UP's chapters, including New York, repudiated Larry's call for violence, but the rhetoric alone raised the stakes. And with that, the press had their juicy hook for covering the June conference: there would be AIDS blood on the streets of San Francisco.

Nearly five thousand articles would be written about AIDS in the four weeks surrounding the conference, and Peter Jennings would host ABC's *World News Tonight* from outside the Moscone Center during its first two nights.

As I and two dozen ACT UP New York members were packing our bags for the trip to San Francisco, I got a phone call from community relations director Dana Van Gorder, the highest-ranking openly gay man on the conference organizing team. He had terrible news: "Vito is in the hospital."

I had heard that Vito had been diagnosed with PCP pneumonia the week before, and that he was recovering on Bactrim. But it was apparently worse than I had heard: his doctors had also discovered that his Kaposi's sarcoma had spread to his lungs.

Like most gay men by then, Dana had made many hard phone calls like this, and he shifted quickly to contingency plans. "We still want an activist to speak at the opening ceremony," he continued. "I know it's last minute, but if you're up for it, we'd like you to step in."

While I was stunned by the offer, I knew it would be best to clear it first with Vito, if I could reach him, and then Larry. "Can I get back to you by later today?" I asked. Dana was fine with that.

When I called Larry and told him about Dana's offer, he immediately pounced, hoping for one last chance to lobby for the speaking slot. "You need to tell them I should speak at this," he said. "You need to tell them that it should be me."

He had pulled rank, and I dutifully obeyed. I called Dana back and made the pitch for Larry. It was a pitch made with genuine conviction. Larry deserved it, and he was intent on moving the audience, both in the room and beyond its walls, to double down on the fight against

AIDS. "I'll give a moving speech for everyone, not just the activists," he had said. "It will make them all cry."

But Dana was a brick wall. "That's a nonstarter," he shot back. "Either you fill the speaking slot or ACT UP loses it altogether."

So I called Larry again and let him know Dana's reply, word for word. "Well, I guess you should say yes then," he said with a heavy sigh. After a few more calls, I got sign-off from ACT UP's planning committee and, most important, got Vito's blessing, as well as his permission to quote from "Why We Fight." I called Dana back, and accepted.

Coincidentally, another thing was peaking as the conference approached: my ego. For better or worse, I had earned a bit of national reputation as an activist by this point. All the fundraising, dozens of gaffe-free interviews in the national press, multiple arrests, and masterminding a couple of ACT UP's most impactful actions had only bolstered my determination to make a dent. If Larry could spark a movement, maybe I could give it a little nudge away from his increasing divisiveness.

From its first days, ACT UP struggled with how to deal with the institutions and the rigid systems it needed to change. With the vigor of youth, we felt like revolutionaries, but with the desperation of dying, we became effective incrementalists. Those contradictions fueled our greatest successes and our most painful rifts.

Take the pharmaceutical industry, for example. We had a vocal minority who dreamed of a purely socialized system, in which the government would bring promising drugs to market, hopefully to a single-payer health care system. Profits, profiteering, and the profit motive wouldn't have a role in this system. It's a nice dream, but it lacks a single historical proof of concept. In countries that removed the profit motive from drug development, their contributions to effective drug therapies over the last century are almost nonexistent.

But even these arguments were moot within ACT UP. The folks with AIDS would remind us, "We don't have time to overthrow capitalism," and that was that. The ticking clock for almost half of our community forced us to adopt hard-nosed pragmatism as one of our guiding forces. We didn't have the luxury of playing a long game, so the smartest path forward was to push current institutions and systems to bend, but not break.

By 1990, our methods for getting the *scientific* establishment to bend to our will were being openly questioned. ACT UP was facing a full-on backlash from leading AIDS researchers, epidemiologists, and biostatisticians who worked hand in hand with the NIH. Our posturing and rhetoric had established an us-versus-them paradigm. When we seized the stage during the opening ceremony of the AIDS conference in Montreal the year before, no one walked out. Initially, we were listened to, and many in the crowd stood and cheered us. But then we went too far.

ACT UP refused to leave the stage. A ninety-minute standoff ensued, and audience members left in frustration. And once the official ceremony finally started, we just made things worse. We booed and hissed during some of the speeches. When Barbados's representative to the United Nations, Dame Nita Barrow, called for compassion for "victims of this disease," our word police pounced and starting hissing. Among US activists, using *victim* when referring to a person living with HIV was a big no-no. *What the fuck are we doing*, I thought. *She's on our side!*

Zambia's president Kenneth Kaunda, one of the first African leaders to speak out about AIDS, had to cut his remarks short, because the ceremony had run way past its scheduled length. Here were mostly White American activists disrupting Black and Brown speakers fighting AIDS in other parts of the world. And we'd go on to disrupt other sessions that week, including scientific presentations.

Less than a year later, ACT UP was protesting at the NIH, demanding a seat at the table at all their scientific committee meetings. Is it any wonder the scientists were resisting? Larry Kramer had just been quoted in the *Wall Street Journal* saying, "I think the time for violence has now arrived. I'd like to see an AIDS terrorist army." Mark Harrington had branded some of the leading AIDS researchers working with the NIH "the Gang of Five."

We were entering dangerous territory. Even though most of our members didn't think this way at all, many of our most public tactics seemed to say, *Only we care about AIDS, and everyone else is a problem, or worse.*

Fortunately, as the conference approached, ACT UP's Treatment and Data Committee had been debating all of this, and we decided to adjust our tactics. We insisted on attending the conference but made a firm commitment not to disrupt the exchange of scientific information, including presentations and Q&As. Any protests we planned inside would have to be nondisruptive.

By repudiating Larry's riot-related comments, and implicitly repudiating our own tactics in Montreal, ACT UP was already pivoting toward fewer confrontations with the scientific community. I viewed my speech as an opportunity to broadcast this change in an emotionally compelling way. We could hit a reset button, right there, at the conference, and test the new relationship over the days that followed.

I knew I'd have to start the speech as any ACT UPer would, driving home some of our most immediate political issues. So I worked with T&D to craft that section of the speech and even build in some audience and activist participation. But I was asked by the organizers to provide a personal perspective as a young man living with HIV, so I told T&D that I would write that part on my own.

Pulling an all-nighter before the opening ceremony, I crafted the second half of the speech as the worried musings of a twenty-nine-year-old who might die from AIDS in the next few years. Instead of looking inward, I would wonder aloud about everyone else in that massive hall, the frontline professionals and the frontline activists who were warily gathered after months of conflict. Kumbaya platitudes wouldn't work with this crowd, but looking squarely at the divide might.

As I finished my mic test at the podium, Dana Van Gorder and his boss, Dr. Robert Wachter, the conference's program director, joined me on the stage. They looked like they hadn't slept in days. Even still, they seemed fully caffeinated, as the moment they had spent a year planning was about to begin.

"Peter, can we have a word?" Dana asked. Wachter had the advance copy of my speech. I had whited out the first few paragraphs that would orchestrate the activism T&D had preplanned.

"We can't allow demonstrators on the stage," Wachter said, pointing to the whited-out space of the speech. Word of our plans had obviously leaked.

"Don't test us," Dana threatened.

The entire front edge of the five-foot-high platform stage was lined with potted flowers. I imagined falling pottery, broken shards, dirt, and crushed flowers covering the stage.

"Excuse me for a sec," I replied, and walked toward the press pen at the side of the stage. I waved over Bill Bahlman, a T&D member who had obtained a press pass. In addition to forging dozens of delegate passes, a handful of ACT UP members had successfully applied for free press credentials to attend the conference on behalf of obscure gay media outlets.

I crouched down and whispered a quick new plan into Bill's ear. As I returned to Dana and Dr. Wachter, Bill left the press pen and passed the word to the activists saving seats in the front rows. He gave me a thumbs up.

"Done," I said, although neither Dana nor Wachter looked convinced. I walked away to reread my speech in quiet before the ceremony started at 4:00 PM.

It seems I gave Dr. Wachter one last scare. As he would later write, "At 3:55, an assistant ran up to tell me that, at the last second, Staley had dropped off a single slide to be shown during his speech. I sprinted to see it. We simply could not allow a slide laden with obscenities or calling for violence to be projected to the audience. Out of breath, I arrived at the projector and looked at the slide. On it was a photograph of George Bush. The opening ceremony began."

Once the opening plenary speakers were gathered backstage, the full weight of the moment sunk in. I was introduced to the other speakers, including the host city's mayor, Art Agnos, a frequent target of ACT UP San Francisco. The scene around us made us all gulp. A massive wall of curtains separated a large area at the end of the hall from the stage and the hall itself. The curtain darkened this backstage area, and as our eyes adjusted, we realized we were far from alone. There were lines of them, in formation . . . almost two hundred police officers . . . in full riot gear. The audience had no idea.

I was gobsmacked. It seemed like a huge overreaction to Larry Kramer's chest-thumping and to the rumors that ACT UP would be demonstrating during my speech. Thankfully, the treatment activists in the audience were ACT UP's most disciplined strategists. If they stuck to our revised plan, these riot cops would hopefully remain hidden. And if they didn't? I tried not to let my mind go there.

The audience applauded nervously as we all took our seats onstage. The conference cochairs spoke first, hitting all the right political notes, openly challenging a new US immigration law banning people with HIV from entering the country. Over a hundred organizations had joined a boycott of the conference in protest, including every ACT UP chapter except New York's (its treatment activists had fought too hard for access to these conferences to ignore the largest one to date), and the International AIDS Society had announced that all future conferences would be held outside the United States.

Mayor Agnos then got the crowd going with a political stem-winder of a speech. "There is something wrong when our nation's leaders would rather debate on how to protect the fabric of our flag than how to protect the fabric of our people's lives," he said, referring to recent congressional grandstanding after the Supreme Court struck down the Flag Protection Act nine days earlier.

With the audience applauding loudly, he continued: "If history should record that this is the last International AIDS Conference in the United States, it should be because we have solved the epidemic and not because some people played politics with human life." All ten thousand seats were filled, and the mayor's face was projected on eight fifteen-by-twenty-foot screens throughout the hall. The crowd roared.

My speech was scheduled about halfway through the two-and-a-half-hour opener, during a section titled "Personal Perspectives on an Epidemic." By this point, eighty ACT UP members had been arrested during the protests outside, and the count was rising. Just before I was introduced, a video montage was played on the big screens with short comments from a diverse group of people living with HIV/AIDS. Larry Kramer, to my surprise, was among them.

"*You* know what is going on and what is not going on, and yet you refuse to use your voices," he said, wearing a Malcolm X T-shirt that read, BY ANY MEANS NECESSARY. "You are coconspirators in this plague, though you think you are heroes."

I saw nothing but stone-faced stares in the crowd, and began to worry that I might get the same reaction. Maybe their feelings toward ACT UP, fueled by fear and frustration, were now unmovable. I'd soon find out.

As the lights came back up and I walked to the podium, a few hoots and hollers from the ACT UPers in the crowd helped settle my nerves.

At the Sixth International AIDS
Conference, June 20, 1990. *Photo
by Anita Armstrong, © International AIDS
Conference*

"In an effort to bridge the gap that now seems to exist between
AIDS activists and you, members of the medical and scientific com-
munities, I would like you to join us in an act of activism," I began.
"Trust me, you'll enjoy this. . . . But first, I would like to be joined *in
front* of this stage by my fellow AIDS activists. Will you all come up?"

The crowd stirred. Dozens of ACT UPers started leaving their seats
and moved toward the stage. Dr. Wachter started to sweat. To my surprise, many in the audience started to applaud. The activists embraced
each other in warm hugs as they gathered in front of the stage. Press
camerapeople swarmed out of their holding area to capture it all.

"At this moment there are others just like us who are trying to
get into this conference but are being barred by the billy clubs of San

Francisco police. And there are still others like us who are trying to get through customs at the San Francisco airport but are being detained instead because they are gay. And these same custom agents are under orders to keep a lookout for AZT in people's luggage. If you're found with any, you're put on the next plane out of the country.

"There is a man that could have prevented these absurdities," I continued, as the slide of President Bush appeared on all the screens to scattered boos. "I ask all of you now—you were asked to stand earlier in silence—we're going to do something different. We're going to stand ACT UP style. If you believe that the present INS policy barring people living with HIV disease from entering this country is useless as a health policy and discriminatory as well, please stand now and remain standing."

I looked out at the audience, large enough to cover three football fields. All the ACT UPers standing by the stage turned around to witness a response. Like a quick and sudden wave from the front row to the back, the entire audience stood up. The ACT UPers went nuts.

"Now, I'd like to ask you to join us in vocalizing our collective anger. Join us in a chant against the man who could bring down the INS barriers. Join us in a chant against the man who has decided to show his commitment to fighting AIDS by refusing to be here today. Instead, he is at this very moment in North Carolina attending a fundraiser for the homophobic author of the INS barriers, that pig in the Senate known as Jesse Helms."

Loud booing and hissing arose from the crowd.

"Join us in this chant: THREE HUNDRED THOUSAND DEAD FROM AIDS, WHERE IS GEORGE? THREE HUNDRED THOUSAND DEAD FROM AIDS, WHERE IS GEORGE?"

The hall filled with a unified chant. I even caught Dr. Wachter mouthing the words.

"Thank you. You can sit down," I said to signal the end of our moment of collective activism.

"You can all now consider yourselves members of ACT UP."

Cheers from the activists. Applause from the audience. Smiles all around. We hadn't burned the place down. We had won them over.

Couched as a series of questions to President Bush, I spent the next few moments slamming various facets of our nation's AIDS response, or lack thereof. These included issues ACT UP had raised during our most recent protest at the NIH, like its terrible record of under-recruiting women and people of color into its AIDS clinical trials. "I ask you, President Bush, is your war against AIDS for White men only?" I added, this time using Bush as a stand-in for many of the leading scientists in the room who ran those trials.

And then I pivoted away from the activist anger the audience had likely expected. I could speak as a twenty-nine-year-old man who might not make it to his thirty-first birthday. I could speak as someone who had been fighting hard for more time but was worried about losing that fight.

"I understand that I'm supposed to give a personal perspective on living with HIV," I started. "As you can tell from the speech thus far, I have never been able to view my situation as just a battle between me and HIV. I have always been painfully aware that in order for me to beat this virus and live, I will need a great deal of help from all of you as well as from my government. Cooperation between all of us is the fastest way to a cure.

"However, recently, I've begun to lose hope in our ability to work together to end this crisis. If anything, the gap that exists between all of you and AIDS activists seems to be widening.

"From your side, we're being constantly told to butt out. In a meeting I went to last week with other members of ACT UP New York's Treatment and Data Committee and NIAID's top brass, Dan Hoth, the director of the ACTG told us that our participation at ACTG meetings, as observers only, could possibly scare the pharmaceutical companies away and bring the whole system crashing down. Robert

Gallo has said publicly that many of his fellow AIDS researchers are talking of leaving the field due to the antics of AIDS activists.

"On my side, the level of anger and frustration is reaching such a point that attitudes claiming that all of you are uncaring and in it for greed are now widespread. I'm being taught to hate the 'Gang of Five'—Drs. Corey, Merrigan, Fischl, Hirsch, and Richman—without ever having met any of them. My good friend Larry Kramer has been trying to talk me into being an AIDS terrorist.

"Is there any way we can avoid all of this? I'm not sure anymore. I do know that we have judged you at times unfairly. I believe that many of you care deeply about ending this crisis and that greed is not your motivation for fighting this disease.

"I also know that you have frequently judged us unfairly, too. Yes, ACT UP has made mistakes, such as choosing an inappropriate target for a demonstration or using an offensive tactic. Communion wafers come to mind.

"But let's be fair here. When we make mistakes, what's the fallout? Some people become offended and begin to hate ACT UP. Whereas when government or the scientific community makes a mistake, such as the now legendary delays in bringing aerosolized pentamidine to market, thousands of people can die.

"While at times we may offend you, remember as well that like you, ACT UP has succeeded in prolonging the lives of thousands of people living with HIV disease. An accelerated drug approval process; marketing approval for DHPG; early access to ddI; Parallel Track; a lower price on AZT; our own needle distribution programs in New York and San Francisco. These are just some of our victories in the war against AIDS.

"Can we all, before it's too late, begin to understand each other? Will we realize that we share similar motivations? Can we try, at least this week, to bridge the widening gap between us?

"I'd like to close with words written by the man that was supposed to be speaking to you now, Vito Russo. Vito fell ill a week ago with PCP, even though he was on aerosolized pentamidine. He's recovering on Bactrim. But now they found KS in his lungs. The following words were spoken by Vito to a crowd of ACT UPers, but it is my hope that they will speak to us all:

> AIDS is a test of who we are as a people. When future generations ask what we did in the war, we have to be able to tell them that we were out here fighting. And we have to leave a legacy to the generations of people who will come after us. Remember, that someday, the AIDS crisis will be over. And when that day has come and gone, there will be a people alive on this earth—gay people and straight people, Black people and White people, men and women—who will hear the story, that once, there was a terrible disease, and that a brave group of people stood up and fought and in some cases died so that others might live and be free.

I had never spoken to an audience of this size, but I could tell from the pin-drop silence that I had tapped into our shared fears. Speaking bluntly about the relationship between the two camps in the room—the scientists and the activists—and not dodging the reality that both sides were angry and even fearful of the other, helped clear the air for something new.

After I ended with Vito's words, the audience responded with a standing ovation.

———————

The days that followed seemed to reveal a new and growing comfort between the two camps.

Tony Fauci, after conferring with the ACTG's executive committee (including the "Gang of Five"), surprised Mark Harrington with some news before a community forum during the third night of the conference. We had been battling Fauci for months over community access to all the decision-making committees within the ACTG. It had been one of our chief demands at the NIH protest a month earlier. Despite months of lobbying, Fauci could never get sign-off from the executive committee for anything more than community "observers" to attend.

"Mark!" he said. "I've got good news. Last night I met with the executive committee and told them they have to let you guys in. The ACTG meetings will be open from now on."

We had finally won our seat at the table. To this day, full community representation has become the norm on NIH committees across all disease groups.

Fauci gave a speech during the closing ceremony of the conference and added his voice to the call for more cooperation. "You heard from Peter Staley representing ACT UP New York in the opening ceremonies in an eloquent, passionate, angry, and poignant expression of his personal fears and frustrations and the frustrations of activist groups," he said. "They do have something important to say, and they can contribute constructively to our mission. Scientists do not need to adhere to every suggestion made by activists, because some may be misguided. However, scientists themselves do not have a lock on correctness. Activists bring a special insight into the disease that can actually be helpful in the way we design our scientific approaches. We must join together, for together we are a formidable force with a common goal."

It was a nice bookend to a remarkable week. I thought I had done some of the best activism in my life, but I was in for a rude awakening back in New York. For all my self-professed political skills, I was wholly unprepared for the blowback headed my way.

ACT UP, the movement, had just entered its fourth year. As a community response to an outside world that seemed to want us dead, we often felt like a joyous and loving family, united in our response. But now that unity was beginning to fray.

Among our members in New York, two camps had started to develop with different visions on strategy. The treatment activists within T&D had been fully leveraging the movement's initial impulse to use inside/outside strategies in tandem. We'd keep up the outside pressure using civil disobedience while simultaneously insisting on a few seats inside, at the table, with the same institutions we sought to influence.

The other camp preferred a more traditional civil disobedience approach, sticking to the streets outside. They viewed inside strategies with suspicion, pointing to the very real risk of being co-opted. Insiders could get too cozy with those they met with, and might concede too much to institutions that needed to change.

As T&D's work became ascendant, both inside and outside, with multiple policy victories grabbing most of the movement's media attention, the old-school activists started to bristle at its lopsided influence. There was a growing sense that the boys in T&D—and with a few key exceptions, we were mostly boys—needed to be reined in.

Our arrogance didn't help. We were young and often lacked the maturity to manage conflict and criticism. During ACT UP's first couple of years, as we were climbing our own learning curves on AIDS research and the government agencies we'd be dealing with, we were mindful of the need to bring the entire membership of ACT UP along for the ride. Full transparency about all our activities was crucial to building internal support. But as our work grew more and more intense, that transparency became increasingly patchy. Early on, it was easy to report on the one meeting with FDA officials that happened every few months, but once we reached a frenzied state of weekly meetings and phone calls with various agencies and pharma companies, we often dropped the ball on fully informing the larger group.

For those who always doubted our inside strategy, this only fed their distrust. The last straw for them occurred when T&D success-fully won a floor vote to attend the San Francisco conference, even though almost all of the other ACT UP chapters had voted to join the boycott and remain on the streets outside.

As one of the perceived leaders within T&D, I was a target for their ire. Even before the conference, my poster-boy status within the movement had placed a bull's-eye on my back. When the *Advocate*, the oldest and most widely read LGBT magazine at that time, did a feature story on ACT UP earlier that year, there I was, all alone, on its cover. Sure, this was the magazine's idea, but as a self-proclaimed media whore, I also leaped at the chance. Maybe it was self-promotion, but I don't remember it that way. At the time, I just wanted to use every skill I had in this fight with the time I had left.

I wanted to lead, and the speech I gave in San Francisco did just that.

But not everyone in ACT UP wanted to follow. ABC's *Nightline* broadcast big chunks of my remarks to a national audience just hours after I delivered them. The speech and the resulting détente between scientists and activists during the conference dominated our press coverage.

Unbeknownst to me, a perfect storm of resentment was brewing back in New York. ACT UP's first Monday-night meeting after the conference was even more packed than usual. After six months of saturated news coverage, including a lengthy profile on the front page of the *New York Times*'s Metropolitan News section, headlined "Rude, Rash, Effective, Act-Up Shifts AIDS Policy," we were outgrowing our space at the Center.

Bill Monaghan, a fiery, heavyset redhead who had become one of the angrier voices among our old-school activists, came prepared to launch an ambush. When the discussion turned to the AIDS conference, he was one of the first to raise a hand to speak. "I'm furious about how we were represented at the opening ceremony while hundreds of ACT UP members from other chapters were getting violently arrested outside," he yelled, then pointed his finger at me. "How could Peter Staley deliver a speech apologizing for ACT UP tactics in front of thousands of scientists and government officials?"

The room stirred with murmurs and tension, and I quickly raised my hand to respond. "You've totally mischaracterized my speech. I strongly *defended* ACT UP. I'll print out the full speech for the back table at next week's meeting so folks can judge for themselves."

Monaghan hadn't sat down and was ready with a knockout punch. He raised a letter and envelope above his head. "And there's this! I just got this in the mail. It's a fundraising letter for Sean Strub's congressional campaign, signed by Peter, with ACT UP's name on the envelope," he yelled even louder. "ACT UP has a strict policy of not endorsing candidates, *so what the fuck is this?*"

The murmurs turned to shaming hisses. ACT UP members routinely hissed when our worst enemies' names were mentioned, like Reagan, Bush, or Helms. It was incredibly rare for a member of ACT UP to be hissed at during a floor debate. That sound, coming from only a small chorus within the room, shattered me. ACT UP was my family, and its meetings in that room at the Center had given me life. How could this be happening here?

I had been standing behind the merchandise table near the front of the room, and asked Charlie Franchino to follow me into a side room behind us.

"What the fuck was that?" I asked him as my eyes welled up.

"I don't know," he replied, "but we'll figure it out. What was that Strub letter he held up?"

"This was the first time I've seen it," I replied. While I was in San Francisco, Sean had called me the day after my speech, asking if he could put my name to a fundraising letter for his congressional campaign. He was a friend, and was also the first openly HIV-positive person to run for Congress.

I said yes, without hesitation. Sean said they'd be rushing it out and asked if I wanted to approve the final draft.

"I trust you," I replied. The letter itself was fine, but I had no idea he would add ACT UP's name below mine with the return address on the envelopes. It was an innocent moment of overeagerness on his part, but it provided perfect political ammo for a guy like Monaghan.

Nevertheless, the letter was my mistake. My name and reputation as an activist were inextricably tied to ACT UP, and if I was going to plug a candidate, I should have made sure it couldn't be perceived as anything more than a personal endorsement. Lesson learned, the hard way.

Charlie suggested that I ask Sean to write something to explain all of this to the floor. "It'll be all right," he said, seeing the pain in my eyes. He knew it was far worse than that, but what else could he say?

Nothing. So he hugged me. I wiped my eyes dry, and we rejoined the meeting, which had moved on to the next agenda item. I tried to look strong as I returned to my spot against the wall, but it felt like half the room was staring in my direction. I couldn't tell which eyes held empathy and which held enmity.

I don't remember the discussion that followed. My head swirled with hurt feelings. I wasn't the seasoned and mature politician that night. I was every bit the twenty-nine-year-old nursing a highly bruised ego.

Fuck this shit, I thought. *This work—our activism—doesn't matter if it destroys us in the process. I want out.*

But how could I leave ACT UP? I had embraced it so thoroughly that it had become my entire life. Maybe this would all pass and things would improve. But what if it didn't? What if it only got worse? For me, something had irreparably broken that night. This surreal, ascendant, and joyous movement had morphed into something else, something painful and joyless. ACT UP was starting to eat its own, and I'd been served up as an appetizer.

I may have been the first, but even then, I could see that I wouldn't be the last. My selfish desire to survive kicked in, and that meant protecting my mental health. From that night on, I would look for a way out.

10

A FEEL-GOOD CONDOM

"**H**OW DOES IT FEEL TO BE the most hated person in ACT UP?" I asked Mark Harrington in January 1991, as we gathered at David Barr's apartment for our newly formed HIV support group.

"You ought to know," he replied, and we both laughed uncomfortably.

Indeed, I did, having been tarred and feathered after my return from San Francisco months earlier. But at the moment, I was more than a little relieved that the personal attacks between ACT UP's two warring camps had been refocused away from me, at least for a while.

Since that terrible night in July, ACT UP's infighting had only gotten worse. I had been maintaining a defensive crouch ever since, keeping my head low as best I could. It was a conscious retreat from the limelight. Where once I would have jumped into any and all debates on the floor, I now largely stayed silent unless there was a need to report on whatever fundraising or T&D work I was involved in. And I was more than fine with that.

Mark started attracting incoming fire at the end of the year, especially after a major kerfuffle in Washington, DC. On December 14, through a fluke of scheduling, key members of T&D had a working dinner with Tony Fauci just hours after ACT UP's Women's Caucus had heckled him at an NIH-sponsored meeting on women and AIDS. The Caucus was there to up the volume on a key demand during ACT UP's demonstration at the NIH earlier that year: the woeful lack of representation of women in HIV-related clinical trials.

When members of the Women's Caucus found out about the Fauci dinner, they went ballistic, viewing it as a betrayal of the outside pressure they were trying to build on Fauci and others at the NIH.

The blowup was also symptomatic of the complete breakdown in communication and trust between these two sharp-elbowed committees within ACT UP. T&D didn't know that Fauci was going to be zapped, and the Women's Caucus didn't know about the scheduled dinner. And once everyone was back in New York, members of the Caucus pounced.

A handy way to attack another ACT UP member was in print, using a weekly single-page, double-sided newsletter called *Tell It to ACT UP*, or *TITA*—our version of the worst online comment sections found on today's Internet.

One of the Caucus's youngest members, Tracy Morgan, struck first. "I would like to know why, after Evil Anthony Fauci treated all the women at the Women and HIV Conference like dirt, Mark Harrington got to have dinner with 'The Big Guy' that same evening?" she wrote. "I find this revolting."

Mark had yet to be cowed like I had been, and gave as good as he got. At a strategy meeting organized by Larry Kramer, Mark said, "ACT UP used to be a safe place to disagree with each other, but it isn't anymore." Referring to the Women's Caucus treatment of Fauci, he said, "We are at a strategic cul-de-sac, mindlessly repeating actions and tactics which may have worked once but aren't working now."

The rift between ACT UP's two camps was widening. What happened next would crack it wide open. ACTG 076—the seventy-sixth proposed clinical trial within the NIH's AIDS Clinical Trials Group—sparked a war between the Women's Caucus and T&D that lasted months and left wounds that, for some, remain unhealed to this day.

A placebo-controlled trial of AZT in HIV-positive pregnant women and their newborns, 076 would test to see if the drug could block mother-to-child transmission of the virus. In 1991 alone, close to two hundred thousand newborns were infected worldwide, and like all the AIDS stats, the numbers were soaring year to year with no end in sight. ACTG 076 was the first trial that would attempt to stem that rising tide.

But it was also the first AIDS trial that focused on women. From day one, T&D and the Women's Caucus had been calling out the ACTG for its seeming disinterest in women with HIV. To have its first proposed trial in women come about because of concern about infected babies, rather than the women's health, rightly caused a furor.

Activists had a tricky choice. They could view it as yet another example of a patriarchal system that cared little about women, and take a hardline stand against the trial itself, demanding that it be stopped. Or they could make a stink about the timing, while still concluding that the trial was essential to do. There were all sorts of ethical concerns about the proposed protocol, especially around how it handled the health of the mothers. Instead of stopping the trial, activists could try to improve it.

This was the choice facing the ACTG's new Community Constituency Group (CCG), the thirty or so activists from around the country who now had a voice, and voting power, on all of the ACTG's committees. These were the activists who won their seats at the table after a relentless campaign by ACT UP's T&D. The CCG was born from the decision by the ACTG's executive committee, during the AIDS conference in San Francisco, to finally let us join the government committees that affected our health and our lives.

The CCG members had been drawn from AIDS advocacy and service organizations around the country. From the beginning, CCG was far more diverse than ACT UP itself, and included leading Black female activists like Saundra Johnson from Chicago, Rochelle Rollins from Boston, and Debra Fraser-Howze, who founded the Black Leadership Commission on AIDS in New York City.

Although fully cognizant of the terrible optics around 076's timing, these activists knew that many HIV-positive women wanted a therapy that would protect their babies should they become pregnant. They knew that the trial was essential. With AIDS treatment advocacy already dominated by gay White men, they, along with the CCG's men of color, also viewed their active involvement to improve 076 as a long-overdue corrective to the movement's diversity problem.

They were also impressed that one of the coauthors of the 076 protocol was an African American woman—the first time this had happened within the ACTG. Dr. Janet Mitchell was chief of perinatology at Harlem Hospital, running the largest prenatal program for pregnant women in New York City. She was legit, and she had personally treated hundreds of women with HIV.

On March 10, 1991, Dr. Mitchell joined other ACTG investigators at the Omni Shoreham Hotel in DC to present the latest trial design for 076. The meeting was packed with other clinicians, NIH officials, and almost all of the activists from the CCG. Just as the presentation was about to begin, members of ACT UP's Women's Caucus stood up in protest, and started reading a prepared statement titled "Stop 076!"

As Mitchell and other investigators pleaded with the protestors to let the meeting proceed, offering to meet with them immediately after, the ACT UP protestors pushed on and began reading their statement a second time. They used air horns to drown out anyone who attempted to speak from the stage. Pitched arguments started breaking out between the CCG activists and the protestors.

Eventually, ACTG administrator Dan Hoth announced that the meeting would have to be postponed, and all hell broke loose. Dr. Mitchell joined various CCG members of color, yelling "Racists!" while pointing at the protestors, who were mostly White lesbians. Clusters of opposing activists screamed at each other, spilling out of the auditorium into the hotel's hallways and lobby.

The non–ACT UP members of the CCG called for an emergency meeting that night, and then asked the members from ACT UP not to attend. They wanted to debate the expulsion of ACT UP members from the CCG, insisting that ACT UP had recklessly jeopardized the CCG's future.

Those ACT UP members went into full damage-control mode. They had been just as caught off guard by the surprise Women's Caucus demonstration as the rest of the CCG. They spent the night preparing a statement condemning the zap, calling it "an act of racist censorship."

By the end of the following day, they had succeeded in patching up the rift within the CCG, but the T&D members who cosigned the statement condemning the debacle had to return to New York to face what seemed certain to be months of rancor.

Within weeks, members of the Women's Caucus brought a proposal to the floor calling for a six-month moratorium on any and all meetings with government officials concerning "women's issues." The proposal called for direct action only—our outside strategy—and explained the need for a moratorium on our inside strategy: "INSTITUTIONALIZED SEXISM in the research and government bureaucracies makes dialogue ineffective for women's issues at this time."

Members of T&D couldn't believe what they were hearing. The CCG had just appointed David Barr and Mark Harrington to a working group (which included many of the CCG's women) tasked with recommending much-needed improvements to the ACTG 076 protocol. Instead of working to improve 076, the Women's Caucus wanted to agitate strictly from the outside to shut it down. Even before the Women's Caucus had been formed, T&D had spoken out often on issues concerning women with HIV, especially around clinical trials. The moratorium was viewed as a blunt instrument to silence that work.

The grueling debate on the proposal lasted for weeks. Once, after a T&D member decried how devastating the six-month moratorium would be, a Women's Caucus member, apparently forgetting her audience, exclaimed, "It's not like it's the rest of your life." Many of the members living with HIV howled in protest—they didn't know if they'd last six months.

Each time the proposal was debated, it would become as heated as the week before and would exhaust everyone in the room until, finally, someone would move to table the motion until the next meeting. Eventually, a vote was taken, and the proposal lost handily, but the damage had been done. The infighting between the two camps simply shifted from issue to issue, tactic to tactic, with no end in sight. Activists on both sides spent almost half their time fighting other activists rather than fighting to end AIDS.

The divide between the two camps was a classic breakdown in communications, fed by growing distrust and the immaturity of a largely youthful movement. But it was much deeper than that, and likely irreconcilable.

Something had to give. One camp wanted to save lives as quickly as possible, a goal that necessitated working within current systems, bending them as quickly as we could. The other camp wanted to focus on many of the systemic issues that fed the epidemic—the homophobia, racism, and sexism that often stifled adequate responses or led to regressive policies. Capitalism and other power structures were all worthy of a full-throated challenge.

Both camps were noble. Both camps wanted to end AIDS. No one in either camp wanted to willfully engage in activism that might backfire and harm people. The differences between the camps never amounted to who cared more or who had the better intentions. For the first few years, both camps had worked together quite well. ACT UP members were encouraged to fight the battles that interested them the most. Some members focused on immediate policy issues, while others focused on broader systemic issues. But once the policy geeks won the access ACT UP had been demanding from day one, and once our monthly street protests started losing their punch after the press decided we were yesterday's news—both happened almost simultaneously in 1991—then our happy marriage quickly unraveled.

As T&D's rapidly expanding inside work kept yielding victories, both small and large, we continued to pivot to a more cooperative relationship with the research establishment. That cooperation was anathema to ACT UP's antiestablishment activists. It only took one specific policy debate that overlapped the stated missions of T&D and the Women's Caucus—the debate over ACTG 076—to blow things up.

While both camps may have had good intentions, that doesn't mean both sides were right. If the Women's Caucus had succeeded in stopping or even delaying 076, it would have cost hundreds of thousands of lives. That isn't hyperbole. If ACT UP had been unified in opposition to 076, in 1991, we had the power to delay it, at the very least.

Evidence of this power was demonstrated thirteen years later by a far weaker chapter of ACT UP, when the movement was weaker overall. In 2004, ACT UP Paris successfully scuttled the first trials that hoped to test whether tenofovir, an antiviral, could work as a prevention drug and block HIV infections. After the collapse of these first trials, the next one didn't start until 2007. This iPrEx study was wildly successful, and Truvada PrEP, the first pre-exposure prophylaxis for HIV, was finally approved in 2012. But the damage by ACT UP Paris had been done. If the early tenofovir studies had succeeded, we might have seen PrEP on the market as early as 2008. Tens of thousands of HIV infections would have been prevented.

The Women's Caucus made the same mistake ACT UP Paris would make years later. They both attempted to stop clinical trials in vulnerable populations without considering the downsides of delay for those same populations. With 076, it was HIV-positive pregnant women, mostly women of color. For the PrEP trials, it was female sex workers in Cambodia and women in Cameroon. All of these trials were branded by mostly privileged White activists as unethical experiments on vulnerable groups before any real dialogue had occurred between the actual stakeholders.

Fortunately, with 076, the stakeholders within the CCG saved the day. They were mostly women of color, and T&D's defense of their newly acquired power within the ACTG proved crucial. ACTG 076 would go on to become one of the most important scientific breakthroughs in the history of AIDS research, proving that an antiviral could block HIV transmission—in this case, from a mother to her child. Within a year of the trial results, perinatal HIV transmission in the United States dropped by almost 60 percent. And ever since, hundreds of thousands of mothers around the world have used antivirals to block HIV transmission to their newborns.

But in 1991, none of this could be clearly predicted, and the positions within ACT UP's two camps had hardened. T&D helped save 076, but the attempt by the Women's Caucus to shut down the movement's inside strategy was rightly viewed by many of ACT UP's HIV-positive members as a mortal threat. In addition, activism work in both camps suffered mightily, as the infighting stole critical time. T&D spent the rest of the year debating how to save the work it excelled at, and even openly discussed distancing itself from ACT UP.

A deep sadness fell over the movement that summer. I was still keeping my head down, cringing with the vast majority of our members who grew increasingly disgusted with the endless debates and personal attacks. But behind the scenes, I started preparing for what I believed was inevitable: the treatment activists would have to split off from ACT UP.

For this, we'd need a new organization. Coincidentally, I wanted to form a new affinity group for another mission-impossible action I'd been dreaming about. Maybe I could kill two birds with one stone.

The dream was simple: target Senator Jesse Helms.

For people living with HIV and for LGBT Americans in the 1980s, few public figures were more despised than Jesse Helms, a hotheaded US senator from North Carolina. He vociferously hated gay people and considered AIDS to be God's punishment for homosexuality, and successfully convinced Congress to pass laws that made the crisis worse.

The ban on allowing HIV-positive individuals to immigrate to the United States, which many other countries subsequently adopted? Thank Jesse Helms. The ban on letting the Centers for Disease Control fund any HIV prevention messaging targeting gay men? Thank Jesse Helms. By 1991, every country in Europe had a science-based HIV prevention plan but the United States didn't. Again, thank Jesse Helms.

During the debate on his amendment to thwart HIV prevention efforts targeting gay men, Helms said, "We've got to call a spade a spade, and a perverted human being a perverted human being." Amazingly, AIDS activists had never targeted this monster in a way he couldn't ignore. We had called him a million names from a distance but had never gotten up close and personal with our anger.

During the summer of '91, I took my first break from ACT UP, and moved full-time to a rental house on Fire Island, splitting shares with Charlie Franchino and a small gaggle of other activists. But I couldn't shake Helms out of my head and kept spinning all sorts of crazy ideas on how to let him know one thing very clearly: we queers had had enough.

First things first: Where did the creep live? One of the many great things about being gay is that we have access to one of the world's largest spy networks. There isn't a single organization, company, or government agency that doesn't have a gay spy willing to share helpful intelligence with their compatriots in the queer underground. And Congress, with thousands of staffers, was crawling with gay spies. So with a quick phone call to one of our spies in the Hart Senate Office Building, I had an address that had never been publicly reported. Helms and his wife lived just outside DC in Arlington, Virginia, at 2820 South Joyce Street.

Address in hand, I started churning ideas of what to do there. My head spun like wheels in a slot machine, looking for the perfect alignment of three matching fruit. The action had to be bold enough to attract national news, but not go so far that it would allow Helms to play the victim. I knew the house would likely be empty during Congress's late-summer recess, so we could do something in front of the house, or even inside, without risking a violent confrontation.

One of my crazier ideas was to break in with a video crew, run upstairs, get naked with one of ACT UP's beautiful boys, and have gay butt-sex on Helms's bed, which probably needed some action. We could later release a carefully edited, R-rated version to the press, titled *Breaking and Entering.* To this day, I find the idea deliciously fun, but my political radar raised obvious alarms. Only a small fraction of the country would enjoy the joke. But boy, that fraction would have howled, which made it tempting.

Ultimately, I wanted to use ridicule to undercut Helms's power. It's not an easy needle to thread. What kind of action would be crazy enough to get everyone's attention, avoid being offensive, yet still provoke a universal chuckle, especially from Helms's fellow senators, all at his expense? Those wheels kept spinning in my head, but it wasn't until late July that three bananas lined up and screamed, "HELLO! Condoms are funny!" Jackpot!

Luckily for me, one of the most brilliant technicians in the world of activism had recently reached out to me, offering his assistance. Twilly Cannon was a beloved member of Greenpeace, designing some of its most visual and challenging actions, and training newbies to pull them off. He had been wowed by our stock exchange incursion, and called me out of the blue with an open invitation to share his expertise for any future actions I had in mind.

So he was my first call after hitting on the jackpot idea. "Twilly, I've got the home address of Jesse Helms. Do you think we could cover his house with a giant condom before the cops arrived?"

He replied simply, "When can we scout out the house?"

A few days later, I drove to DC, camera in hand, picked up Twilly, and slowly drove past the senator's home. We parked farther down the quiet, tree-lined street, then tried our best to look like we belonged there, leisurely walking down the block while admiring the manicured lawns.

Helms's house was blessedly small: a simple two-story colonial, with only a short bit of lawn between it and the sidewalk. But the house's side-gabled roof had a steep pitch down the front and back sides, which would make our action risky.

Twilly told me we'd only need one picture of the house, which I took from across the street on our second pass, returning to the car.

"Are you able to eyeball the house's measurements?" I asked.

"The picture is all we need," he replied. He explained that there was a standard door size for traditional American housing. The width might vary, but the height was almost always eighty inches. Using a ruler on the front door in the picture, and some basic math, we could make decent estimates of the house's measurements.

Back then, there were only a handful of mom-and-pop shops in the country that made custom inflatables—those oversized gorillas or

Uncle Sams or Santa Clauses found in front of used car dealerships. For reasons I still don't understand, most of these shops were located just outside San Diego, California. But they all had fax machines, the barely convenient electronic communication method of the day.

Twilly and I sketched out some specs for a boxy-looking condom. Like a Hollywood set, it wouldn't have to be real or complete. The press would get video and pictures of the condom from one angle while standing on the street. If our condom completely covered the front of the house, including the front-sloping roof, then voilà—a condom-covered house!

We needed a huge inflatable section for the front roof, which would tower above the house, including a reservoir nipple at its peak. This would be seamlessly stitched to a giant sheet of the same material to cover the front of the house. For extra realism, an inflatable tube would be stitched to the bottom of the sheet, representing the unrolled base of the condom sitting on a lawn of green pubic hair. Two electric blowers, powered by a portable generator, would quickly inflate the roof and lawn balloons. Long lines would reach out from every edge of the roof balloon, to be secured in place with stakes hammered into the lawn in front and back.

I faxed the specs for our house condom to three San Diego companies, telling each that I was doing an outdoors AIDS benefit at my home on Long Island and hoped to cause a big media splash with a condom-covered house to promote safe sex. They all loved the idea.

I gulped when the pricing estimates came back. The first was $15,000. Even the lowest quote had me worried—$3,500. That's a pricey condom.

When I revealed all the details of my crazy plan to my then boyfriend, Kevin Sessums, he started to panic. We had a huge argument one morning at the house on Fire Island. He was convinced I'd end up in jail for decades if I put a condom on a powerful senator's house. I told him he was being silly, and he stormed off.

Kevin was one of the best-known cover-story writers for *Vanity Fair*, doing profiles on Hollywood's royalty. He had introduced me to entertainment mogul David Geffen soon after we started dating. Geffen had a house on Fire Island that summer, and I started to stew, fearing Kevin had run to Geffen to cry on his shoulder. I imagined Geffen saying, "I warned you he was crazy." I pitched a lonely towel on the beach, hoping the sun would burn away my hurt feelings from the fight. Then up walked David Geffen with Kevin lagging behind.

"Here," David said, handing me a very thick wad of hundred-dollar bills.

"What's this?" I asked, stunned.

"It's for your $3,500 condom," he said, smiling. "Don't you ever tell anyone where you got this money. Now you two make up."

Kevin explained later that Geffen took my side, telling Kevin, "This is who Peter is, and you have to trust that he knows what he's doing."

Two weeks later, the hundred-pound condom arrived in a huge duffel bag, complete with two blowers. We tested it upstate on another rich gay guy's lawn hidden in a well-wooded area. The roof balloon took seven minutes to fully inflate—the same exact amount of time Twilly estimated it would take for the police to get from their Arlington station house to the Helms address.

In addition, we hoped it would take at least two minutes for one of the neighbors to figure out that we were up to no good and call 911. That meant we probably had very little time to unload everything from our rental truck, set up a twenty-eight-foot extension ladder to the top edge of the roof, start the generator, set up the extension cords, haul the heavy condom and the main blower up to the roof, unroll the entire thing, and hammer lines into the lawn. It was a lot, but if we divided all of these tasks among seven activists who trusted each other like comrades in battle, it might just work.

I quickly recruited some of the most fearless members of T&D: Sean Strub, Garance Franke-Ruta, Mark Allen, Derek Link, Jim Serafini, and Jason Childers. Dan Baker, who had been my coat-and-tie-wearing media spokesperson for the invasion of Burroughs Wellcome, agreed to reprise his role in front of the house. And my most recent ex, Robert Hilferty, signed on to be our videographer. He wanted to create a short film that would include the planning, practicing, and doing. You can find it on YouTube.

We'd call ourselves TAG, the Treatment Action Guerrillas, a new affinity group of ACT UP. But I had quietly registered the name as a nonprofit corporation in New York State, so we were the first and only ACT UP affinity group to have its own checking account. It was my hope that if and when T&D decided to split off from ACT UP, a new organization's name, paperwork, and checking account would be ready to hit the ground running.

At around 8:00 AM on September 5, 1991, we loaded all of our equipment into a U-Haul outside our cheap motel rooms in Arlington.

Local television network affiliates and newspaper photographers had been told only that ACT UP would be doing something spectacular at a senator's house, and started to arrive on schedule.

A line of press vehicles followed our truck to South Joyce Street. As soon as we stopped the truck, the choreography began. Four of us wrangled the ladder to full extension while the other three fired up the heavy generator.

Sean and I hauled the heavy duffel bag to the top right corner of the roof, then slowly crawled toward the middle to unfurl the condom. We switched on the main blower a little more than three minutes after we parked, a minute and twenty seconds over our target time. It was going to be close.

As the main sheet of the condom rolled over the roof and down to the lawn, our carefully stenciled message was revealed in huge black letters:

A
CONDOM
TO STOP
UNSAFE POLITICS.
HELMS IS DEADLIER
THAN A VIRUS.

By this point, a neighbor had appeared and was yelling at us to get off of the senator's house, warning us that she had already called the police.

When the first cruiser pulled up, camera crews swarmed around it. The cop behind the wheel craned his neck to get a full view of the reservoir nipple, half erect and visibly bending upward into its final position, an exclamation mark screaming, *TA-DA!* Then I saw it, the reaction I had dreamed about: the cop started laughing. His partner, a female cop, got out of the car and joined in, saying, "I haven't even had my coffee yet."

Two more police cruisers arrived. My TAG team quickly huddled for a big group hug and cheered, our mission accomplished. Dan Baker drily explained to the cops that some AIDS activists from New York had put a giant inflatable condom over Senator Helms's house. The cops stared at the condom and its stenciled message for a while, then one of them turned to Dan, pointed his thumb over his shoulder, and asked, "You wanna take this off?"

I told the cops we'd be glad to take it down if they'd allow us back on the roof, hoping we'd get to keep the condom if we helped them out. To my surprise, the cops agreed. As the deflation commenced, the commanding officer was on his radio. For a while. They were waiting to see if Helms wanted to press charges and have us arrested. About fifteen minutes later, the condom and all our gear were back in the U-Haul, and the cops asked for our driver's licenses, which they wrote down. Another cop wrote out a thirty-five-dollar parking ticket for our truck for facing the wrong way.

"The senator will decide later if he wants to bring charges," the cop in charge said. "You can all head home." Helms never brought charges against us, knowing we'd love the extra publicity.

The networks sent out the footage to their affiliates, and dozens of them ran short stories that night. If you were queer, no matter where you lived in this country, AIDS was then a heavy weight in your life, and it seemed like it would never let up. Folks like Helms had beaten you down with hate, and it was hard not to feel defeated. But for a moment, if you saw that giant condom, you rejoiced. You pumped your fist and barely suppressed screaming, "YES!"

We weren't defeated. We were still fighting back. And in such a gloriously queer fashion.

Fuck you, Jesse Helms. We're here, we're queer, get used to it.

11

TAG

ACT UP WAS IN CRISIS. The two camps that had developed more than a year earlier were locked in battle. T&D's most active members were desperate to find a way to continue what they considered increasingly effective inside work—and, frankly, both camps needed to get back to the activism they loved. The only feasible way to do this was a formal split. So the core members of T&D decided to continue their work under a new banner.

In January 1992, I filed a doing-business-as application to update the Treatment Action Guerrillas' name to the Treatment Action *Group*, primarily for fundraising purposes. TAG's first major donor was Dr. Mathilde Krim, founding chairwoman of the American Foundation for AIDS Research, better known as amfAR. She suggested the name change before she sought out other donors, and her stamp of approval helped launch us.

The dozen or so T&D members who made the leap to TAG had no idea if our new group would survive beyond its first year. Leaving the ACT UP mothership was a gamble, ditching a brand name that was internationally recognized and opened doors. But we could also ditch some of ACT UP's strictures and habits and find other ways to make change happen.

Case in point: TAG started paying its busiest activists. Mark Harrington and his new boyfriend, Gregg Gonsalves, were paid a small stipend to read and categorize every single AIDS grant approved by the NIH during the prior fiscal year.

Gregg had first showed up at T&D meetings in 1991, as an import from ACT UP Boston, along with Derek Link and a few other young gay men from Beantown who wanted to join the founding chapter. With a Portuguese father and Sicilian mother, he had a painfully flawless combination of gorgeous looks and whiz-kid smarts.

TAG boys (clockwise from upper right) David Barr, Gregg Gonsalves, Mark Harrington, and me. *Newsday*

Mark and Gregg were quite a duo. After their relationship ran its course, no one was surprised that they each, individually, won a MacArthur "Genius Grant," the only AIDS activists ever to earn that honor.

TAG's first project was highly ambitious: proposing a total reorganization of how AIDS research was done at the NIH. ACT UP had successfully guilt-tripped an entire country and two Republican administrations to dramatically increase its AIDS research budget. But as that budget approached $1 billion a year, it still hadn't made a dent in the rising AIDS death toll.

TAG wanted more bang for those bucks. The AIDS research budget was being split among seventeen of the NIH's institutes, with little coordinated oversight and direction. Shouldn't we be setting priorities and shifting funds accordingly?

After some friendly cajoling of Mark's NIH contacts, three huge boxes filled with reams of paper detailing more than three thousand grants were shipped to his apartment. Two months later, Mark and Gregg emerged from their East Village cubbyhole with a two-part, 154-page report.

AIDS Research at the NIH: A Critical Review was a damning indictment of our government's current efforts to find lifesaving treatments for people with HIV. But more importantly, all the documented shortcomings were paired with well-reasoned recommendations on how to fix them. Folks noticed, especially the policy wonks at key national AIDS organizations.

Proving our worth, TAG tried other strategies ACT UP had rarely attempted. We asked for help from these more established AIDS organizations and worked with them on the messy give-and-take of turning our hopeful recommendations into actual law. TAG was an unknown on Capitol Hill, but amfAR, AIDS Action Council, and the Pediatric AIDS Foundation didn't have that problem. Congress knew exactly who they were and respected them.

This new coalition handed the report to key staff members of two of the most powerful forces in public health in Washington, Congressman Henry Waxman and Senator Edward Kennedy. And then we all got lucky. Bill Clinton won the 1992 election, denying President Bush a second term, which meant the Democrats would control the White House and both houses of Congress come January.

Tim Westmoreland and Michael Iskowitz—two gay men who wrote almost all of the major AIDS legislation ever passed for their respective bosses, Waxman and Kennedy—set to work. They translated our recommendations into legislative language, slipping it into the NIH Revitalization Act of 1993.

It was introduced as Senate Bill 1 on January 21, the day after Bill Clinton's inauguration.

And that's when our trouble really started. A fierce opponent emerged, one of the institute directors: our friend and sometime adversary Dr. Anthony Fauci, the director of the National Institute of Allergy and Infectious Diseases. The T&D gang had tangled with him before, and even grew to respect and like the guy, but now he wanted to stop our reforms.

Fauci's institute received about half the NIH's AIDS research budget, and we wanted to strengthen the NIH's existing Office of AIDS Research (OAR) so that it could review and oversee how that money was spent and move money for AIDS research from one institute to another. But Fauci wasn't keen on being overseen, and definitely didn't want his huge AIDS budget messed with. And in a final insult, we proposed that the director of the newly empowered OAR couldn't be one of the institute directors, since that would cause an obvious conflict of interest.

Yup, Tony Fauci, NIAID's director, was also the director of the current, largely powerless OAR. He was wearing both hats, and Senate Bill 1 would force him to hand over one of those hats to someone else.

Fauci fought back, hard, and for months. I still find it deeply ironic that one of the central charges against the T&D camp during

ACT UP's split was that we were too close to and even co-opted by Fauci. And yet the first thing TAG did after the split was go to war against the good doctor.

The months-long legislative battle between TAG and Fauci at times felt like hand-to-hand combat. Both sides would lobby Fauci's superiors—the outgoing NIH director, Bernadine Healy, and the new Health and Human Services secretary, Donna Shalala. We convinced Healy to remain neutral, and Shalala became a crucial ally.

Before key committee votes in the House and Senate, TAG and Fauci would lobby for public endorsements of their respective positions from various AIDS experts. Fauci got some of the professional medical societies to recommend against the new language. They used his suggested counterattack to our proposal for an empowered OAR, claiming that it would add an unnecessary layer of bureaucracy. We, in turn, got hundreds of AIDS researchers to write their own letters to Waxman and Kennedy, endorsing the lawmakers' proposed language for strengthened oversight and coordination of the NIH's disparate AIDS research efforts.

As we were winning Democrats to our side, Fauci lobbied Republicans. At one critical juncture, a Republican-sponsored amendment was introduced before Waxman's committee that sought to strike the OAR's new budget authority. Thankfully, it was defeated: twelve votes for it, thirteen against.

In the end, after Fauci lost all the committee battles, the NIH Revitalization Act was approved by huge majorities in both the House and the Senate. President Bill Clinton signed it into law on June 10, 1993. Every AIDS researcher in the country now knew TAG's name and respected our role as advocates for better AIDS research, Dr. Fauci included.

"Do we know what we're doing here?" I asked, clearly worried.

"We are so right about this," Spencer replied with total confidence, before launching into one of the most convincing arguments I've ever heard.

It was August 1994, and Spencer Cox had just had his picture plastered on the cover of *Barron's* magazine under the headline Do We Have Too Many AIDS Drugs? His extensive quotes in the article hadn't said any such thing, but the damage was done. He was now the most hated AIDS activist in the country.

Spencer had only been twenty years old when he walked into his first T&D meeting in early 1989, having dropped out of Bennington College to pursue a possible acting career in New York City. Like me, his HIV diagnosis pushed him away from his initial goals and instead toward full-time activism.

Within T&D, only Garance Franke-Ruta was younger. And yet, in gay years, Spencer often seemed a generation or two older than the rest of us. He was all southern twink on the outside, with his lean frame and devilish grin. But when he spoke, an old classic theater queen was revealed, with an encyclopedic knowledge of every line Bette Davis ever delivered. And the constant cigarette between his fingers, hand raised, elbow tucked in, was just like Bette, and offered a visual bridge between his boyish and older personas.

Spencer seemed always to be performing, and he found an adoring audience within ACT UP and TAG. But behind his campy exhibitionism was a sharp intellect. In short order, he became a leading treatment activist.

A month before our conversation, his signature was included among eight activists, including Mark and Gregg, on a letter to the FDA that marked a radical shift for AIDS activism. It recommended, shockingly, against the quick approval of an AIDS drug. Prior to this, AIDS activists had always pushed the FDA for faster and faster drug approvals. In fact, it had been an organizing principle of ACT UP.

The drug in question was saquinavir, which was being developed by pharma giant Hoffmann–La Roche. Roche was in a race with at least three other companies working on a new class of antivirals called protease inhibitors. The company asked the FDA for accelerated approval based on limited data in less than three hundred patients.

Previously, AIDS activists had won two major victories in reforming the drug approval process at the FDA: Parallel Track in 1989 and Accelerated Approval in 1992. The latter allowed a company to bring an HIV drug to market with only limited data, like a small trial showing improvements in CD4 cells, with a promise to the FDA that larger trials would still be done to prove that the drug prolonged lives. Theoretically, the FDA could later pull the drug from the market if these larger trials didn't pan out as hoped.

TAG had tangled with Roche before. The company had a drug similar to AZT called ddC, which got an accelerated approval in 1992. In the months before this, Roche ignored pleas from activists to expand access to the drug through a parallel track program, and then it failed to launch larger trials after the drug was approved.

By 1994, we had four approved antivirals—AZT, ddI, ddC, and d4T—and yet the yearly death count from AIDS kept climbing. Accelerated approvals were giving us earlier access, but without larger trials, we had little evidence on how to use those drugs to prolong our lives.

Many HIV-positive gay men in New York and San Francisco, mostly White, had access to the most informed AIDS doctors and the latest research literature. Their docs attended all the AIDS conferences and would help them craft slightly effective combinations of drugs, adjusting doses to avoid toxicities. It was highly personalized care, and for many, it bought some time. But at best it was a sophisticated guessing game. The quick drug approvals left patients and doctors in the dark as to which drugs to try first, when to start them, and in which combination. There just wasn't enough information to formulate a standard of care to guide them.

TAG became convinced that companies like Roche were abus-
ing the new accelerated approval regulations that AIDS activists
had fought so hard for, and instead did the bare minimum the regs
required, while still raking in the dough on these big-ticket drugs.

Our "not so fast" letter to the FDA about Roche's protease inhibitor was cosigned by some of the same coalition partners TAG had
during the OAR campaign. Still, it was out of step with the views of
the wider community, which always argued for faster access to drugs.

Roche was livid and decided to quietly stoke intracommunity
warfare, hoping to stifle TAG's influence with the FDA. The company
faxed our letter to dozens of AIDS organizations, followed by *Can
you believe this?* phone calls, playing the victim.

At that point, a very public fight broke out among AIDS advocates. Many of the ACT UP chapters screamed bloody murder, as did
other more mainstream groups like Project Inform. Their attacks were
simplistic, claiming TAG was against Accelerated Approval.

We weren't. We were against the abuse of this relatively new
approval system by companies like Roche. The system had loopholes,
and Roche had used all of them.

And then the *Barron's* article hit the newsstands. Angry diatribes
were delivered during ACT UP's Monday-night meetings, calling for
open warfare against TAG. A mention of Spencer's name would elicit
hissing.

So when I called him after hearing about the uproar brewing
within ACT UP, asking if we knew what we were getting ourselves
into, he sounded ready for the coming debate.

One of the charges heard on the floor of ACT UP was that TAG
was an elitist group of activists unmoored from the larger community
of people living with HIV, advocating a policy shift that would harm
folks by reducing their access to lifesaving meds.

Spencer responded to my doubts with one of the most convincing sermons I've ever heard. TAG's position was *anti*elitist. ACT UP

was defending a system that only satisfied the privileged demands of well-connected gay men in New York and San Francisco for immediate access to experimental treatments. To these defenders of the status quo, if that immediate access came at the expense of data that could help formulate a standard of care for everyone else, including the overwhelmed HIV clinics serving people of color in Harlem, Newark, Miami, and Oakland, so be it. The defended status quo was personalized care from AIDS docs serving mostly gay White men. And standardized care for everyone else would have to wait.

"TAG is saying, 'Fuck that shit,'" Spencer told me. "TAG is fighting for everyone, not just those in the community who have led the policy discussions from day one." And besides, TAG wasn't against accelerated approval. It just wanted to close the loopholes Roche and other companies had used.

Few of our critics had noticed the fix we put forward in the letter to the FDA. TAG proposed that Roche and other protease inhibitor developers launch a kind of large, simple trial that hadn't been used in AIDS research before. If the FDA insisted that these trials be up and running before granting accelerated approval, we'd likely see similar approval times compared to the first four AIDS drugs.

These large, simple trials would let patients take whatever AIDS drugs they were already on, a kind of real-world standard of care. Two-thirds of the patients would get different doses of the protease inhibitor, while the final arm of the study would get a placebo. With few if any entry restrictions, such as requiring patients to stop their current treatments, enrollment would be easier and faster than previous trials, and the larger sample size in all three arms would typically lead to quicker results. Researchers would also get *more* results, such as which combinations of AIDS drugs worked best with the experimental protease inhibitor.

These types of trials had been successfully used in cancer and heart disease research, so why not AIDS?

———————

Two months after our letter, the FDA scheduled a special hearing to review the accelerated approval regulations before its Antiviral Drugs Advisory Committee. TAG was outnumbered by various community groups saying the regs were working just fine. But the scientists on the committee, along with FDA leadership, took our suggestions seriously.

Roche was encouraged to launch larger trials before applying for accelerated approval. Spencer helped Abbott Laboratories design a large, simple trial for its protease inhibitor, ritonavir, becoming the first AIDS trial to allow patients to keep taking their current background regimen. The ACTG enrolled two thousand patients into a trial looking at Merck's protease inhibitor, indinavir.

In the end, Roche won the approval race but lost the data and marketing races. Saquinavir was approved in December 1995, but it was the weakest of the protease inhibitors and would soon be outclassed by its rivals.

In February 1996, tears rolled down Spencer's face as scientists presented the stunning data from Abbott's protease inhibitor at a conference in DC. Those receiving ritonavir plus standard of care had 50 percent fewer deaths than those receiving placebo plus standard of care.

"We're going to live!" he exclaimed.

This was the moment—the breakthrough we had all been fighting for for so long.

The FDA approved the drug on March 1. Merck's protease inhibitor, the strongest of the bunch, was approved two weeks later. The first HIV viral load test, which could measure exactly how much virus was in a patient's blood, was approved three months after that.

By July, it all came to a head. At the International AIDS Conference in Vancouver, results from multiple trials using the new viral load test conclusively showed that triple-drug regimens with the new protease inhibitors appeared to fully control HIV in patients. After a few months on the regimens, most had undetectable viral loads, meaning only very low amounts of the virus remained, just below the lower limits that the test could measure.

Spencer's ethical arguments proved true. With data from larger trials, treatment guidelines emerged and were updated regularly. By the late 1990s, a newly infected gay White man living in Manhattan's Chelsea neighborhood, regardless of his wealth, would start the same regimen as an African American single mother diagnosed at a crowded clinic in Queens. As everyone started the new triple-drug regimens, deaths from AIDS plummeted in this country, falling two-thirds in just three years.

But at the 1996 AIDS conference in Vancouver, before this miracle panned out, the activists who had witnessed so much death over the previous fifteen years had difficulty imagining the full import of this turning point. We had grown cynical after winning so many political battles only to see deaths rise year after year, unabated.

As with most of the AIDS conferences, many of us added some vacation time to the trip. This time I ended up on a Vancouver Island beach with David Barr. Then and now, David has been a constant comrade in the fight against AIDS and closest of friends. Born and raised in Brooklyn as a pink diaper baby—with Jewish lefty parents who had never joined the Communist Party, one shade over from a red diaper baby—David inherited their patient skills for community organizing, a huge asset for AIDS activism. He also has a heart of gold. When the infighting in ACT UP began taking its toll on all of us, David organized a self-run HIV support group for his closest comrades, imploring us all to take care of ourselves while fighting for the lives of so many others. Spencer jokingly called us the HIVIPs.

Mark, Derek Link, and Gregg Bordowitz rounded out the group, and we kept meeting monthly for home-cooked meals, rotating among our apartments. This got us through the worst years of the crisis, right up until the amazing news at the conference in Vancouver.

After lathering on our suntan lotion and smoking a little weed, we both stared out at the ocean's waves and endless horizon. "So, is this real?" David asked. "We're not going to die horrible deaths soon?"

"Wild, eh?" I replied, slightly taken aback. "We might actually survive this."

12

SURVIVING SURVIVOR'S GUILT

ONCE WE RETURNED FROM VANCOUVER, almost every HIV-positive comrade I knew added a protease inhibitor to their two-drug regimens, hoping the same miracle they saw on those slides at the conference would happen to them.

I did the same. One by one, all of us became undetectable within one to three months, meaning our virus was under control for the first time since being diagnosed. I found out I was undetectable on my eleventh diagnosis anniversary, November 15, 1996.

Though it was wonderful news, not one of us celebrated. How could we? So many had died just months earlier, cruelly missing the second chances we'd been given. The death toll in the previous few years had been unrelenting. Bradley Ball, ACT UP's first administrator, who singlehandedly and meticulously managed our inner workings—budgets, elections, note-taking, contact lists, etc.—died in 1995. He was only thirty-four.

Bob Rafsky, who had famously heckled presidential candidate Bill Clinton, prompting his "I feel your pain" reply, died in 1993. He had joined many of my actions with a passion and eloquence that few in ACT UP could match.

Lee Arsenault died while we were planning the Helms condom action. He was a founding member of the Power Tools, invading Burroughs Wellcome and shutting down trading on the New York Stock Exchange.

Personally, my most heartbreaking loss was Griffin Gold, who died in 1989 at the age of thirty-three. He was the first HIV-positive person I met after my diagnosis, and he had introduced me to activism.

These names and so many more excluded any possibility of victory laps in 1996. I've often compared it to coming home from a horrifying, unpopular war, like returning from Vietnam in 1975. It was a time of unprocessed grief, unrecognized accomplishment, and unfinished business.

Mainstream LGBT rights groups pivoted from AIDS to gays in the military and gay marriage so quickly and thoroughly it felt like the surviving activists, our history, indeed AIDS itself had been purged. There were plenty of logical reasons, like the falling death rate, a shriveling fundraising landscape, mental burnout from all the previous trauma, and more. But it still felt like the community turned its back on those of us who survived. They also abandoned unfinished work, since HIV infections were still rising in people of color. AIDS organizations like the National Minority AIDS Council and the Black AIDS Institute tried to pick up the slack, but often with little support from an exhausted LGBT community and its mostly White leadership and donors. Instead, the community moved on to other battles, using all its newfound power that AIDS activism had awakened. I wish it had done so with more balance and grace.

I've often wondered how many of us who got infected in the early '80s made it to 1997. The longest-running AIDS trial offers a clue.

The Multicenter AIDS Cohort Study (MACS) enrolled nearly five thousand gay men from Baltimore, Chicago, Pittsburgh, and Los Angeles in 1984 and early '85, and has been following them ever since. Of the original enrollees, 1,814 tested HIV positive on entry, around 40 percent of the total. I assume I was infected in 1983 and found out in late '85, so those HIV-positive men were a near-perfect cohort of my peers.

If all you've ever heard is "AIDS killed everyone" in the 1980s and early '90s, then you might be surprised to learn that 30 percent of those eighteen hundred men were still alive in 1997.

One of the biggest misunderstandings about HIV is that it kills someone in about two to three years. Many think this because most patients in the '80s found out so late in their disease and then died within months or, if they were lucky, a couple of years. But in fact, untreated HIV infection takes an average of eight to ten years to kill someone. After the infection takes hold, there is usually a multiyear latency period when the virus remains somewhat dormant, ever so slowly undermining the immune system. The Hollywood version of HIV/AIDS never portrays this often lengthy period of chronic, asymptomatic infection.

So even without treatments, some percentage of the MACS cohort from 1984 who had been recently infected lived slightly longer than the average and made it to 1997. Many were likely infected years earlier; we know now that HIV was spreading in the United States during the late 1970s.

Even so, many of those who made it to 1997 limped over the artificial breakthrough line the year before. More than a few had experienced an AIDS diagnosis, along with one or more serious illnesses, and the early AIDS drugs had come with heavy side effects. These guys were pretty beaten up. Tests had shown that their bodies and minds more closely matched a typical male ten years older. Living with HIV this long had prematurely aged us.

By 2019, only 410 of the HIV-positive MACS men were still alive—23 percent of the original group. Though I'm not in this study, my history matches the original cohort. Of my still-living, HIV-positive peers, are there circumstances or things we did that helped us survive? One thing for sure: multiple studies have shown that socioeconomic status affects outcomes in HIV disease. These social determinants of health are made obvious across all disease groups in the United States, with its patchwork health care system, income inequality, systemic racism, and antigovernment political bias.

My odds of joining the 23 percent were greatly increased by unbroken access to high-quality health care, uninterrupted housing, and a monthly stipend from wealthy parents once I stopped working.

My privilege—or was it luck?—also extended to the religion I was born into. Sadly, the odds of having your family support you after coming out as HIV positive and gay are often determined by how religious your family was. I'm an American rarity—a born Unitarian. Unitarian Universalism is the least doctrinaire religion in existence. You can be an atheist, like I am today, and still call yourself a Unitarian. Up until very recently, almost every other organized religion in history has been the bane of queer people.

Most everyone I knew in ACT UP had been mentally tortured by family members touting religion. Many had to start their adult lives without family support of any kind. I got a lucky pass. My mom's dad, Dr. James R. Killian Jr., paved the way. Dedicating himself to a life of science starting at MIT, he broke from his Southern Methodist upbringing to join the Unitarian Universalists, eventually becoming the national church's Moderator, its highest lay position.

Thankfully, my dad, probably with a shrug, deferred to my mom's religion, adopted from her father's. And thus, the Staley kids started as Unitarians and remain unscathed, at least directly, by the kind of religious hatred that destroys families.

Beyond the privileges I started with, my treatment history after being diagnosed might also have bought me some time. I benefited from the highly personalized antiviral choices my doctor and I made over time through trial and error.

When AZT was approved in early 1987, I held off using it until my T4 cells dropped to 351 that fall. The initial dose was 1,200 mg a day with a brutal dosing schedule: 200 mg precisely every four hours. I got anemic almost immediately, causing me to look visibly pale and nod off at my trading desk. A month later, I gave up. Stopping the AZT left me feeling defeated and more than a little anxious about losing the only option available at the time. Nine months later, my T4 cells fell dangerously low, to 103.

Dr. William started me on Bactrim, a strong antibiotic that could prevent PCP and toxoplasmosis, which the lowered T4 count put me at a real risk of getting. But I also pitched him a desperate idea: What if I tried taking just a little bit of AZT, like 300 mg a day, to see if I could tolerate it? There was no data showing that taking a quarter of the recommended dose would have any effectiveness, but I was out of options.

At that point, William was losing so many patients that he likely shared our sense of desperation. If we came to him with what-the-hell treatment ideas, he'd often sign off on trying them as long as their known side effects were mild and manageable.

I had no issues at all with the lower dose. It was like a different drug compared to 1,200 mg, so I stuck with it. We both marveled as my T4 counts rose to 216, then 305, then 514, and finally, a year later, peaked at 702. Most patients on AZT monotherapy only got a few months of improved health, including increased T4 counts and weight gain. Luckily, less medication proved to be more for me, and I got a year's worth of gains.

The effectiveness of any therapy can always be plotted on a graph with a bell curve. If the vast majority of patients improved for three to six months while taking AZT, they'd fall under the peak of the bell curve. But a smaller number of folks got no benefit at all, falling on the left edge of the curve. By pure luck, I fell on its right edge, with the small percentage of patients who did extremely well.

Shortly after I topped 700 T4 cells, the FDA cut the recommended dose of AZT in half, to 600 mg a day. The label eventually said that an even lower dose of 400 mg could be used for patients weighing less than 60 kilograms. I weigh about 62 kilograms. My wild guess of 300 mg a day wasn't far off the mark.

In late 1990, a year after my T4s peaked, they had fallen back to the mid to low 300s. By this time, the second experimental AIDS drug, ddI, was looking promising in larger clinical trials. It was the first drug to be widely distributed through the Parallel Track program ACT UP had advocated for, and twelve thousand patients were taking it by then. Yet only those who had failed AZT could enroll in the expanded access program.

Dr. William and I both thought AZT was still helping me. I asked him if he was OK with me adding a low dose of ddI if I could get my hands on some. He said sure.

Getting some ddI turned out to be quite easy, thanks to the buyers clubs the community had set up to find and distribute experimental drugs. Some of the sickest patients who were shipped a three-month supply of ddI died before, or just after, they could start the drug. Their friends or loved ones would then donate the unused drug to their local buyers club. I was getting my ddI from the recently deceased. And though it sounds creepy, I viewed it as a collective strength—lifesaving, caring, and efficient.

Once every few months, I'd visit the offices of the People with AIDS Health Group, New York City's buyers club, and pick up free boxes of the drug. Based solely on my low-dose success with AZT, I decided to add just a half dose of ddI. It had its own toxicities, and I hoped to avoid them as well. Sure enough, I had few issues, and my T4s started climbing again. By March 1991, they hit 606. I coasted on this dual regimen all the way until the breakthrough news about triple-drug regimens with the protease inhibitors.

A year before HIV viral load tests became commercially available, doctors in the know could send their patients' blood to Roche Biomedical Laboratories for the experimental test. So in early 1995, while I was still on low-dose AZT and ddI, my first viral load result was 19,120 copies in a milliliter, or about half a thimbleful, of blood. That sounds like a lot, but if your virus becomes fully resistant to the treatments you're on, you can have a viral load of over 1 million per milliliter of blood.

I would find out a few years later that my HIV had only mutated enough to become partially resistant to AZT and ddI, even after I had been taking them for six years. Once again, if there was a bell curve for how folks did on dual therapy, I fell on the very lucky end of it.

I made it to 1996 without a serious illness or a diagnosis of AIDS. When discussing long-term survivors today, I'm careful not to claim membership in its most resilient fellowship: those who survived AIDS itself. AIDS is considered the end stage of HIV disease; you'd get the diagnosis only after your immune system was so weak that one or more opportunistic diseases or cancers would hit you.

While my T4s got dangerously low a couple of times, they didn't stay there that long, and I never got a major secondary illness. In 1993, the Centers for Disease Control revised their case definition for AIDS to include a T4 cell count less than 200, but this came well after my two dips below that threshold in the late '80s. I was never diagnosed with AIDS.

Those who were suffered far more, physically and mentally, than those of us who were diagnosed with AIDS-related complex or were just HIV positive. When I think of survivors of the early AIDS years, I think of them and am awed by their resilience.

While I luckily avoided an AIDS diagnosis, I shamefully avoided witnessing its often brutal death. I feared that death so much, I shunned hospitals and funerals when I could. I even avoided the shame of this by rationalizing the avoidance. I imagined myself as a soldier on the front lines who couldn't retreat from his foxhole to visit wounded comrades in the field hospital. I would stay focused on the job at hand and just kept fighting.

This is bullshit, of course. I wasn't pinned down in a foxhole. When Griffin Gold was hospitalized a final time, I could have joined his care team and still made it to all my ACT UP meetings. But I rationalized my behavior. Griff had a solid care team of loving long-term friends, Michael Lesser and Ray Balsys, plus his mother. I would be the newcomer. Besides, I knew I sucked at empathy. I was raised in a family of WASPy stoics conditioned to ignore our emotions, and even better at avoiding those of others. Years later, I'd partially break these bad habits, but not then.

So I stayed away.

Griff died in March 1989. He had requested that I play the piano at his memorial, so I refreshed one of the pieces I used a decade earlier for my audition to Oberlin's Conservatory: Brahms's Intermezzo in A Major, op. 118, no. 2.

I played it well. As the eulogies were delivered, the loss finally hit me. I cried hard through most of them. Fear was in the mix. At that moment, compartmentalizing my mortality was impossible.

Today I look back and feel shame at not doing more for Griff during his last weeks. But I understand the flawed and frightened young man I was back then, who did what he thought he had to do not to fall apart.

I've talked to hundreds of people who survived those years, both HIV negative and HIV positive, and none of us were saints. We all have regrets about the corners we cut for selfish reasons, which includes self-preservation. We all deserve a process toward self-forgiveness.

But for the most part, I wasn't burdened by some of the rampant and unwarranted shame that often came with an HIV diagnosis. I suppose some people saw that as detachment or, worse, lack of emotion. In reality, though, I think my self-confidence was my armor. All in all, I'm proud of my Spock-like devotion to logic and reason; it has served me well.

And, in the final analysis, my diagnosis stemmed from a virus that had no moral valence, just relentless marching orders from its RNA. If the virus was my sentence, then my only crime was being human. That was so true on my first night with Curtis Randall, the bartender from the Duplex, who sent a drink on the house my way and then swept me off my tipsy feet. I look back on that now and I can only smile. Zero regrets.

Even though I was deeply closeted, being gay never shamed me either. My closet was a logical reaction to society's unforgiving condemnation of something I had no control over. Whatever my desires, they were obviously innate. Indoctrinated homophobia was the shameful part of the equation, not my intrinsic and beautiful gayness.

Don't get me wrong; I'm not immune to shame. I spent my early forties processing plenty of it during a twelve-step program. But something in my constitution fortified me from feeling unjustified shame—the kind that many bear for things they either can't control or never fully avoid while living a decent life.

I also avoided another scourge that occasionally accompanied an HIV diagnosis: denial. I could have compartmentalized the virus itself, retreating into inaction or, worse, self-destruction. Instead, I immediately sought out everything I could find to learn more about the disease, looking for ways to buy some time.

I don't think I was special in this regard. It seemed to me that the vast majority of those diagnosed with HIV worked hard to stay alive as long as possible. And a subset of us became activists.

A few scientific studies have indicated that optimism leads to better health outcomes, and pessimism leads to worse. It stands to reason that being highly proactive, in my case as a full-time activist, likely helped, at least on the margins. I know for sure that my mental health thrived during ACT UP's first few glory years. I remember how dark it felt during those sixteen months between my diagnosis and the moment I stepped into that first-floor hall at the Lesbian and Gay Community Services Center for my first ACT UP meeting. Everything changed in an instant, like a dark stage suddenly bathed in warm hues. I entered a surreal protective bubble that became my entire life for the next few crucial years.

That bubble was a wildly empowered and loving community. All of our emotions were heightened and intense, frustrating and beautiful at the same time. It was a bubble filled with demonstrations, endless meetings, nights of ecstasy and dancing, nights of wheat-pasting, hospitals and memorials, boyfriends, new friends, breakups, phone zaps, phone trees, shame-free sex, sex between proud sluts, sex that was political, that said fuck-you to the haters, more endless meetings, kiss-ins, kissing hello on the lips, kissing lesbians, selling T-shirts and buttons, covering an entire city in SILENCE = DEATH stickers, heckling presidents, getting arrested with your best friends, chanting, laughing, crying, hugging, lots of hugs to fight off fear and tears, and a beautiful surge of creativity, artistry, and genius that synergized among us.

I have never felt more alive and protected. I do not believe in god, but I witnessed something profoundly spiritual in those years: the power of collective empathy. Each of us is capable of it, possibly instilled by evolution. When members of a support group tap empathy together, wounds can be healed and lives can be saved. When a community taps it while under siege, history itself can be bent toward righteous victories.

So yes, I lean toward believing that the emotional payoffs of fighting back within a glorious movement helped save my life. But only on the margins. The ACT UP bubble was still no match for the virus. During the darkest years of the crisis in the early '90s, ACT UP was losing about twenty members a year to AIDS—more than one funeral a month.

The things I tried and any advantages I may have had were not unique. Many others took the same meds but didn't make it. More than a few had the same or greater privileges but still died. We don't know why some lived, and may never know, so we call it luck. There were no magic strategies or circumstances that consistently saved any of us.

My friend and comrade Gregg Bordowitz, who helped me disrupt trading on the floor of the New York Stock Exchange, was recently asked during an interview (*Brooklyn Rail*, July–August 2020) about those years:

> By '93, I was really sick. . . . I was home with a nurse. Most of my friends thought that I was going to die. I was prepared to die. I somehow recovered from that and hung on until '96. Many of my friends did not. I did not do anything different than what they did. I still don't understand it. Luck and privilege are the only reason I am alive.

I share Gregg's baffled conclusion. And I marvel at being alive today. But it is a haunted joy.

13

FIGHTING TINA

———————

'M NOT GOING TO PIN MY ADDICTION to crystal methamphetamine on survivor's
guilt. Many HIV-positive gay men who survived the plague years
got tangled up in the surging popularity of meth in the late '90s and
early aughts, and some attributed it to the challenging transition we
shared after our death sentences were lifted.

And I'm not going to connect it to unprocessed self-loathing,
or an addictive personality, or a troubled childhood. Only the latter
might apply, but I had processed most of that long before. My mom
had nothing to do with this.

My addiction was more superficial than those tangible narratives.
It was prompted by a somewhat standard gay man's midlife crisis,
with youth, looks, and easy sex slipping away. I stumbled upon meth,
and it felt like one last ticket to ride all three.

Then again, there's no doubting that I had a rough transition
leading up to it. My final few years in TAG were frustrating. Mark
and Gregg were doing the bulk of the policy work, while I handled
all the administration and fundraising. Even though I was skilled at
both, they hardly got my blood flowing each day. After ten nonstop
years of AIDS activism, I was feeling burnt out.

On top of that, my ego was rearing its ugly head. At the 1996 AIDS conference in Vancouver, I distinctly remember feeling like a has-been. Six years earlier, I had opened the same conference in San Francisco with a speech that I thought made a huge difference, nudging activists and scientists toward collaboration instead of conflict. But in Vancouver, with that alliance in full bloom, I was doing grunt work, reduced to searching for the cheapest printer to copy TAG's press releases, which were filled with quotes from my fellow activists.

One year later, I resigned. Mark and I had been getting into increasingly bitter spats over silly issues involving organizational turf. I was pretty controlling over how things should run administratively—shocker, I know—and he started pushing back.

We laugh at it now, but the last straw was over Mac versus PC. Back then, the two computing platforms were far less compatible than they are today. Most organizations picked one or the other. I wanted TAG to go all PC, and Mark wanted a new Mac.

Embarrassingly, our board of directors had to end the dispute; they sided with Mark. That gave me my last excuse to look beyond AIDS activism toward a new career that would excite me again. My resignation letter to the board included this hopeful sign-off:

> TAG will continue to thrive. TAG will continue to benefit and save the lives of people living with HIV. For this, I feel very proud, as should everyone who has been involved with this unique group.
>
> I have been an AIDS activist for over ten years, and have known a life with HIV for nearly twelve. It has truly been a wild ride. Now, while I seem to have the time, I want to pursue some dreams that I had put on hold. Some of them are pretty crazy, so wish me luck.

My resignation relieved much of the internal tensions caused by the infighting between Mark and me over the previous year. TAG *has* thrived, and I remain immensely proud of it.

———————

Some of those crazy ideas I had for the next chapter of my life were entrepreneurial, possibly opening my own business. Or maybe I should try teaching, a profession I greatly admired.

The plan was to give myself a year to figure out this next chapter while enjoying some much-needed time off. But after a year and a half passed, I was in a panic. None of the ideas I mulled over during the previous eighteen months lured me into action. In fact, they all seemed a bit scary. The gap between the surreal existence I had been living and the real-world existence I hoped to reenter seemed too daunting.

Being a full-time activist with only a few years to live had some distinct upsides. It was kind of nice not having to worry about the future. I hadn't had a boss in over a decade—my life was totally my own. I got to choose which activist projects to work on and how to fill my day. In a sense, I was spoiled. My status quo was too damn comfortable. The real world had become daunting in comparison.

Eventually, a dear friend of mine, Laura Pinsky, threw me a lifeline. As a counselor at Columbia University, Laura had been doing AIDS activism since before ACT UP, launching the student-run Gay Health Advocacy Project in 1985. Through her years of experience in academia and activism, she seemed to know everyone in New York. One of the people she knew had just started his own career counseling business, so Laura played matchmaker.

Bruce Hermann had recently left a high-pressure career at PepsiCo. He had ditched corporate America to try something entrepreneurial and was now picking his own clients and setting his own hours. I liked his thinking.

A good career counselor needs to be a good shrink, and Bruce was one of the best I've seen. Each week I laid all my emotional baggage on the small table between us, especially my fears of trying to build a future I never thought I'd have.

His process was methodical, always keeping small, doable goals in front of me so that I wouldn't lose hope. After fully examining what I liked and disliked during previous jobs, vocations, and hobbies—everything from a summer job at Burger King cooking fries and onion rings to trading bonds on Wall Street to being TAG's founding director—we created two short lists of what I wanted, or wanted to avoid, in a new career.

We both looked at my lists with raised eyebrows. I wanted a career that wasn't 24-7, allowing for lots of free time. That nixed most business start-up ideas. I also wanted total control. That ruled out working for anyone. And I wanted to make a comfortable living. Easy, right?

While Bruce and I spent months exploring options that might thread all these needles, my body was changing in a way that terrified me. The HIV meds that were saving my life were also melting away otherwise healthy layers of subdermal fat in my legs, arms, buttocks, and face. At the same time, my upper abdomen distended a bit from fat accumulating around my organs. It's called lipodystrophy, and it seemed to be happening to just about everyone taking the first generation of HIV meds. The new marker of being poz was deep grooves carved in our faces. We had been saved only to be marked.

Since this was 1999, I browsed the newish and rapidly growing Web for answers. There were only a few HIV-related websites at the time, and they mostly posted all the treatment-related newsletters from various AIDS organizations, acting like online libraries. Wading through it all was a bit overwhelming, even for an experienced AIDS activist.

I knew that the newly diagnosed needed help climbing the steep learning curve involving the virus itself, complex treatment regimens, side effects, various blood test results, and possibly a dual diagnosis with an opportunistic infection. But the Web was missing an easy-to-read guide that provided some hand-holding up this learning curve, written by those who were in the same boat and constantly updated with the latest info. A business idea was born.

I discussed all of this with Bruce, and after a few more months of research, I registered a new domain name called AIDSmeds.com. The business model for the website was built around unrestricted educational grants from pharmaceutical companies. The industry recognized that patients trusted community-based education far more than pharma ads and websites, and that well-educated patients were more likely to start treatment.

I recruited two fellow AIDS warriors, Spencer Cox and Tim Horn, to write the site's easy-to-read "lessons." Tim had been an editor of the *AIDS/HIV Treatment Directory* at amfAR during the '90s, overlapping my thirteen-year stint on its board of directors. Together, we started building AIDSmeds.com into one of the most well-respected online resources for people living with HIV.

My role was administrator, fundraiser, and coder in chief. One feature that I was particularly proud of allowed users to input all the meds they were on, and a comprehensive third-party application would return all possible interactions. Along with Check My Meds, we built Graph My Labs and the busiest HIV-related community forums on the Web. My inner geek was in heaven.

All the while, other parts of my inner self were hurting. Even though I was successfully launching a new career, some bad decisions risked it all.

I was turning forty, an age I never thought I would see. When I looked in the mirror, I winced. Lipodystrophy had dug those deep grooves in my face, and while I'd always been a lean guy, I felt that I now looked gaunt. So I did what every other self-respecting-if-a-little-vain gay man was doing: I hit the gym. Hard.

At the time, I was living in Brooklyn with my partner, Gary, and our relationship was open sexually. His nonprofit work sent him to San Francisco monthly, and those business trips inspired very different trips of my own—typically, a night on the town, starting around midnight at the Roxy, the biggest gay dance club at the time, and ending at the West Side Club, the city's newest bathhouse, which opened in 1995. A single hit of ecstasy flooded my body with enough serotonin for a full night of dancing and no-strings-attached sex.

As Gary's trips became more frequent, so did my benders. The mornings after—sometimes several mornings after—were brutal. The serotonin crashes knocked me on my ass, and they seemed to be getting worse. I moaned about this to a gym buddy, and he said four words that changed my life:

"You should try Tina."

Crystal meth—it was cheap, plentiful, and my gym buddy had experienced few if any issues bouncing back from it the next day. That last bit of info turned out to be wildly off the mark, unless you stopped after a single snorted bump on the dance floor.

I got my first taste of Tina a few nights later, snorting a small bump. Meh, I thought. Ecstasy was so much better. But the next time, a few weeks later, was like night and day. The other guy had a pipe, and said it worked much better when you smoked it. I became hooked immediately.

So this is the part of the addiction narrative where I get on the roller coaster of higher highs and lower lows, where the things that I thought were permanent are suddenly made fragile, where implausible bargains for pleasure make fortunes crumble and relationships falter, where the heat of the high renders your values from your soul, leaving nothing behind but a glass pipe.

But I'm going to spare you the details. It's not out of shame, although I'm not exactly proud of a lot of things that I did to myself and other people. I've shared the details quite often during interviews and in front of audiences, but always at a cost to those closest to me. Besides, the details are no different from those you'll find in dozens if not hundreds of addiction memoirs. After sharing my story again and again, I began to feel like the car wreck that everyone turns their heads to see while passing slowly on the highway.

An outline will do. It took me over two years to get sober, after some tough love from Gary and even tougher love from the Realization Center off Union Square—an outpatient drug rehab program that had support groups for gay men.

My story differs from most in one respect: I knew I had a problem almost immediately. Drug use was not new to me, but addiction was. The third time I used meth was unplanned, and that shocked me. The second time had been amazing, but the crash was hard, so I scheduled some relaxing time with friends the following weekend. Those plans were thwarted by a burning desire to relive the wild ride I had just experienced, and I disappeared for another binge instead.

So I started seeing a shrink with experience helping addicts just four months after my first hit. Boaz Dalit has my eternal thanks for helping me process each lower low until I hit hard bottom and started climbing back.

And community saved me too, as it had before. Boaz slowly convinced me to give a twelve-step program a try. In the fall of 2001, I sat in the back rows of a huge beginners' meeting at the same LGBT Community Center where ACT UP once met. I was instantly reminded of those first glorious years when a community came together to take care of our own. The same kind of brotherly love was in the room all these years later.

But I still struggled, and a year later, I hit a spiritual bottom that scared me more than any moment before, including the years I thought AIDS would kill me. I finally entered an outpatient program.

I had been trying to get sober for a year and a half, but I was backsliding instead. I had a sponsor and was working the steps, slowly. The time between relapses was shrinking, not growing. I lost all hope of digging myself out. My self-confidence was destroyed. It felt like a permanent trap, a rewiring of my brain that I couldn't undo. Maybe I'd live for many more years, but they'd all be joyless, each worse than the one before it.

Walking into the Realization Center was an act of desperation. Almost immediately, it clicked. The twelve-step program I had been using, with its lack of cross talk or confrontation, gave me too much slack to avoid the serious work of getting sober. But the counselors and group therapy at the RC weren't shy about verbally smacking me around if I offered up excuses, because they'd heard them all before.

Their tough love was exactly what I needed. It complemented the fellowship I found in my twelve-step program, which I continued using for its loving, communal embrace.

After a year and a half of constant group therapy meetings at the RC and completing the twelve steps with a sponsor's selfless direction, I was a changed man. I had wanted to get sober, but had not expected the personal growth. I had gone through life thinking I didn't need to change. From my early teens, I had felt more mature and self-assured than my peers. This hardened into a kind of snobbery by which I avoided the less assured or those who seemed wounded. I became cocky and arrogant and fully self-aware of both. Preoccupied with my own thoughts, my listening skills atrophied, and ultimately sucked.

I was convinced all of this worked just fine for me. I knew my flaws, but they had protected and served me well. In my head, the forty-year-old me was little changed from the confident and talented young pianist and teacher's pet in sixth grade.

All of this was challenged in group therapy and by working, with profound openness, through the twelve steps. Meth destroyed my self-assuredness, my belief that I could dig myself out of any hole. It was slowly rebuilt, this time with some humbling perspective, by the love and empathy I experienced among gay men leaning into each other for support and healing. I not only felt restored, I felt remade.

This old dog was taught new tricks—the most useful of which was focused listening. I spent hours every week completely tuned into what others were saying. Our shared pain and fears reeled me in, though my own tears caught me off guard. I had avoided other people's pain my entire life, thinking it would pull me down. But now, by embracing it, I was being pulled up. I listened to these gay men as they became friends and then brothers. I cried with them, dared to offer advice that might help, and then marveled when, every once in a while, it did.

Rich DeNagel entered the program just before I did. He was younger than I was by seven years and had his own battle with a terminal disease: he was born with cystic fibrosis.

Some men didn't last long in our meetings. Others, like Rich and me, managed to hang in there for months, eventually becoming the old-timers. We were both hard-core stoics. Rich had tried rehab before and had grown cynical about its potential to help him. That didn't stop him from offering advice with a weary been-there-done-that attitude, which would always make me chuckle.

Rich was a rule-breaker whose boyish charm often prevented repercussions. He violated RC rules at least twice. The center had a zero-tolerance policy for relapses, and we marveled at his I-don't-deserve-to-be-here, broken puppy retelling of how a bottle of beer turned into a weekend meth binge. The counselors would boot anyone else for this, but they let him stay. Months later, Rich slept with a guy in our group—another huge no-no—and instead of them both being banished, the smooth-talker convinced the center to let both of them remain.

He had me at rule-breaker.

I found myself instantly gravitating to Rich, much like I had to Griffin Gold at that HIV support group meeting I joined the year after my diagnosis. They both came off as tough as Bea Arthur on *The Golden Girls*, with a great sense of campy humor. More importantly, they both had levels of empathy and listening skills that I aspired to.

I still don't come close to either of their higher powers. But I've been a changed man since being saved by so many other flawed men, facing ourselves, sitting in circles of folding chairs. Every relationship in my life since recovery has been enriched by the tools these men taught me. I no longer flee from wounded friends. I no longer defend long-lived traits that have blocked any chance at personal growth. I've ditched the self-defeating stubbornness of *I am who I am*.

My addiction and recovery pushed me toward a new type of activism. During months of outpatient and twelve-step meetings, I realized I was witnessing a new health crisis among gay men in New York City. But outside those transformative meetings, no one was talking about it.

It felt like early AIDS all over again, with politicians and public health officials ignoring an uncomfortable new reality. Rising meth use among gay men was fueling an uptick in HIV infections. Meth targets the brain's chemistry in a way that makes inhibitions vanish, often leading to increased risk-taking during sex. As an upper, it can fuel marathon binges of unprotected sex, sometimes with multiple partners.

My work with AIDSmeds.com kept me in close contact with front-line HIV docs, many of them gay. They were seeing newly infected patients with multiple health issues whose lives were falling apart.

These gay doctors, like those of us attending increasingly crowded twelve-step meetings, were all witnessing a private hell. But the world at large wasn't noticing or, worse, wasn't caring.

I was also witnessing a blitheness about meth among gay men outside the meetings. It had become the party drug du jour in New York City, and news of the wreckage it was causing among many gay men on the West Coast hadn't quite reached us yet. I'd hear guys laughing about their friends' crystal meth binges, as if they had hilariously fallen down drunk. "That girl loves her Tina"—ha-ha-ha!

All the while, I was witnessing its widespread wreckage. It felt like silence equals death all over again, and my anger built. My head began spinning with familiar thoughts of activism—maybe I could break the silence.

I brought all this up at my RC group, using them as a sounding board and for much-needed encouragement, which I got every step of the way. I knew that any activism I launched to raise awareness around gay men and meth would carry far more weight if I came out about my addiction, just as my openness about my HIV status had empowered my AIDS activism.

I was now nine months sober, and on a warm August night in 2003, I walked by a phone booth along Eighth Avenue in Chelsea, the city's newest gay ghetto. An advertisement on the side of the booth was backlit, making its picture of two sexy men embracing light up the sidewalk. The ad was promoting GAY.com's personals and chat-rooms, the leading pre-Grindr hookup site for finding sex in the early aughts. It triggered an a-ha moment.

The GAY.com ads were perfectly and efficiently targeted—just a few of them getting thousands of cruising looks from the avenue's nightly flow of preening gay men. *I didn't know advertisers could pick specific phone booths in specific neighborhoods,* I thought. *Why couldn't an activist do the same thing?*

Five months later, just before sunset on a below-freezing January night, I shivered in front of another phone booth. I had removed all my winter coverings for a *New York Times* photoshoot. The ad behind me had a ripped male torso clad only in tight underwear, reposed, legs spread wide. The model seemed headless, his face digitally replaced by a mirrored disco ball. Surrounding him were screaming headlines in bright neon colors: HUGE SALE! BUY CRYSTAL, GET HIV FREE! Next to the word "crystal" was a picture of a small ziplock baggie of meth.

More offensiveness followed. A smaller headline next to the model's crotch surrounded a picture of a glass crack pipe, saying, BONUS SPECIAL: BUY THIS HANDY ACCESSORY PIPE, GET A LIFE-TIME ADDICTION FREE!

Six of these ads had gone up that morning along Eighth Avenue in Chelsea, each one costing me a thousand bucks for a month's run. I had trusted a gay reporter at the *Times* Metro desk with an exclusive story. With the help of Vincent Gagliostro, one of ACT UP's best graphic designers, we filled the ad with bright colors, hoping to grab the attention of the Metro Section's cover editor. Back then, the *Times* was using color printing only on the front page of each section.

It worked. A few days later, Gary picked up the paper outside our apartment door before dawn, walking it back to our bedroom. "Um, it seems the *New York Times* has decided you're *the beast* in the bathhouse," he said with a mixture of shock and annoyance. He held up the unfolded Metro Section before me. The picture was huge, taking up almost a third of the page. The unfortunate headline above the picture said, THE BEAST IN THE BATHHOUSE.

Thankfully, the subheadline clarified things: "Crystal Meth Use by Gay Men Threatens to Reignite an Epidemic." The reporter, Andrew Jacobs, did an amazing job, with quotes from the city's health commissioner, various experts, frontline AIDS docs, and recovering addicts.

The Metro Section

The New York Times

The Beast in the Bathhouse

Crystal Meth Use by Gay Men Threatens to Reignite an Epidemic

By ANDREW JACOBS

Bob looked haggard but was feeling fabulous. Chewing gum at a manic clip, circling the labyrinthine halls of the West Side Club on a recent Sunday afternoon, he had been awake since Friday, thanks to a glassine pouch of crystalline powder he had tucked beneath the mattress of a room he rented in this Chelsea bathhouse.

The powder, known as methamphetamine, or crystal meth, had helped Bob conquer a half-dozen sex partners during a 35-hour binge. Like many of the men cruising the two-level club lined with closet-size cubicles, Bob, a 37-year-old advertising copywriter, was "tweaking," high on a wildly addictive stimulant that has been sweeping through Manhattan's gay ghettos.

"The stuff is a wonder," he said, taking a pause from his prowling, his scrawny frame wrapped in a white towel. Asked about condoms and the niceties of safe sex, Bob shrugged. "Whatever," he said, turning away.

At the club, there were plenty of condoms for the taking, courtesy of the

Associated Press

Methamphetamine, or crystal meth, can be smoked, snorted or injected.

management, but in conversations with a dozen patrons who acknowledged using crystal, only two men said they were following the rules of engagement in the age of AIDS. "Some guys just throw you out of the room if you pull one out," said one of the men, James, who, like everyone else, would not give his full name. "To them, rubbers are a killjoy."

Health officials say a sharp increase in the number of syphilis cases in the city indicates an increase in unsafe sex, which they fear may lead to a resurgence in H.I.V. transmission.

For now, researchers say, crystal meth use in the city is largely confined to gay white men in Manhattan, although they fear its eventual spread to the wider gay population and beyond.

There are no numbers, however, to show what health care workers say is the growing role that crystal meth is playing in transmitting H.I.V. Although the evidence is anecdotal, health officials say that crystal, which erases inhibitions and spurs sex marathons with multiple partners, is helping to spread the virus.

According to the city's largest private clinic for lesbians and gay men, Callen-Lorde Community Health Center, two-thirds of those testing positive for H.I.V. since June acknowledged that crystal meth was a factor in their infection.

Dr. Howard Grossman, one of the city's best-known AIDS specialists, said more than half the men who test positive in his private practice blamed methamphetamine. "This drug is destroying our community," he said. "It

Continued on Page B5

Lucian Read for The New York Times

Peter Staley, an AIDS activist and recovering crystal meth addict, beside an ad warning against using the drug. Mr. Staley spent $6,000 of his own money to place the ads on public phones in Chelsea. "My goal is to get the drug the reputation it deserves," he said.

Syphilis on the Rise

The number of reported syphilis cases in New York City has increased sharply. Health officials associate use of crystal meth with unsafe sex.

PRIMARY AND SECONDARY
SYPHILIS INFECTIONS

'96 '97 '98 '99 '00 '01 '02

Source: New York City Department of Health and Mental Hygiene

The New York Times

Cover of *New York Times* Metro Section, January 12, 2004. *New York Times*

Before its publication, I spent an extra thousand dollars on a public relations freelancer, hoping she could fully leverage the *Times* piece into more coverage. By that afternoon, I was doing back-to-back interviews with all five local TV stations in front of the same phone booth. In each interview, I explained that the ads were meant to be a political provocation. I hoped they might move the needle, nudging the gay community toward an open discussion about this hidden health crisis, and hopefully nudging our city's health department to react.

While I had speculated both would happen to a degree, it was thrilling to see how fast and extensive the reactions turned out to be. All the city's gay and lesbian politicians spoke out and called for action. The city council held a full hearing and promptly appropriated $600,000 for community-based public health messaging around meth, the first time any such messaging targeting gay men received public funds in the United States.

San Francisco and Los Angeles soon followed, forming government working groups and appropriating similar funds. For a good three years, everywhere gay guys looked in these three cities, they saw ads.

But from the moment I went public about my addiction, doing activism around meth felt lonelier and more vulnerable than any activism I had done before. There was no protective ACT UP cocoon, no safety in numbers, to build one's courage and fend off emotional challenges.

Coming out as an addict is no picnic. I was branded a "meth-head" or "meth-whore" in online comments. I was accused of spreading HIV, even though I had remained undetectable on my HIV viral load tests during my meth use, never missing a dose of my HIV meds—I always packed enough for a weekend binge.

Thankfully, I wasn't completely alone once the activism got rolling. Even before the *New York Times* story, I found comrades to work with. Two HIV-negative gay men with little to no prior experience in activism had organized a huge community forum at the Center in November 2003, titled "Challenging the Culture of Disease: Why Are New Infections Increasing Among Gay Men Again?" Dan Carlson, who worked in PR, and Bruce Kellerhouse, a psychologist, managed to pack the third-floor auditorium, successfully luring Harvey Fierstein to moderate the panel discussion. And a film crew from *60 Minutes* was there, working on a profile of Fierstein.

Dan and Bruce asked me to be on the panel. It was still two months before my phone booth ads would appear, but I decided to use the moment to come out to my own community about my addiction, before the big national coming out occurred. I barely slept the night before, and almost canceled from a serious bout of cold feet. When I finally got personal during my turn as a panelist, the crowd seemed stunned. As I finished my plea for a larger community discussion around meth, I struggled to read the audience. Had I tapped into shared frustrations, or were they embarrassed by my disclosure?

I got my answer during the Q&A, as the discussion turned almost entirely to meth. Everyone had a story of a friend in crisis. A bubble of undiscussed fear and frustration was bursting.

Dan and Bruce organized another huge community forum centered on meth after my ads came out. The three of us went on to form the Crystal Meth Working Group, designing ad campaigns with some of those city health department contracts for the next three years.

After the second forum, the backlash came. *Genre* magazine ran an article titled "Monsters, Inc.," which ripped me a new one. The author, a club-scene blogger who bravely used an alias rather than his real name, accused me of airing the gay community's dirty laundry in public. He claimed that my ads demonized users and that there was no proven connection between meth use and rising HIV infections.

In fact, there *were* studies then that showed a connection, and there have been dozens since.

We shrugged it off. But there was a kernel of truth to the charge of demonizing users. Many in the harm-reduction community were horrified by our approach. From the day I came out about my addiction, I made every effort to narrowly focus on how the drug itself, not its users, deserved a more accurate reputation. Too many guys thought it was a harmless party drug. But when you stir that pot, it gives ammo to those who want to stigmatize users.

I had recently been a user, too, and none of us deserved society's shaming. The Crystal Meth Working Group walked a fine line during the months that followed, trying to work with harm-reduction activists to get it right. Looking back, I think we crossed the line at times, especially with an ad that quoted from Larry Kramer's 2004 speech "The Tragedy of Today's Gays." It was some of Larry's worst shaming rhetoric, and we shouldn't have gone anywhere near it.

Our defense at the time was always "As long as we get gay guys talking to other gay guys about meth, that's where the harm reduction really happens." On that front, I do think we made a difference.

In 2004, the CDC's ongoing National HIV Behavioral Surveillance program added a question about crystal meth use to their surveys of gay and bisexual men. When our activism started, 14 percent of gay and bisexual men in New York City reported using meth during the previous twelve months. It was even worse on the West Coast, with 28 percent of the surveyed men in San Francisco saying they used, and 15 percent in Los Angeles. But when the survey was done again four years later, all three cities reported huge drops. San Francisco and L.A. fell to 13 percent. New York went from 14 percent to 6 percent. Each stat dropped a couple of points more in 2011, with New York dropping to around 4 percent.

These numbers represented saved lives. The activism we did was painful and far from perfect, but for a time, at least, it mattered.

Sadly, in recent years, they've been ticking back up, with New York close to 10 percent. I hope another generation of activists will pick up our playbook and not repeat our mistakes.

––––––––––––

For ACT UP's alumni, the saddest loss of all was Spencer Cox. His addiction started after mine, and it quickly destroyed the well-funded not-for-profit he had launched to examine the issues gay men faced as they got older, especially those who had survived the worst AIDS years.

Things spiraled from there. He ended up in the hospital twice with PCP pneumonia, admitting both times he had stopped taking his HIV meds. When asked why, the question would make him uncomfortable, and he'd just shrug. Between the two hospitalizations, he had a drug-related arrest. Eventually, most of his friends were pushed away.

Spencer's death from AIDS in 2012 was a wake-up call to all of us. We thought he was bouncing back, having returned to New York after a few years in Atlanta with his mom. Instead, he had stopped his meds again and was rushed to the Allen Hospital with pneumonia and sepsis. His viral load was 300,000, and his CD4s had dropped to 30. He died three days later.

It matters little that Tim Horn and I were there to witness his final hours. It was too little, too late. Our community had failed to save him.

Spencer became a symbol for the unhealed scars from the early AIDS years, for the isolation and depression faced by some of its survivors, the few who remained from a decimated generation of gay men. His death sparked much change, but not nearly enough. Forums were held, support groups formed on both coasts, and AIDS organizations launched new programs focused on the isolation felt by many older people living with HIV.

I still can't let go of the part meth played during the last years of his life, especially the walls it erected between Spencer and those who loved him.

Meth still has a grip on me, and always will—a permanent rewiring of some corner of my brain that will never untangle itself. I've had some one-off relapses since my meth activism wound down around 2006. Thankfully, each one was more distant from the one before it. But my scars from the early years weren't as deep as Spencer's and others', and my friends sustain me now.

I'll be OK, and there's joy in that.

14

DALLAS BUYERS CLUB

DAVID FRANCE, A gay journalist whose byline had caught my interest since the ACT UP days, arrived on time at my Brooklyn apartment on a cold Monday morning in December 2008. He had recently written a piece for *New York* magazine describing the tragic downfall of a once-beloved AIDS doctor who, like me, had developed an addiction to crystal meth after witnessing the worst of the plague years.

Dr. Gabriel Torres had run the AIDS ward at St. Vincent's Hospital in Greenwich Village—ground zero during the height of the city's plague. France's evocative description of those years had moved me deeply, yanking me back to those surreal times. He had another project in mind that involved the early years of ACT UP, and it was comforting to know he understood the emotional roller coaster we had ridden.

France wanted to direct a documentary about the treatment activism within ACT UP and TAG that led to the first protease inhibitors, changing the epidemic's course. His film would cover approximately ten years, from ACT UP's birth in 1987 to the treatment breakthrough in 1996.

Like me, he believed an account of this medical breakthrough would also be a story about highly effective activism. Like me, he considered it ACT UP's greatest achievement, a largely untold story worthy of inclusion in our country's history books.

"Have you worked on other documentaries?" I asked.

"No. This would be my first," he replied.

My heart sank, just as it had sunk after all the other pitches I had heard over the previous decade—ACT UP documentaries that had fizzled into unfulfilled dreams. But, just as I had during these other pitches, I offered France my encouragement.

"How can I help?" I responded.

"Can I borrow your videotapes from those years?" he asked.

I had a five-foot-wide bookshelf of VHS tapes from various sources, including most of the original content that ACT UP's video collectives had created. I also had some one-of-a-kind recordings of TV broadcasts that no longer existed on tape, including that *Crossfire* episode after the FDA demo. We browsed through my library, sometimes popping an unmarked cassette into my player to see what was on it. "So which of these do you want to borrow?" I finally asked.

"If possible, I'd like all of them," he said, promising their safe return along with an added bonus. He'd digitize the entire collection and give me a set of DVDs with the returned tapes.

As he left my apartment with two doubled-up Macy's bags filled with my most valued memories, the only thing I thought would come of it was some handy digital files of my dust-covered videotapes. But four months later, he surprised me, e-mailing a three-and-a-half-minute video of teaser footage set to music: Queen's "Bohemian Rhapsody." It was his pitch video for possible funders of the documentary, which now had a working title, *Brightness Falls*.

I wasn't prepared for this glimpse of what France was on course to create. There was a reason my videos were covered in dust. Most of us who had survived those years did our best to avoid reliving them. We hadn't processed the relentless and extraordinary waves of loss. We hadn't been allowed—our own community, exhausted from years of defeat, pivoted quickly to easier battles once AIDS no longer appeared in newspaper headlines.

The video left me in tears. "OMG, so many memories," I wrote back. "This is the time to finally remind the world what we did. It might also serve as a much-needed catharsis for all us survivors of the plague—a way to finally mourn and remember."

France soon found a generous executive producer, a seemingly gentle but radical-loving lesbian on GMHC's board of directors, Joy Tomchin. But I didn't hear anything from them for months and months, as their expanding research team uncovered hundreds of hours of archival footage.

Finally, in August 2010, France asked me to sit for a lengthy interview for the film. Many of my ACT UP comrades got the same call. I cabbed out to a studio deep in Brooklyn and tried my best to answer dozens of France's questions, straining to recall actions and moments that were now over twenty years old.

By this point in my life, I'd done dozens of recorded interviews, sometimes with masters of the art like Phil Donahue, Anderson Cooper, and Ed Bradley. I had never once teared up. That's nothing to brag about—just the outcome of remaining focused on delivering my talking points, trying my best to be calm and controlled but firm.

David France managed to break my record of feigned control. Keeping me on one stool under bright lights for four hours certainly helped. But it was the amount of remembering that began to overwhelm me. It was one thing to briefly recall those times, but it was quite another to recount those years for hours, blow by blow.

"We're almost done," he said. "For you, what was the worst thing in the plague years?"

"Just surviving, when so many others didn't," I replied, almost as a question, as if asking him for permission to say this. And then

I quietly lost it for a moment. France welled up too, and I felt newly vulnerable to internal damage, long suppressed. I tried to talk through the tears. "Um, you know, just losing, and uh, just so many, hmm, so many good people. And uh, you know, like any war, you wonder why you came home."

France, along with his brilliant editors Woody Richman and Tyler Walk, used that last confession late in the film during a montage that often stunned audiences. Close-up moments from our 2010 interviews are revealed one at a time—a few of the young activists viewers had been watching for an hour and a half were now men in their fifties. They had survived.

Less than two minutes of my four-hour interview were used in the film. France's research team unearthed more than 700 hours of archival footage, and he and his editors stitched them into a gripping ten-year story arc spanning 110 minutes. The film team shot nearly 100 hours of contemporary interviews but ended up using only a few minutes of them. The result was genius, giving the audience an emotional sense of what the activists lived through for many years, not knowing who among us, if any of us, would be alive to witness the fruits of our activism.

I finally saw the finished documentary, retitled *How to Survive a Plague*, less than one week before it premiered at the Sundance Film Festival in January 2012. It was almost too much to process at first. The emotional wounds that France had opened within me during the interview were now fully exposed—hopefully, to be partially healed in time.

The screen was filled with beautiful ghosts, our lost heroes: Stephen, Vito, Ray, Keri, Lee, Jim, Ortez, Keith. Each clip from a demonstration or Monday-night meeting would reveal a few more, all fighting gloriously for victories that would eventually, after their own deaths, save millions of lives.

The reaction to the film at Sundance was rapturous. Sundance Selects / IFC Films bought the distribution rights four days before the closing ceremony, and a slew of film festivals requested it immediately. France asked me to tour with the film on the festival circuit prior to its expected theatrical release later that year.

I had no excuse timing-wise, having left AIDSmeds.com and its new owner, *POZ* magazine, after my contract expired the year before. I was again seeing Bruce Hermann, the career counselor who pulled me out of my post-TAG rut, and we were both trying to figure out the next chapter of my life.

My initial hopes for the film now seemed realizable. It was strong enough to reach two audiences that needed to see this history. First, those of us who had lived through and been deeply impacted by it needed a worthy remembrance, a tool for catharsis. And we deserved an accessible monument if not dozens, be they movies, books, or memorials, to reverse our growing fears of being lost to history.

The second potential audience that could be impacted were younger generations, especially LGBT folk curious about history and looking for inspiration. I had a powerful memory from my first year in ACT UP, when I was being enveloped by a new queer movement making its own history but was clueless about what had come before.

One of the older activists had suggested I watch *The Times of Harvey Milk*, which had won the Oscar for Best Documentary Feature in 1985, just two years earlier. I found it at my local video store and sat alone on my couch, sobbing as a sea of gay people holding candles marched through the night down Market Street after Milk's assassination. I learned about a queer community that had come together into a political force powerful enough to defeat a statewide voter proposition that would have banned gay teachers. I also felt the rage of gay protestors who later torched over a dozen police cars outside San Francisco city hall after Milk's assassin was given a lenient sentence.

I had been ignorant of all this history, and now it was grounding me as an activist. I was part of something far larger than ACT UP. We were standing on the shoulders of thousands of brave warriors who came before us. And by the end of the film, I knew that queer people were some of the fiercest on earth. Collectively, we could do anything.

After a few more viewings at Sundance, I was convinced *How to Survive a Plague* could do for today's young, budding activists what the Milk documentary had done for me. It also succeeded in the other way I had hoped, setting me on a path toward full remembrance and catharsis while lifting my fear that what we did back then would become forgotten history. I told France that I was all in for helping to promote the film.

Touring with it was a blast. The festival circuit is its own little world, and I enjoyed its warm embrace. We kept seeing the same directors and documentaries on that year's circuit, and France and I would often deconstruct each festival's events and personalities over late-night cocktails back at our hotel bar.

Since then, watching David blossom into one of the best documentarians of our era hasn't surprised me at all. I've witnessed firsthand his dogged approach to filmmaking, which for the faint of heart can go too far at times yet never crosses an ethical line. I've come to know the underlying goodness of the man, even while critics have taken potshots at his work. I won't give those critics space here, mostly because they always involve a competitive grievance disguised as contemporary identity politics. I remain in awe of his work and thankful for his friendship.

As much as I enjoyed traveling with David and the film, I became more and more uncomfortable with a question that was often asked during audience Q&As. Folks inquired about what I was up to now or wanted to do in the near future. I'd honestly reply that I was "in transition," having recently ended a ten-year stint at AIDSmeds.com, which was mentioned in my where-is-he-now title card at the end of the film. But I wouldn't admit that I wanted a break from AIDS activism, much as I had after leaving TAG fifteen years earlier. Bruce Hermann and I were actively looking at next-chapter life options that didn't involve activism. I was in a been-there-done-that burned-out state of mind.

Little did I know that something would fall into my Outlook inbox and slap me upside the head, trashing my what-next plans.

On October 11, 2012, while I was packing for a flight to Norway for the Bergen International Film Festival, I got an e-mail from a Hollywood talent agency:

> Hi Peter,
> We are casting a film called Dallas Buyers Club about the story of Ron Woodroof with Matthew McConaughey set as Ron. The director, Jean-Marc Vallée, was deeply moved by the documentary "How To Survive A Plague" and asked us to reach out to you as he is interested in you for a role in the film. The film will begin shooting in New Orleans in early November. I have attached a copy of the script. I believe he wanted to speak to you about playing IAN or MICHAEL. I have given him your contact info and he will be calling you to discuss.

My first thought was *How fucking cool is that?* I had heard about the film project for years, as various actors and directors were attached to it, but it never actually came together. I knew the real-life story of Ron Woodroof, the founder of the buyers club in Dallas. It was loosely modeled on New York City's People with AIDS Health Group, the first buyers club for experimental AIDS treatments.

I hadn't known Woodroof personally, but one of my best friends, Derek Hodel, had been the founding executive director of New York City's buyers club, and had crossed paths with Woodroof often.

Before boarding my flight to Oslo, I opened the script and did a quick search for scenes with IAN or MICHAEL. The two characters were described as "a conservative gay couple in their 40s," and they had two scenes with Ron Woodroof. Ian has AIDS, and Michael is desperately trying to find experimental treatments to save his partner's life.

In the first scene, they are in Ron's office at the buyers club, hoping to sign up Ian as a client, listening to Ron's pitch to new members. In the second scene, they offer an empty house to Ron after the FDA closes down the club's first office space. Michael has six lines in total. Ian just has to look sick and worried.

That the person with AIDS seemed incapable of speaking for himself should have been my first red flag, but all I could think about was how cool it would be to shoot two scenes in New Orleans with Matthew McConaughey. And I'd get a SAG card, the highly coveted proof of union membership in the Screen Actors Guild!

I wanted to read the entire script before answering the e-mail, but Bergen monopolized my attention for a week. Finally, on the flight home, I started reading what sounded like a very made-for-Matthew-McConaughey opening:

EXT. RODEO STADIUM — DALLAS — TEXAS — DAY 1

Ambient sounds of the CROWD, RODEO, SEX, and a strange
RINGING fade in along with BLURRY IMAGES of...

A COWBOY riding a BULL in an enclosed RODEO ring.

RON WOODROOF, early 40's, handsome, long sandy hair, denim
clad, worn snakeskin boots, dusty, cowboy hat, mirrored

aviators, is engaged in wild SEX with a WOMAN. He watches the
rodeo through open slats in a BULL STALL as the STEER throws
the COWBOY violently thru the air; he lands hard on the dirt.

Another WOMAN snorts cocaine and offers some to Ron as he
switches over to having SEX with her.

Well, that's strange. I thought Woodroof was gay. My friend Derek
certainly thought he was. But it was true he wasn't out about it. Friends
had said he told the local press he had gotten HIV from injecting drugs,
thinking *that* carried far less stigma than gay sex, at least in Texas.

But as I read on, it didn't take long before my jaw was in my lap.
I knew the real Woodroof had tried AZT early on and, like many,
including me, had to stop taking it because of the anemia it caused. He
joined the AZT-is-poison crowd but went on to become the country's
biggest buyers club supplier of bootleg ddC, an equally toxic sister
drug of AZT. Logic wasn't one of his strong suits.

The script was predictably filled with AZT-bashing, but there was
an entire storyline added on top of this that had nothing to do with
Woodroof's actual story. Ron has a sexy doctor and potential love
interest, Eve Saks, the role snapped up by Jennifer Garner shortly
before shooting started. Page 59:

INT. DALLAS MEMORIAL HOSPITAL — HALLWAY — NIGHT

Eve walks down the hall, in mid-conversation with Dr. Sevard:

> EVE
> Dr. Peter Duesberg — the molecular
> biologist — he says HIV is a harmless
> passenger virus.

> DR. SEVARD
> Based on what?

                    EVE
That women aren't contracting AIDS at the
same rate as men. Not to mention no one
has been able to infect an animal with
AIDS. The point is we don't know for
sure if HIV is the cause.

                  DR. SEVARD
I'm not going to debate HIV with you.

                    EVE
            (holding out a file)
Ron Woodroof has a low T-cell count but
other than that he's healthy as an ox--

For the uninitiated, Peter Duesberg, a professor of molecular and cell biology at the University of California, Berkeley, was the founder of one of the most deadly conspiracy theories in history. In 1987, he claimed that HIV was a harmless virus that doesn't cause AIDS. The theory's ability to offer false hope to those who tested HIV positive helped birth what soon became an incredibly dangerous movement: AIDS denialism. All sorts of quack ancillary theories were offered to explain the rising deaths from AIDS, including that the drugs to treat it, like AZT, were responsible, not the virus.

A couple of journalists tried to make their names promoting AIDS denialism. Websites were launched. And a nutty millionaire funded a slick documentary that claimed to expose the scientific fraud around the "harmless virus" HIV.

But most enraging of all, South Africa's president, Thabo Mbeki, became a denialist and kept antivirals out of his country from 2000 to 2005, until finally its supreme court intervened. An estimated 340,000 lives were lost and 35,000 babies were infected because of Mbeki's denialism.

And now here was a script in which Duesberg, the denialists' founding nutjob, was an off-screen hero. Accordingly, Woodroof becomes a denialist, then convinces his doctor to become one too. Dr. Eve immediately pulls all her patients at Dallas Memorial Hospital off AZT, because she becomes convinced the drug itself is killing AIDS patients. Her patients start doing better after she rescues them from AZT.

Whatever is making Woodroof sick, an experimental drug called peptide T seems to help. It even helps his ailing dad with his Alzheimer's!

Page 78:

INT. DALLAS BUYERS CLUB APARTMENT — LIVING ROOM — NIGHT

Music plays. Rayon, extremely sick, holds a bottle of
POPPERS, watches Sunny dance around the room amongst the
stacked moving boxes. Rayon starts coughing into a
handkerchief, pulls it away, it's covered with BLOOD. Sunny
stops dancing.

One page later, Rayon is dead. The scene includes a major dog-whistle for the AIDS denialist movement. One of its earliest ancillary theories was that gay men were dying from AIDS because our immune systems couldn't handle all the party drugs we were using, including poppers. To drive this point home, another scene has Ron picking up a pamphlet from a literature table during a mostly gay community meeting on AIDS that says, "POPPERS STUDY: POSSIBLE CAUSE OF AIDS."

The Rayon character is described as "a cross-dresser in his early 30s," and is fictionalized. But the real Ron Woodroof, by most accounts, didn't need an oppressed queer business partner to constantly challenge his nonexistent homophobia. And the trans community probably didn't need another cisgender male actor playing this part. (Just before shooting started, Jared Leto signed on for the role.)

By the end of the script, McConaughey is riding bulls again, happier and healthier, having empowered Dallas's gay community to live longer lives by bucking FDA advice and using alternative therapies. This is followed by two final title cards:

> Ronald Woodroof died on September 12, 1992, six years
> after he was diagnosed with the HIV virus.
>
> Fluconazole and Peptide T are now F.D.A. approved.

More dog whistles. Early in the script, Ron is told immediately after his diagnosis that he only has six months to live. In the title card, he hasn't died of AIDS; instead, he has survived six years beyond a misleading diagnosis. Oh, and after multiple studies, peptide T turned out to be a worthless drug that was never approved for anything.

The script was a horror show for AIDS activism. We had done a fairly good job in recent years of snuffing out the impact of AIDS denialism, especially after what happened in South Africa. Whenever the denialists' slick documentary was added to a film festival's program, we'd bombard the organizers with pro-science how-could-you's. They'd pull it from the program every time.

But there were rumors the movement was trying to get its claws into a Hollywood project. If the script I had just read made it into theaters with a roster of A-list stars, AIDS denialism would be reborn. And people would die unnecessarily as a result.

I returned from Norway on October 21. The next day there were stories out of Hollywood reporting that Matthew McConaughey had already lost thirty pounds to play the part. Filming was scheduled to start on Monday, November 12—exactly three weeks away.

I e-mailed Professor John Moore, a Cornell University virologist and cofounder of the group AIDSTruth, a collective of scientists and activists who actively fought AIDS denialism with truth and science. He immediately cc'd others in the group, including Nathan Geffen, a South African activist who had spent years fighting Mbeki and the denialists; Gregg Gonsalves, who was earning his doctorate at Yale; and Richard Jefferys, director of the Basic Science Project at TAG. Richard had been sued by a denialist for libel and won a resounding victory against the accuser in court.

AIDSTruth shared my alarm at the script. I asked if we should go public with our concerns as a way to pressure the film's creative team, but they advised against this. They had learned the hard way that fighting denialists in the press often backfired. Conspiracy movements thrive on all public mentions, including scathing ones. As long as their theory gets mentioned, there will always be one person out of a thousand who becomes intrigued and Googles the theory. All press, including bad press, helps a conspiracy movement grow.

John Moore suggested an alternative strategy. "We've got three weeks to work with, and you've got an in with the director. Let's try to push them to fix the script," he told me. "We need to find out how the denialism got added to it. Was it just some innocent Googling by one of the screenwriters, or is there a full-on denialist within their creative team?"

We aimed to find out. I needed to bait a hook to quickly grab the director's attention. All I had at that point was the talent agency's e-mail, so I sent them a short reply:

> I finished reading the script this week. I know Ron Wood-
> roof's story pretty well, and there are some major threads
> in this script that had nothing to do with Ron and would
> infuriate the AIDS community—activists, researchers, you

name it. I'm more than willing to help Jean-Marc and the writers fix the main problems in order to prevent a huge backlash down the road.

By not describing the problems, the e-mail would hopefully prompt an inquiring dialogue.

It worked like a charm. My phone rang five minutes later. It was Jean Marc Vallée.

Vallée was a French Canadian director who had done a few well-reviewed art-house films. He had a distinct visual style, often holding his own always-in-motion camera during shoots and adding music from up-and-coming artists for a final cut that audiences embraced. His best known film at that point, *C.R.A.Z.Y.*, was a story about a young French Canadian boy coming to terms with being gay. I had seen it already and remembered loving it.

If only *C.R.A.Z.Y.* had been autobiographical. Alas, Vallée is straight, and I would quickly learn that his knowledge about HIV/AIDS was extremely basic—what you'd expect the average progressive straight guy from outside New York City or San Francisco to know, which isn't much.

After some very kind words about my activism as documented in *How to Survive a Plague*, he asked me about the problems in the script. I tried to explain the history of AIDS denialism, which meant describing quite a bit of overall AIDS history as well. Without this larger knowledge of the crisis, it would take him time to grasp how serious the script issues were.

Thankfully, he immediately made clear that he wanted to get things right. "I want this film to be beautiful, and I want it to be true," he kept saying. But I could tell that most of his knowledge about AIDS came from the script itself, which he was led to believe was Woodroof's real story. He immediately suggested setting up a four-way conference call with me, him, and the two screenwriters, Craig Borten and Melisa Wallack.

Richard Jefferys helped me furiously Google everyone involved with the film, but we had found very little info on the screenwriters. Both were apparently L.A.-based and in their forties. Borten had no prior screenwriting credits. Wallack had one previous project, having written and directed *Meet Bill*, a 2007 film starring Aaron Eckhart.

Vallée was already in New Orleans, living in a rented apartment as he scouted possible sites for shooting the film. He suggested a Skype call for later that night. Borten wasn't available then, so we did the call with Vallée, me, and Wallack.

After friendly introductions and niceties, I once again started to explain AIDS Denialism 101, starting with Duesberg and finishing with Mbeki. I pointed out that Ron Woodroof was not a denialist. After being asked about AZT's toxicity, Woodroof was quoted in a 1992 *Dallas Morning News* article saying, "I don't see how anything can be more toxic than HIV itself."

They let me ramble on for ten or fifteen minutes with only one or two questions from Vallée. I had no idea what Wallack was making of any of this history, but once she finally weighed in, everything became clear in an instant.

"Well," she said, "I can't believe you'd say disparaging things about a genius like Peter Duesberg."

DING-DING-DING! My eyes widened. My nostrils flared. Our denialist had just revealed herself. Within seconds we were screaming at each other. "You can't be serious," I yelled at one point.

"I've met and interviewed Duesberg, along with other experts who agree with him," she yelled back. "Their story is hugely important to tell!"

Our screaming match escalated even further. Vallée looked stunned, not quite understanding what was happening.

And then the AIDS gods intervened: the Skype call went dead. Vallée called me back immediately on his cell phone. The power had gone out in his apartment. He offered to use three-way calling on his cell phone to get Wallack back on.

"No, no, no," I replied, "I never need to talk with her again. Jean-Marc, Melisa is an AIDS denialist, and she added denialism into your script, even though it was never part of Ron Woodroof's amazing life. The number-one drug that his buyers club distributed was bootleg ddC, a very similar drug to AZT. Ask Melisa why her script doesn't mention ddC. I'll tell you why: because it would destroy her denialist storyline."

I could tell he was a bit frozen at this point, not knowing enough to pass judgment either way.

"Jean-Marc, I know this is a lot to take in, but what you do next could make or break this film," I continued. "I implore you to reach out to any and all opinions you can find in the next twenty-four hours—find others who lived through the early AIDS years and know its history. Find some doctors or experts. Reach out to some national AIDS groups. If you want a truthful film, you have one job in front of you. Don't just trust me or Melisa, because one of us is right and the other one is crazy, and you need to figure out which of us to listen to."

I could tell his bubble on this project was still pretty small, and I was banking on Hollywood's deeply felt experience with AIDS. It would likely take only a few phone calls before he'd get advice that backed me up.

He agreed to make some calls the next day.

It worked. Vallée set up a call with John Moore, me, and his other screenwriter, Craig Borten. Wallack had been sidelined.

But we worried about Borten too. He had written the original script after interviewing Woodroof shortly before his death in 1992. By 1996, that script almost got made, with Woody Harrelson set to play Woodroof and Dennis Hopper directing. But then the production company that bought the script went under.

In 2001, Borden's agent suggested pairing up with Wallack for a script rewrite. I can only speculate, but the in-depth research she claimed to have done for the script may have started with Googling AIDS, right around the same time Mbeki did, and from there she went down the denialist rabbit hole.

Rewrite in hand, they sold it to Universal, with Brad Pitt to star and Marc Forster to direct. When that fell apart, Ryan Gosling signed on with director Craig Gillespie. Financing slowly killed that pairing as well. Eventually, McConaughey and Vallée signed on, and everything finally fell into place.

Before the call with Borten, e-mails were exchanged among all of us. Moore's e-mails deconstructing denialism were key. Vallée e-mailed his new leanings before the call:

> Let me reassure you that my intentions are to make this beautiful project a truthful and respectful one, one that serves Ron Woodroof's story and what he was fighting for and against. It might read now as a pro-denialist script, as Peter was putting it, with some inaccuracies, but it won't be the case once I start shooting. I intend to address and attack every single problem of the script.

We now had fourteen days until filming started. Multiple calls and e-mails followed. Borten seemed willing to pull most of the references to Duesberg, but grew increasingly worried at how this was impacting his anti-FDA, anti-pharma narrative. Most of the denialism was baked into Jennifer Garner's character, which kept shrinking with each edit.

On November 8, just four days left before filming started, I e-mailed Vallée and Borten a highly annotated PDF of their most recent script, outlining thirty specific lines or scenes that still needed fixing, including one remaining mention of Duesberg. I couldn't believe that things like the poppers scene were still in the script, and let loose about it in the e-mail:

> The poppers theme was debunked once the virus was discovered. Having your lead gay character hanging around with a friend, just snorting poppers, then being rushed to the hospital where he dies, is an offensive scene. For one thing, that's not how gay men used poppers. If you insist on having your only lead gay character remain a cross-dressing effeminate drug user whose life spins out of control—and the only character to die in the film—then how about a line of coke in that scene instead? "Rayon" is still a sad cliché (Vito Russo would be spinning in his grave), but at least the audience won't wonder if poppers killed him.

We jumped on a phone call a few hours later. Vallée voiced exasperation that I had cc'd folks at amfAR on my e-mail. *Mission accomplished*, I thought, as I had hoped it would bring even more pressure on him to relent on the thirty remaining issues. Borten seemed resistant to further changes, so I called Vallée separately for one last appeal.

"What you saw in *How to Survive a Plague* was a story of good versus evil, heroes versus villains. The story you didn't see is the decades-long battle between AIDS activists and AIDS denialists, another story of heroes versus villains," I said. "If your film even hints at denialist theories, they'll use Matthew McConaughey and Jennifer Garner's characters as fodder for their lies. Every AIDS activist in the country will condemn your film. No matter how good your directing of McConaughey's acting is, no one will be nominated for any Oscars."

Vallée told me he'd fix all the remaining issues and send me a final script. He asked me again to join the project as IAN or MICHAEL. He even offered a producing credit. I politely declined.

He never sent me the final script. I'm guessing he got spooked, worried that I'd never be satisfied, and he didn't want me to have something to take to a media outlet. But he assured me in a final e-mail that *Dallas Buyers Club* would be "a beautiful film that doesn't support denialism."

Pictures and video of an emaciated McConaughey on set started appearing on *Access Hollywood* and other TV programs. After filming wrapped and months went by, I remained in the dark as to what the final product contained. In April, press reports announced that Focus Features had bought the distribution rights. The film would have its world premiere in September at the Toronto International Film Festival, followed shortly thereafter by a theatrical release.

And then in June, the AIDS gods intervened again. A friend of mine from the ACT UP days, Mark Aurigemma, who now did public relations counseling for UNAIDS and various AIDS conferences, sent me an e-mail saying Focus Features had reached out to him. They wanted to hire him to manage community relations for the rollout of *Dallas Buyers Club*.

Mark had heard through the grapevine that I had had some problems early on with the film, and he wanted to hear why before taking the job. I filled him in on everything that had happened and sent him the first damning script as evidence, along with the near-final script with my thirty suggested edits.

Focus was going to let him see the film before he decided whether to sign on. By mid-July, he reported back that he had seen the film and, from his perspective, denialism had been completely scrubbed from it.

"Can you ask Focus if I can see it?" I asked. On August 7, I sat down for a private screening of the film with John Moore and Rowena Johnston, amfAR's director of research, in an otherwise empty fifty-seat screening room in downtown New York. Vallée had found out about our screening only days before, and offered to Skype into the theater to introduce the film. The Skype idea fell through, but he told us he'd be standing by on his cell phone for our feedback afterward.

We liked what we saw, with two exceptions. That damn final title card still said, "Ron Woodroof died on September 12, 1992, seven years after he was diagnosed with the HIV virus." But he died of AIDS, and dodging those three truthful words was an insult to all the families and friends and lovers of those who wanted this truth known when they died.

Vallée agreed to change it to say, "Ron Woodroof died of AIDS on September 12, 1992, seven years after he was diagnosed with HIV."

But we still had a bigger issue. As the film then stood, it may as well have been a giant billboard saying, "AZT is POISON." Yet AZT was still being used by pregnant women around the world to block HIV transmission to their babies. If the film convinced only one of these women to forgo this preventive therapy, it would be one too many.

I asked Vallée if we could add a final title card that spoke to AZT's later usefulness. This would also have the added effect of becoming a one-sentence inoculation against any denialist hoping to use the film as propaganda.

Vallée said the film length was set in stone, but he could squeeze in a four- to five-second title card, which translated into about fifteen words. We all exchanged about thirty e-mails trying to find one short sentence that would do the trick.

The final film now ends saying, "A lower dose of AZT became widely used in later drug combinations that saved millions of lives."

Dallas Buyers Club opened to very strong reviews. Six Oscar nominations quickly followed, including one for Best Picture. McConaughey and Leto both got nods. Vallée was nominated for his editing. And to my utter disbelief, Craig Borten and Melisa Wallack were nominated for Best Original Screenplay.

Someone I knew at Focus Features later told me that Borten and Wallack were no longer talking to each other. She had been sidelined since our intervention before shooting began but enjoyed the award circuit regardless.

Just before Oscar voters filled out their final ballots, I had to intervene one last time. Borten and Wallack had done a podcast called *The Q&A with Jeff Goldsmith*. Wallack had offered up her most homophobic denialist theory to their baffled host and his studio audience:

> AUDIENCE QUESTION: It was interesting to see . . . um . . . the different manifestations of the different stages of AIDS, you know, based on the lesions that are seen, the other symptoms that are seen, and the weight loss obviously was apparent as well. And how much of that was research versus Jean-Marc, versus once you got it with hair and makeup people deciding, like, for stages and stuff like that?
>
> MELISA WALLACK: I think that it was everything. I mean the research that we did about that—it's called Kaposi's sarcoma—when you get the lesions on your face . . . um . . . that men were getting from using poppers . . . um . . . in nightclubs . . . um.
>
> GOLDSMITH: They were getting lesions from poppers?
>
> WALLACK: Well they were putting poppers through the . . . um . . . ventilation systems, so it's a toxic . . . it's toxic, and it was going in their bodies every single day so, it was coming from . . . anyway, so that was just one of the sources of them, but yeah, it was crazy.
>
> GOLDSMITH: That's some intense research, I've never heard of poppers going through the ventilation systems. Wow.

WALLACK: Yeah, they were putting them in all the . . . literally in all the nightclubs, they would just dump them in so that every single person in there was breathing them all night long, so you'd have like these incredible rushes of . . . so I don't know if you know what poppers are, but . . . um . . . but really, they sell it under stereo head cleaner.

GOLDSMITH: Interesting.

WALLACK: Yeah.

I shot off an angry e-mail to Wallack, cc'ing everyone I could, including senior staff at Focus Features:

Your remarks during the interview below about poppers and KS are factually incorrect and deeply offensive. This is classic AIDS Denialism claptrap and comes from their canon of deeply homophobic theories around HIV/AIDS (namely that gay men died because of all our recreational drug use, including poppers, and not because of HIV). There is no connection between AIDS and poppers or KS and poppers. Poppers were never put in the ventilators at dance clubs. This is just crazy talk.

You are dishonoring the memories of hundreds of thousands of gay men that died from AIDS with a KS diagnosis.

I'm not sure what to ask of you at this point, except for restraint. . . .

DBC is a beautiful film, but your theories almost destroyed it. The film was thankfully saved by Jean-Marc and his drive for truthful storytelling.

I'm pretty sure Focus reined her in quickly, because I couldn't find any interviews with her after that.

With Jean-Marc Vallée, and with Jared Leto during the Oscar campaign, 2014.

McConaughey and Leto won their Oscars. So did Adruitha Lee and Robin Mathews, the film's makeup and hairstyling team. Truth be told, their KS lesions looked like the real deal.

But Jean-Marc Vallée deserves all the credit. I put the man through hell and back, but he kept his promise to seek truth in his filmmaking. He told me in an e-mail that in all his films, he tries to "capture humanity and reveal the beauty behind it."

Bravo, Jean-Marc, and thank you. You reminded me how much I love activism.

15

DINNER WITH TONY

MY HIGH-PRESSURE ACTIVISM against the creative team behind *Dallas Buyers Club* left me with two convictions: I love this work, and I'm good at it. So I've been doing it ever since.

After looking at my finances and using one of those retirement calculators, it looked like I might have a chance at coasting without an income until Social Security kicks in. I'm not rolling in cash, but I invested my savings wisely, freeing me to do whatever activism gets my blood flowing without being tied to a salaried job at any one organization.

I call it freelance activism, and it has felt like a daily blessing. While *Dallas Buyers Club* may have resparked my activism, the roll-out of *How to Survive a Plague* provided much of the fuel and still does. Since the film premiered, a day hasn't gone by that I haven't received a message via social media from someone who's just watched it and been inspired. I know dozens of them who have since joined the fight in some way.

Several long-dormant ACT UP chapters have been relaunched or revitalized, usually by new activists in their twenties. AIDS history courses have sprung up, offered by college professors across the country. A mini-wave of documentaries, books, plays, and TV series like *POSE* look back at the early days of AIDS. These projects may have happened regardless, but *Plague* felt like the door cracking open.

This new chapter in AIDS activism has helped end what Dan Glass, a thirty-year-old who restarted ACT UP London, called "the second silence": when the gay community turned its focus away from AIDS after the protease inhibitors came out. We focused on gay marriage instead, while ignoring rising HIV infection rates. (The first silence was exemplified by President Reagan ignoring a quickly rising body count during the plague's early years.) The second silence was broken by a new generation of HIV prevention activists, mostly young, HIV-negative gay men who demanded wider use of pre-exposure prophylaxis, widely known by its acronym, PrEP. *How to Survive a Plague* came out the same year that the first PrEP regimen was approved by the FDA, in 2012.

These millennial activists have been demanding wider access to a once-a-day pill that blocks HIV nearly 100 percent of the time. It's a miracle drug, and these activists, having watched some of their friends become HIV positive, are livid about PrEP's slow rollout, especially among gay men and trans women of color. The activism they are doing today ranks right up there with ACT UP and TAG's best.

Besides launching a new wave of activism, *Plague* filled my own sails as well. I hadn't lacked my own voice or platform, but the film handed me a much bigger bullhorn and the inspiration needed to use it.

David France's decision to focus on a handful of personal storylines from a movement that eschewed formal leadership turned out to be awkward for the film's primary subjects. It reopened old wounds around the internal controversies that had divided ACT UP. The treatment activists in T&D and TAG were getting all the screen time again, just as we had gotten the lion's share of press back then.

Once again, a journalist was focusing on what many considered ACT UP's greatest success. If that's true—and I believe it is—then it still leaves all of ACT UP's other successes on the cutting room floor. ACT UP had dozens of leaders and hundreds of equally important followers. Each activist derived power only through the collective.

I was no exception. ACT UP was not one or two heroes but *a movement* that saved millions of lives, including my own. That truth is in my bones, and I preach about that righteous collective power every chance I get.

But I can also support, without reservation, France's decision to focus on personal narratives, rather than the subtleties of ACT UP's structureless structure. It is how the best documentaries, the ones that stick with you and inspire you, are always made. My card was one of the lucky few drawn by France. My poster-boy status in ACT UP resulted in a trove of footage over many years, which undoubtedly led to more screen time.

Regardless, I had a choice of how to handle the film's focus. I could simply appreciate the documentary and go on with my life as if nothing had changed, or I could use that bigger bullhorn France was handing me. If you love winning activist battles as much as I do, it wasn't even a close call. Take the bullhorn.

I've been using it ever since. If something pisses me off, I work toward changing it. But, just like during ACT UP and TAG, or the model of activism I patched together for *Dallas Buyers Club*, I never do it alone. Every project I've worked on has been done within a coalition of activists. Sometimes that coalition already exists. But often I reach out to various activists to form a tight group willing to work on the issue. Usually, some of them are with established organizations that can offer ongoing institutional support.

Early on in this newest phase of my work, I joined with other prevention activists to take on the budding morality debates within the gay community that threatened uptake of PrEP. Our main opposition, the AIDS Healthcare Foundation—the McDonald's of AIDS, with HIV clinics throughout the US and around the world—used anti-science and homophobic arguments to try to block PrEP, including recommending that the FDA not even approve this prevention breakthrough. Then, after its approval, AHF, at the direction of its demagogue CEO, Michael Weinstein, spent millions of dollars—profits derived from their own pharmacies—on advertisements in gay magazines claiming that PrEP would actually increase HIV infections by giving a false sense of security to gay men who wouldn't use it as prescribed. They also claimed PrEP was toxic and labeled it a "party drug" that irresponsible gay men were using to have "unprotected sex."

Can you imagine? A daily pill, about as nontoxic as aspirin, was found to block HIV close to 100 percent, better than almost every vaccine that exists today, and there were nutjobs trying to discourage its use! If scientists had discovered this pill back during ACT UP's first few years, we would have burned down the FDA headquarters if they tried to block it.

After a concerted, multiyear effort by prevention activists, Michael Weinstein has effectively been silenced on this issue, and will rightfully join the AIDS denialists as historic villains in the fight against AIDS.

———————

In 2014, I was asked to join Governor Andrew Cuomo's Ending the Epidemic Task Force, an initiative hoping to dramatically cut HIV infections in New York State by 2020. Our resulting blueprint pushed the city and state governments to spend an additional $130 million a year to fight AIDS. Infections have been dropping by a double-digit percentage each year since.

In 2015, I formed an ad-hoc group of PrEP advocates to start pressuring Gilead Sciences on growing access issues around their drug Truvada. Later that year, Gilead responded by lifting some restrictions on their copay assistance programs, but not to the extent we requested. Thus began a frustrating game of misfired attempts by the company to placate the community, always offering too little, too late. I've been battling the company, always in conjunction with other activists, ever since.

In 2016 I joined fellow ACT UP alumnus Charles King to organize an effort to force AIDS into the Democratic presidential primary. Charles was the CEO and cofounder of Housing Works, New York's largest AIDS organization, and we had gotten into an online spat over how damaged Hillary Clinton was after some profoundly baffling remarks she made about Nancy and Ronald Reagan's AIDS legacy during an interview with Andrea Mitchell. I was a Hillary supporter and Charles was a Bernie Sanders supporter. I suggested we stop arguing online and turn the moment to our advantage. Hillary was suddenly vulnerable on the issue, and Bernie took advantage of it by quickly releasing a simple AIDS plan on his website.

We felt we could demand that both of them do better. Given how competitive the race had become, we could play them off each other, pushing for public meetings and firm promises. Months of activism ensued. During the height of the primaries, they both met individually with a coalition of twenty AIDS activists and dramatically strengthened their respective AIDS plans. Sadly, our dreams of working with the next president, fully briefed on AIDS, were dashed by the election of Donald Trump. But it once again proved the power of AIDS activism: when we demand to be heard, it's almost impossible to ignore us.

Gilead Sciences is learning that the hard way. They continued to drag their feet on even the most reasonable requests from PrEP advocates around access issues. Worst of all, each year they hiked the price of Truvada by three or four times the rate of inflation. My guess is that they no longer viewed AIDS activists as a threat. There was some truth to that, especially after many years of the second silence.

But the company seemed unaware of the new awakening the movement was having—or maybe they assumed that without the ability to launch huge protests, we could be ignored.

When a handful of millennial PrEP advocates asked me to join them as a founding member of the PrEP4All Collaboration in early 2018, work was already underway to overcome Gilead's intransigence.

And now? Let's just say Gilead has learned not to underestimate AIDS activists. PrEP4All helped launch a massive antitrust lawsuit in federal court against Gilead and three other pharmaceutical companies over their efforts to monopolize HIV treatment and prevention. I signed on as lead plaintiff, along with five other AIDS activists. The case has a catchy name—*Staley v. Gilead*—and is heading to trial in 2022.

On top of this, PrEP4All convinced the Trump administration, amazingly, to launch its own lawsuit against Gilead. We discovered that the CDC had patents on PrEP but wasn't enforcing them. Gilead had never done any research on PrEP and had openly resisted getting involved beyond agreeing to donate some Truvada for the clinical trials. Yet now they rake in over $3 billion a year selling PrEP, an invention they had nothing to do with. *United States v. Gilead* seeks to change that.

We didn't need large demonstrations to take on Gilead. AIDS activists had perfected their inside game during TAG's first years; we just needed to dust it off and try new tricks, like using the Internet, courts, and Congress. PrEP4All was barely a year old when Gilead's CEO was dragged before the House Oversight Committee and grilled by its chairman, Rep. Elijah E. Cummings, and then embarrassed by a viral moment as Rep. Alexandria Ocasio-Cortez brilliantly exposed the company's gross profiteering.

I find today's AIDS activism thrilling. Unlike the early years, when we doubted if we'd live long enough to see the fruits of our activism, today's activists have the scientific tools to save lives in real time. Our work is propelled forward with a kind of frustrated optimism. The scientific tools for treatment and prevention provide the optimism. When applied, they can dramatically lower deaths and infections. But the frustration comes from society's unwillingness to fully implement those tools, to spend a few bucks now to save many more bucks later, along with many lives.

Today's activism is about using every political tool we have to nudge those in power to do the right thing. As always, it involves tons of strategizing. After PrEP4All's first meeting in March 2018, that strategizing was in overdrive. As we looked for ways to bring down the price of Truvada to a level that would allow health departments to provide instant and free access to PrEP, we explored a couple of government regulations that could be employed. One option, called march-in rights, would allow the NIH to ignore the exclusive license it granted Gilead to sell Truvada in order to license it to a generic manufacturer as well.

David Barr and I were the only two old-timers in PrEP4All, and we thought it would be great to explore these options with our old trusty comrade Tony Fauci, who was still running the NIH's National Institute of Allergy and Infectious Diseases. Besides, it had been a couple of years since we had organized an activist dinner with Fauci, like the now-historic ones during T&D's glory days in ACT UP. Back then, Fauci had welcomed members of T&D into his NIAID office to hear our ideas on reforming various FDA and NIH policies, long before most government officials would even talk to us on the phone. He even went a step further by inviting us to dinner from time to time.

We knew full well that these dinners were strategic for him, and probably attempts at appeasement. But we would have been fools to decline the invites. Tony Fauci was in charge of the government's AIDS research, and prying him for information and opinions would prove essential to our activism. His everyman charm, delivered with a Brooklyn accent, coupled with his evident openness and affection for gay humor, worked on many of us for sure. But not to the detriment of our goals.

We came to respect Fauci, and even like him, but it never stopped us from confronting him. Case in point, we used one of these dinners to inform him that ACT UP was gearing up for a massive demonstration at the NIH over several issues he hadn't moved on quickly enough. The early warning was a common tactic to gain possible concessions before a demo. Fauci was shocked and pushed back, but the demonstration still happened.

The debates during those dinners have been well chronicled, especially in the companion book to David France's documentary *How to Survive a Plague*. Some of those debates are fading from my memory now, but the location where we dined is still crystal clear.

At first, Fauci didn't risk inviting a bunch of radical AIDS activists into his home, but he had a savvy alternative that would allow us to break bread and still assure total privacy. His right-hand man at NIAID, Dr. James C. Hill, lived in a town house near the Capitol Building with a large first-floor dining room. And conveniently, he was an excellent cook. Even more conveniently, he was gay. This offered Fauci a blatantly obvious neutral zone to wine and dine us.

Various T&D members, including David, Mark, and Charlie, still share fond memories of piling into my brother Jes's freely loaned bimmer and driving all afternoon down to Hill's place in DC. We'd savor Jim's cooking with Fauci and finish off multiple bottles of wine, then deconstruct the entire dinner on the long late-night drive back to New York.

Thirty years later, David and I were on the same roads again, heading to DC for PrEP4All's first dinner with Fauci. He was no longer the young scientist recruited to run NIAID in 1984, just after the virus that caused AIDS was discovered. In those early years, he was a tentative leader, unwilling to rock the boat. The more established virologists then insisted on slow and methodical research, even during a crisis, even if lives were lost—and some were—by being too methodical.

But now Fauci was the country's preeminent disease fighter, counselor to presidents, and a calming voice on TV whenever a new bug struck. He helped convince one of the worst presidents in American history, George W. Bush, to create an international AIDS program that has saved tens of millions of lives. He crafted President Obama's extraordinarily effective response to the 2014 Ebola outbreak. And against remarkable odds, he survived President Trump and kept the country informed during the coronavirus pandemic.

Now, in our later years, I feel blessed to call Tony a good friend. In April 2018, for the PrEP4All dinner, he invited us to his home in a tree-lined neighborhood of DC. His equally busy wife and confidant, Dr. Christine Grady, was there to cohost.

Tony Fauci and me, 2014. *Courtesy of Friends of the Global Fight*

David and I didn't come alone. We had started to jokingly refer to the guy sitting behind us in the back seat as "our secret weapon." James Krellenstein was the twenty-seven-year-old HIV-negative gay man who founded PrEP4All. With degrees in physics, natural science, and mathematics, James had previously worked as a research assistant in molecular biology and pharmacology at the Yale School of Medicine, Icahn School of Medicine at Mount Sinai, and CUNY School of Medicine.

Simply put, James is freaky smart. He's also wonderfully warmhearted and more than a little weird, with an endearing frenetic energy. When he was sixteen, he almost burned down his high school when one of his lab experiments exploded. He was trying to test whether DNA damage to certain cancer lines could be lessened by priming the cells with a small dose of ionizing radiation before delivering a much larger dose. You know, stuff most sixteen-year-olds try. Instead, he suffered burns on 18 percent of his body, including third-degree burns on one of his arms that required skin grafts.

During his stint at Mount Sinai, he read a CDC report in the *Journal of the American Medical Association* that shook him to his roots. It showed that tens of thousands of gay men were still becoming infected every year, the same unrelenting levels seen since the early '90s, accounting for two-thirds of all infections in the United States. Like many gay men his age, he had been living under the misperception that HIV/AIDS was an epidemic in decline.

By the time he formed PrEP4All, James knew of three friends his age who had become infected, even though PrEP was on the market. Why were so few at-risk Americans on PrEP? Like the geeks in T&D before him, self-educated experts on AIDS treatment research, James quickly became a leading expert on HIV prevention.

And he's not alone. The future of AIDS activism is now in the hands of hundreds of millennials, both HIV positive and negative, who have taken up the fight with a shared belief that they can end this crisis. They are a deeply inspiring lot, and it was time that Tony Fauci witnessed their power in person.

After James got a quick tour of Tony and Christine's house and backyard, we gathered around the kitchen island, wine glasses in hand, while Tony prepared his signature pasta dish. James, whose stream-of-consciousness conversing style speeds up when he's slightly nervous, started peppering Tony with questions about his current lab research at NIAID. Beyond managing the government's AIDS research efforts, Tony has coauthored a record number of studies that have helped define the basic science around HIV. His most recent research has focused on monoclonal antibodies that might work as future vaccines or treatments against HIV.

Once James was questioning Tony on the chemical structures of his most promising monoclonal antibodies, Tony shot David and me a side glance, the look we had been waiting for: a big grin, a quick raised eyebrow, and then a wink to punctuate his wordless message. *Well, well, look at what you guys found*, his glance said.

The conversation quickly turned to one of the big asks we planned to drop on Tony. The NIH had never been willing to use march-in rights against any pharmaceutical company since the law that allows it was written. If we petitioned the NIH to use its march-in rights against Gilead's monopoly on PrEP, would he support the effort?

"Sure," he replied. Now David and I were exchanging raised eyebrows. We had not expected such definitive support for a policy that is still considered radical. While PrEP4All ultimately decided to push for alternative ways to break Gilead's monopoly, Tony's willingness to challenge Gilead would later percolate up within the Department of Health and Human Services, leading to the huge lawsuit *United States v. Gilead*.

As the conversation moved to the dining room, the wine kept flowing and the brainstorming started. How could we dramatically lower HIV infections in the United States? Tony told us he was making progress selling his fifty-county AIDS plan to the new HHS secretary, Alex Azar. He also hoped the new CDC director, Dr. Robert Redfield, would be amenable to the idea.

Fauci had pitched the plan during the last year of the Obama administration but ran out of time building support for it. His idea was to do a hard public health push with PrEP, HIV testing, and treatment access in the nation's fifty hardest-hit counties, where most of the HIV transmissions occurred each year. Tony figured if they fleshed out a modestly funded, long-term plan that had the potential to dramatically lower HIV infections nationwide, then Azar could sell it to Trump before his next State of the Union address. It sounded like a Hail Mary pass to us, but one worth trying. Amazingly, it worked, and we now have a national HIV prevention plan with hundreds of millions of new federal dollars backing it.

After we downed our second servings of Tony's delicious penne with spicy Italian sausage, trying to leave room for dessert, I asked Tony how his memoir was going. He marveled at how skewed our own memories had become, and that most of the research he did for each chapter kept proving this.

"Actually, can I indulge you all with a short chapter I wrote?" he asked sheepishly. The three of us urged him on, eager to hear some possible insider dish from one of his many Oval Office visits over the years.

Tony stepped out of the room for a bit and returned with a few printed pages and a small picture frame. He handed me the picture, asking, "Do you recognize him?"

"Oh, wow, it's Jim," I replied. I handed the picture to James, saying, "This is Jim Hill, Tony's right-hand man during the ACT UP years, the guy we told you about on the drive down." As James passed the photo to David, I said, "Tony, remind me what year it was when Jim died."

"Ninety-seven," he replied. "I tried so hard to save him, but ultimately his liver gave out. I wrote a short chapter about Jim if you want to hear it."

To David and me, this was a beautiful gesture. We both adored Jim but never really knew his and Tony's backstory.

Jim was an Arkansas farm boy with a love of science, eventually getting his doctorate in microbiology from the University of Arkansas. On a whim, he stopped into a navy recruiting station and asked if they had any research positions. Within months, he was a commissioned navy officer at the Naval Biological Laboratory in Berkeley, and from there ended up at the Naval Medical Research Institute in Bethesda, just across the street from the NIH. Five years later, Jim was working at NIAID.

Tony started bumping into him at NIAID conferences in the early '80s, and they hit it off almost immediately, sharing a sense of humor and a love of politics. Tony also appreciated Jim's work ethic, so when he got the top job at NIAID, he asked Jim to join his team as a special assistant and, ultimately, his deputy director.

"You need to know that I'm a somewhat closeted gay man," Jim told Tony after being offered the job.

"Jim, I knew that you were gay from the moment I met you, so cut the shit and say yes to my offer," Tony shot back.

As Tony read on, his deep affection for Jim began to shine through. It turns out they were travel buddies, too. Jim would tag along with Tony for all his speaking gigs around the world, keeping him on schedule and organizing meetings and the like. From Tony's telling, they sounded like TV's Odd Couple, with Jim's anal compulsive scheduling often driving Tony nuts. To keep the peace, Tony caved to Jim's insistence on getting to the airport hours before a flight. Month after month, Jim would be waiting in a cab outside Tony's home at a very dark four in the morning for their eight o'clock flight.

As he turned another page, Tony's voice got slightly quieter. He was describing a day at the office in 1991. Jim asked him if he could shut the door and speak privately. He had bad news. He had recently been diagnosed as HIV positive. "I feel like I've let you down," he told Tony.

As Tony read those words to us, his voice started shaking. He paused. And then he started to quietly sob.

All of us teared up. David put his hand on Tony's shoulder and looked over at me, wide eyed. We were both stunned, having never seen Tony reveal vulnerable emotions. He had always been the calmest and steadiest one in the room, with a great sense of humor. Laughs would come easy but never tears. Yet here he was, raw and sharing his pain from the plague years.

"I'm sorry," he said.

"No, it's OK, Tony," we replied. "Keep going."

He kept reading, once again with a steady voice, just softer, all the way until Jim's death from AIDS-related liver failure. Tony was now rereading the eulogy he read at Jim's memorial service. And then his voice cracked again. A second quiet sob.

As I looked across the table at this man I have respectfully and unemotionally tangled with for decades, I remembered the thousands of patients he was in charge of at the NIH hospital during the worst of the plague years. How easy it was to forget that he had been a frontline doctor, first and foremost, during those years. He had tried to help hundreds of AIDS patients in their last months, with few tools to save them. I had avoided deathbeds. He saw hundreds die.

There is a bond among all of us who survived those years. Not just those of us with HIV but also our friends, family, lovers, researchers, civil servants, nurses, and doctors. We all carry the memories of those we lost, a deep scar that will never heal.

We go on with our lives, enjoying new friendships and routines, but then a moment catches us and our bond is revealed, the weight of all those memories of friends lost.

Tony finished the chapter, and we shared our own memories of Jim. And then we all helped stack the dishes and hugged Tony and Christine good-bye. On the drive to our hotel, we tried to process what had just happened.

James was almost speechless at first. He was fully aware we had all just witnessed and participated in another little moment in AIDS history. None of us were ready to call it a night. We bought a six-pack at the hotel bar just before it closed and talked, laughed, bickered, and strategized until the beer ran out.

As I watched James get excited about the work ahead, I was reminded of those late nights in ACT UP's first year, those post-meeting gatherings at Woody's—the deconstructions, the strategizing, the beer, and the laughs.

History was threading forward into a final chapter for AIDS. I intend to witness it.

EPILOGUE

MY APOLOGIES FOR STARTING this postscript with sad news, but just as this book was heading to the printer, my mom, Kit Staley, died at the age of ninety. Thankfully, she had lived life to the fullest up until recently, with only three weeks between a diagnosis of abdominal cancer and death. I witnessed her last breaths. After my diagnosis and coming out, she was there for me when I needed her most. I can only hope that I partially returned this great favor by being there for her at the end.

I started writing this book a few months before that 2018 dinner at Tony Fauci's home in DC, and decided the very next morning that the emotional evening would make a great final chapter. But a lot has happened since that night, namely the worldwide COVID epidemic.

Like most of the AIDS activists I know, I became a COVID activist within days of the first reported case in the United States. James Krellenstein shot off an e-mail to Tony on February 2, 2020, cc'ing David Barr and me, pressing him on issues around the CDC's failing COVID tests. Within weeks, a bunch of us had cofounded the COVID-19 Working Group–New York, launching a frenetic pace of activism—using the same hardball inside game honed by TAG and PrEP4All—well into the Biden administration's first months.

AIDS activists can be easily triggered when a new epidemic hits. Politicians repeat the same mistakes—the avoidable mistakes that killed so many of our friends during the early years of the plague. And since our old-gen and new-gen activists are now so integrated into the public health establishment, we are uniquely qualified to advocate on the experts' behalf. Pushing politicians to do the right thing is what we do. And if they don't, we are fine with raising hell.

That's why Tony Fauci found us knocking on his digital door just as COVID hit. After James's e-mail, we've kept his inbox pretty busy ever since. But as Tony's friend, I worried about him as well. By late February, he was at the White House every day—Trump's White House—and I knew he'd experience a crazy kind of pressure like he'd never faced before, through five prior presidents and multiple epidemics.

"You holding up OK?" I texted after watching him on TV, standing behind Trump, caught putting his hand to his face in a failed attempt to hide his OMG reaction. To my surprise, Tony called right back. He needed and wanted to vent. During the three decades I've known Tony I made it a habit of telling him, often to his face, what I thought his faults and mistakes were. To his great credit, my pull-no-punches approach only strengthened our friendship rather than ending it.

"Do you want to hear what I liked and didn't like about your comments at the mic?" I asked.

"Of course," he replied.

As the White House's reality-TV-like daily press conferences became bigger and nuttier shitshows—"Tonight on *Big Brother*, Donnie embarrasses Debbie yet again!"—my calls with Tony became more frequent. I gave him instant feedback on most of his public remarks, including some harsh reviews. We'd then brainstorm on better responses to similar questions from the press, or assholes like Senator Rand Paul and Rep. Jim Jordan, the next time they were asked.

We also strategized how to navigate the various personalities in the White House. Tony had a camp of supporters among the president's team, as well as a camp of detractors, some of whom became outright haters. The haters fell in the batshit crazy category—the anti-mask, anti-testing, pro-hydroxychloroquine, it-will-magically-disappear-because-of-herd-immunity crowd.

I loved strategizing with Tony, to help him not only navigate this hornet's nest but survive it as well. It reminded me of my career dreams long before HIV changed the course of my life. If I couldn't be president someday, my second choice was being a close adviser to a president. Now, perhaps even more on-brand for me than my previous aspirations, I found myself being a close adviser to the president's nemesis!

Through it all, my respect for Tony only grew. Here he was, about to turn eighty years old, working at a pace that would destroy men half his age—and doing it with unflagging determination and decency in such close proximity to madness. After taking Tony and Dr. Deborah Birx's shutdown advice for about six crucial weeks, preventing a million deaths by midsummer instead of the still horrifying 150,000 we hit in July, Trump pivoted, pushed by his state media network, Fox News, and put a bull's-eye on Tony's back. The death threats flooded in, not just for him but for his wife and daughters as well—including from Trump's Lord Voldemort, Steve Bannon, who called for Tony's beheading. The situation necessitated a 24-7 Secret Service detail that followed him everywhere.

I've been blessed with a few friendships that have grown stronger over not just years but decades, and there's a kind of love and protectiveness that sets in. But you also learn each other's faults, and just like all of us, Tony has his share. While I may have spent half my time worrying about him in 2020, the other half was spent feeling pissed off that he wasn't doing more.

Regardless of how much power Tony has obtained over time, he has always stubbornly stayed in his own lane—running NIAID and explaining new bugs and how to fight them to presidents and the public alike—while scrupulously avoiding the politics of it all. I lost count of how many times I told him during COVID that he was "a lousy activist." Activists try to grab every bit of power they can and leverage it for a greater good. Tony often underestimated his own power during his battles inside Trump's White House—or, worse, didn't use his power to push hard for non-NIAID-related policy initiatives.

But I'll be the first to admit that if Tony had started throwing his weight around on policies his institute wasn't directly involved with, he would've racked up twice as many enemies. And much of his power was derived from a public reputation for *not* being political—for not being an activist. He's a brilliant scientist, especially with infectious diseases, and knows how to explain that science to laypeople, a rare talent.

By methodically and instinctively staying in his lane, he's saved millions of lives, especially when he's convinced a president to get serious about fighting an epidemic, like Trump instituting a COVID shutdown, or with Bush Jr. providing AIDS drugs to Africa. And yes, indeed, these moments rank as activism. I just wish there were more of them.

That said, I'm still immensely proud of Tony. He survived Trump. America watched as the press accurately reported how at odds the two men were. Again and again, Tony corrected Trump's falsehoods right in front of him while cameras were rolling, even interrupting him at one point to do so. Within weeks, Trump was retweeting the #FireFauci hashtag, and his political team began efforts to muzzle Tony. But Tony outmaneuvered them every time, using Web-based conference appearances and Instagram interviews, all replayed on national TV news programs as if they were live.

By July, the White House attempted to take down Tony by releasing a laughable unsigned statement outlining all the times he was supposedly wrong about stuff, only to be ripped to shreds by every major news outlet (ignoring Fox News, which should always be ignored) for getting everything wrong in the statement itself. Tony's understated fuck-you response got more coverage than the original statement: "I think they realize now that that was not a prudent thing to do."

By November, Trump openly insinuated during a campaign rally that he'd be firing Fauci after the election, as his MAGA cultists chanted "Fire Fauci! Fire Fauci!" But guess who was still at his government desk on January 20, 2021?

Helping Tony survive Trump was one of the greatest honors of my life. I still pinch myself that he trusted me enough to ride that political bronco with him, and after that wild year, my love and respect for the man could not be any deeper.

One of the hardest calls I had with Tony during the early months of COVID was when I broke the news to him that Larry Kramer had died. Larry had only recently entered a hospital with aspirated pneumonia, but the last I had heard, he was bouncing back. Ever since his liver transplant in 2001, Larry had always recovered, triumphing over one close brush with death after another as his body was failing him, overwhelmed with various comorbidities.

Tony and I were caught off guard, not just by Larry's passing but also by how deeply this loss hit. Even though Larry was eighty-four, we thought his anger was the fuel that would keep him alive forever. We choked up as we shared memories of our fallen friend, his annoying faults, and his profound legacy.

Larry and I had butted heads over many issues after TAG split off from ACT UP, especially around PrEP (he was initially against it), but I will be forever thankful for his righteous rage. It helped launch GMHC and ACT UP, the two best examples of the LGBT response to AIDS—how we took care of our own and how we fought back.

Larry Kramer, Dr. Mathilde Krim, and me, 2000.
Courtesy of amfAR © 2000

Larry taught us the power of anger, and our community has maintained a posture of righteous indignation against anything less than full equality ever since.

Larry's death felt like a final bookend of loss while I was writing this memoir. Shortly after writing the first chapter in late 2017, I witnessed my dad's last breath. Paul Staley was eighty-eight.

Even though he was a lifelong Republican, my earliest memory of his political views was how he described Martin Luther King as one of the greatest American heroes of his lifetime. By today's progressive standards, I know that his I-have-a-dream version of MLK would be judged simplistic, but it became the foundation on which I built my own progressive views growing up. I've met too many racist peers, including gay men, not to realize how lucky I was to have parents who taught me that this country's diversity is its greatest strength.

All his children hit their rough passages, but my dad always worked relentlessly to smooth them out, guiding us back to a safer place. In my case, coming out to him as gay and being diagnosed with AIDS-related complex was a gut punch. Imagine the Republican CEO of a multinational chemical company with its conservative Main Line board of directors seeing his "radical homosexual" son on the national news and on *60 Minutes* being led away in handcuffs from pharmaceutical companies and the New York Stock Exchange. I was able to share all of this with him in real time, asking for his best advice on ACT UP strategy and bringing home a string of crazy boyfriends each Thanksgiving dinner. If he ever had any qualms about my activism, he never let me see them. So many of my comrades were abandoned by their parents, but my dad was there for me from day one. This was my dad's greatest gift to me.

And my greatest gift to him? Somehow managing to outlive him, forestalling his terrible fear of having to watch one of his children die.

Ten days after my dad died, the AIDS community lost its most beloved heroine, Dr. Mathilde Krim. As cofounder of amfAR, she raised millions for AIDS research and used her expert credibility to relentlessly push back against the stigma, racism, and homophobia that seemed joined at the hip to this deadly virus.

After my speech at the San Francisco AIDS conference, she had asked me to join amfAR's board. In a close vote, the board rejected her nomination of me, fearing my perceived radicalism. She was furious and spent the next six months lobbying a few members for a planned revote. Krim was known for her persistence. I joined the board in 1991 and witnessed that persistence while growing from her mentorship for the next thirteen years.

During the last decade of her life, as her public appearances became less frequent, those of us who witnessed them got to participate in beautiful outpourings of love and respect. Whenever she was introduced to an audience packed with gay men who survived the early AIDS years, the standing ovation seemed to last forever. We made sure she knew our profound thanks for fearlessly standing up for us from day one.

Between Mathilde's death and Larry's death—both losses softened by the full lives that preceded them—I lost my best friend, Rich DeNagel. He was only fifty, and he suffered greatly in his last weeks after all our hopes were raised by a double-lung transplant, only to be dashed by infections his body just couldn't handle.

When I met Rich in 2002, his lungs were at constant war with cystic fibrosis but still breathed at 70 percent capacity. Just before his transplant in 2019, they were at 20 percent. His illness had stripped away any possibility of continuing his career as a schoolteacher. And then it robbed him of travel, and finally short outings for a meal or a movie with a friend.

But at the beginning of the friendship, we embarked on a multiyear conversation that intensified over time, further cementing our bond. Rich was fascinated by the early AIDS years, grilling me about how gay men his age dealt with sickness and the very real possibility of death. We shared a deep admiration for the self-empowered way these men chose to spend their last years or months, and how their gay brothers and lesbian sisters stood shoulder to shoulder with them to defend that self-determination.

While I was often afraid of these conversations during the plague years, Rich just rolled his eyes at my survivor's guilt. He instinctively guessed I'd remain calm and unafraid about discussing his illness and his possible death. We both agreed that the only reason I survived the plague years was luck. Thousands of gay men fought a perfect fight to beat the odds, as have thousands of those born with cystic fibrosis, but a virus or a genetic mutation is incapable of mercy.

It's all a crapshoot, and the brutal odds Rich faced stripped away life's typical luxury problems, leaving much harder questions for us to discuss. How can he buy himself another year or another month?

When do his increasing burdens of illness outweigh the narrowing window of his life's occasional joys?

Rich asked me to be part of his care team after the transplant—a blended family of his two sisters and three of his queer friends. The first two weeks were filled with hope, followed by five weeks of misery, buffered only by love. Every minute of it was a lesson in grace and perseverance.

And what gifts he left me. The clear-eyed appreciation for what matters and what doesn't. The power of forgiving ourselves, our faults, and the very human faults of others. The letting go of our own pushable blinking buttons as we realize their insignificance.

At sixty, I look forward to my last decades. Will some activism be in the mix? Undoubtedly. I'd love to keep fighting until that day when some sort of gene therapy removes all traces of HIV from my body, and a vaccine is available to block its further spread. I want to witness and celebrate the end of AIDS.

But truth be told, that's not where I find meaning these days. Instead, I wake up each day trying to live like Rich lived, cultivating quality time with those he loved.

I'm amazed I've lived this long. It feels like I've climbed a well-earned peak of serenity, defined by moments with family, pets, and good friends. This peak leaves me with a single, modest ambition: to walk along its ridge and enjoy the view for as long as my mind and body allow.

ACKNOWLEDGMENTS

FOR THE THREE PAINFUL YEARS of writing this book, I only half-jokingly referred to it on social media as "my fucking memoir." My problem was that I hate writing—like, a serious lifetime loathing of it. I've selected jobs and careers that didn't require writing, such as bond trading or running a website (where I paid other people to do it). But I did have this nagging desire to write down all these stories in my head. Maybe the process, with a generous one-year deadline from my publisher, would break my stubborn animus toward humanity's most creative form of communication.

No such luck. After I blew through multiple deadlines and a laundry list of anti-procrastination hacks, I'm pretty sure I hate writing more than ever. This will be the first and last book I ever write.

That said, I'm proud of the final product and that I never caved by using a ghostwriter. These are my stories told the way I've told them to close friends. But, god, I needed help. Here's an incomplete list of folks who now carry "I owe you, big time" cards, signed by me, to use against me the rest of my life.

First and foremost, my good friend Bruce Francis. If the IOU cards I gave to everyone else are laminated paper, Bruce's is gold with embossed lettering. About a year into writing, I had only two chapters to show for it, and I couldn't tell if they were any good. I needed some serious hand-holding by someone who knew me well and knew good writing, and Bruce reached out his hand. Like Rich DeNagel, Bruce has been battling a life-threatening illness for many years, which keeps him mostly homebound in San Francisco. He offered to be my daily sounding board, reading everything, offering quick edits, and, most important, brainstorming during long phone calls, figuring out *how* I'd tell these stories. A friend that can remain critical and not lose patience when those critiques piss you off is precious indeed.

And then there's my COVID pod—a thruplet of three happily-single-as-long-as-we-have-each-other, getting-older-together friends—with Laura Pinsky and Robby La Fosse. Along with Bruce Francis, we all met three decades ago on Fire Island and just got closer each decade. Laura and Robby rent a place near my home in the Poconos, and we spend every weekend together, which turned into every night during COVID. Misery withers in loving company, and they were my company throughout. Let's just say they are thrilled I finally finished the damn thing. Their unflagging cheerleading played a huge role in its completion.

During the last three-week crunch of editing, AIDS activist Shawn Decker spent every night adding spit and polish to my occasional lazy prose, with only my thanks as payment. However, he'll likely smile when he spots his spit and polish throughout. When I wrote the first chapter for the book proposal, author/speaker/warrior goddess/badass Amy Ferris offered to be my daily sounding board to get things in motion.

I blame Anderson Cooper and my literary agent, Robert Guinsler, for convincing me to tackle this project. They've been great cheerleaders and even better friends. My editor at Chicago Review Press, Jerry

Pohlen, has had to suffer through all my insufferable moments and somehow not kill me in the process. I feel like we walked over hot coals together, but he led the way calmly and never let go of my hand.

I lost track of how many folks I got on the phone to fact-check my memories—dozens, at least. Everyone who is still alive got back to me and opened their own memories, some of them painful, to help me get it right. They have my deepest thanks.

Finally, beyond the book, I want to thank all the shrinks in my life. They got me through thick and thin, and I'm sure I'll be back to see one of them after this book's first bad review. In chronological order: "Dr. Freud" (sorry I've forgotten your name), Albert Ellis (yes, *that* Albert Ellis, for all you psych majors), Dixie Beckham, Rosemary Caggiano (whose practice became packed with ACT UP's busiest and most stressed), Bruce Hermann (great career counselors require good shrinking skills), Boaz Dalit, Marilyn White (founder of the Realization Center), Dave Schwing, and Sylvie Acoulon (who helped me avoid memoir-related suicide).

If you've never seen a shrink, please start. Your friends will thank you.